Trans-Per Understanding Human Communication

Kenneth K. Sereno   **Edward M. Bodaken**

University of Southern California

Cover and illustrations by Ken Maryanski

Houghton Mifflin Company   Boston

Atlanta   Dallas   Geneva, Ill.   Hopewell, N.J.   Palo Alto   London

Printed in the U.S.A.
Library of Congress Catalog Card Number: 74-20113
ISBN: 0-395-18701-X

Contents

Preface

Perhaps the most important feature of our text is its development of the Trans-Per model of communication. We've been careful to present our model in such a way that it serves as the reference for *all* our statements about communication and in such a way that it gives the text continuity and structure.

Trans-Per is a simple model of the fundamental process of human communication. It was designed to be simple so that students can understand it early in the course and then have time to test and use it. It was also designed to be flexible so that students can apply it to all communication, including their everyday experiences, and not just to class assignments or textbook exercises.

Besides being useful and accessible to the student, we believe the model makes up for a deficiency in the communication field. Communication writers seem to agree that communication is a transactional experience, yet the transactional nature of communication is not depicted in a meaningful and consistent way throughout most texts. Similarly most communication texts deal only superficially with the perceptual process of communicators. We argue that communication is perceptual in nature and that the way we select, organize, and evaluate stimuli is directly tied to communication behavior. Because we believe that the transactional-perceptual assumptions are so important to an understanding of communication, we have used them in a consistent and central way to build our model; we combined the first syllables of each term to title our model Trans-Per.

In addition to the model and its role in "cementing" chapters of the book together, there are a few other things about our text that we think will be helpful. We've attempted to write a text that is comfortable for students. Some teachers may be disturbed with our conversational language or perhaps our student-life examples. Obviously we can't please everyone, but generally we believe that we've written a jargon-free book that is pleasant to read and easy to understand. Along these same lines, we've refrained from filling the pages with footnotes or citations. One reason is that many of the ideas are our own (and nobody else will claim them). Another is that most students are interested in a book's content and not the text or journal that a particular piece of information happened to come from. But we've added a bibliographic section at the end of the book for instructors or students who choose to do research in any particular area. The sources we've listed are the ones mentioned by author's name and year of publication in the text; and we consider them major research references for the communication field. Also at the end of the text we've placed a glossary to give students easy reference to essential terms and definitions. At the end of each chapter we've included several annotated sources for the student who wants to go into greater depth or read a different point of view on ideas we've discussed; and we've provided several exercises that can be used to test and develop ideas discussed in the chapter.

Trans-Per is the way we've come to understand the complexity of human communication. We hope Trans-Per will be as meaningful to you.

Kenneth K. Sereno
Edward M. Bodaken

Acknowledgments

It is clearer now than ever before that books or meanings are not created by authors alone. There are significant external elements we'd like to acknowledge:

Denny Rea for giving us the encouragement to initiate this project

Adolph Coors and Cutty Sark for concentrated assistance when words were scarce and comfort was needed

Janice Rushing for demonstrating that our ideas could indeed be exorcised

Katy Connor and Mike Fahs for research assistance when our ideas were too crude even for us to understand

Our final reviewer, Paul Nelson, for perception and turn-around that will not be forgotten

Our departmental secretary, Thelma Larkin, for sensitivity and competence that we often didn't deserve

Our graduate students in communication theory who tolerated the many distractions and research down-time this work created

One wife and eight kids for tolerating living habits projects like this make necessary

C. David Mortensen and John R. Wenburg: professional colleagues who encouraged and stimulated our thinking in many different and meaningful ways

Gerald R. Miller for initially stimulating us to think about the significance and potential of the field of communication

The 901 Club for providing an environment in which ideas could be nurtured, destroyed, and drowned

Our typist, Barbara Kadlec, who converted scratches and errors into a final manuscript

Reviewers who kept reminding us of our sex and our locale

And each other for a friendship that seemed to become more meaningful as meaning was discussed

Trans-Per Understanding Human Communication

CHAPTER • 1

Studying Human Communication

In a real sense the study of human communication is the study of human behavior. A person's ability to communicate with himself, with others, within institutions, or across cultures is what makes him human. The drive to survive, to destroy, to move from one place to another, to breed new generations—all these are things that a person shares with animals. But to communicate, which involves giving meaning to events, objects, and behavior—that's what makes a person different from any other living thing.

Possibly because communication is so much a part of being human, people come to take it for granted. Despite all the time spent in communication, people usually take little effort to study it—to learn more about it. They go from day to day generally content to describe communication in terms of its effectiveness. In a classroom discussion a student who argues strongly for his position—that, for example, Shakespeare found more evil than good in the world—considers his communication successful if he persuades others to believe his point of view. The supervisor on the assembly line is considered to be a good communicator if production stays the same or increases. The teacher judges his communication successful in terms of how well his students know the material. And parents look at their children's actions to see if they were successful in communicating their ideals to them. Although quite a common one, the assumption that communication should be looked at primarily in terms of its effectiveness doesn't help much in understanding the *nature* of communication. In this book you'll be looking at the workings of human communication—not so much how *well* people communicate as *how* and *why* they do.

We think a study of the nature of human communication should be preceded by two things: first, the value of such a study ought to be considered; second, the general framework of the study should be presented before it is used.

Why Study Communication?

Maybe this class satisfies a requirement for your major. Or maybe in glancing through the course catalog, you read the course description, liked what you saw, and signed up for it as an elective. In either case the course is probably described in the catalog as "an attempt to understand the communication process." But why try to study formally something that you do all the time? After all, you don't spend any time in class studying how to walk or eat—similar basic behavior.

To Understand Yourself as a Social Being

To begin with, communication is a significant *social* experience: communication occurs in all of your relationships. Through communication you get to know others, and you let others know you. Through communication you are able to move from the level of acquaintance to friend and from stranger to lover. Human communication provides you with the capability not only to create relationships but also to develop or destroy those relationships. The study of communication can bring to your attention the various strategies you may use in your own communications to help you work better with others and to make mutually beneficial compromises—helpful for everyone involved. In addition the study of communication can help you understand, and possibly change, the attitudes of others by describing for what basic reasons people hold their attitudes. To sum it up, you cannot consider your life as a social being without considering the importance of communication; all social behavior either directly or indirectly is tied into human communication. It seems reasonable, then, to learn more about communication than that it happens and to let it go at that.

To Understand Yourself as a Person

In addition there's the need to study communication for *personal* reasons. The study of communication helps you to know yourself better. It points out and thereby brings to your attention some of the possible reasons you hold some of your own positive or negative attitudes toward a given topic or issue or person. It helps you understand that you hold your favorite attitudes—whether you are conscious of it or not—to satisfy certain inner or psychological needs; and it points out that individuals have a need for consistency, balance, and inner harmony in their attitudes. The study of communication helps you understand how your oral conversations and written messages *reflect*—and convey to others—your positive and negative attitudes. It may give you insights into the effect of your communication on others; it helps you become aware of possible motives, purposes, and goals of others in their communications with you. In other words this study should be a consciousness-raising process for you—in an area of supreme importance. Our point is quite simple: the study of communication will give you help in understanding and improving your day-to-day living with yourself, with friends, with groups to which you belong, and with those with whom you work. Shouldn't you spend some time getting to know a little more about it?

Frameworks for the Study of Communication

Recall how each day begins for you. You can probably describe a fairly predictable pattern. You generally wake up at the same time, get dressed in similar ways, take the same roads or transportation to school and work. Because of your routine—whatever it is—you've grown to expect things to happen in a certain way. You carry with you images of how you expect the world to operate. These mental images influence the way you approach each day and each event.

Similarly you've probably come to have certain expectations of your communication with yourself and others. Can you point out features of mental images you have, of the way you look at your own methods of communicating—at your world of communication? If you can, you're the exception for, as we said earlier, communication is usually taken for granted.

The study of any process as complex as communication demands that you have some systematic means to guide what you do. On the following pages we want to acquaint you with a general framework—a mental image—of communicating behavior. Our approach may be consistent with yours or it may be just the opposite. Whatever your reactions while reading, keep in mind that this is the way that we, Sereno and Bodaken, look at the communicating world. Hopefully, as you move through this book, you'll find this framework as useful as we do and will apply what you have learned to your own communicating.

Our approach draws on and uses behavioral theories and empirical research as aids in attempting to describe communication. Empirical findings come from detailed and repeated observations of communicating behavior. This doesn't mean that our framework is research-oriented in the sense that we'll ask you to set up or perform experiments or to collect statistics. Instead we'll rely on well-established research and theory of psychologists and be-

haviorists to provide some basic working material from which we can operate. At the end of the book we identify these sources by author and date.

Before we describe our framework and its basic components, we want to
comment briefly on two other ways of looking at communicating behavior,
which some researchers have found useful.

Communication as a One-way Action

One particular view of the nature of human communication suggests that
messages are transmitted in one direction—from one person to another. For
example a person has some information: he selects an audience, delivers that
information to the audience; and communication is said to have taken place.
(The term *audience* can refer to another person as well as to a group of people.) In many organizations the general notion of communication is this
one-way, one-time transmission of information from one person to another.
Basically this approach to communication as an individual *one-way action*
holds that a "source" originates a message and that the message ends, hopefully, in the mind of a "receiver." But isn't it possible that, as one person is
listening to another, he is also communicating with the source? Perhaps
with his facial expression of interest or disinterest, perhaps with his tone of
"really?" or "uh . . . huh." The one-way action framework or orientation
to communication leads to the conclusion that if there is some breakdown,
the fault is the source's. The assumption is also made that, if the source
would refine his skills in communicating, the problem could be elimi-
nated. So a person is told to be more dynamic, to adapt to his audience, to
reinforce the telephone instructions with a written memo, and so on. All
these are strategies designed to reinforce a one-way notion of communication, and often they also reinforce the problem because the source is dis-
suaded from hearing the receiver sending. In sum, the action framework is
deficient, for it tends to oversimplify communication by treating it as a
one-way or linear activity.

Communication as Interaction

A second framework frequently applied to communication is *interaction*.
In contrast to the one-way action framework, this view holds that communication is a string of causes and effects or actions and reactions. A person speaks, another nods, the first speaks again. In other words one person
sends some information to another and in turn receives something back.
Interaction is thought of as two-way—with each communicator equipped
with an on-and-off switch. Each is either sending or receiving. This is, of

course, a more sophisticated perspective on communication than the one-way action framework, for it adds the notion of feedback. Nevertheless this framework fails to account for the possibility that people can send and receive at the same time.

But is it possible for an individual to be only a source *or* a receiver during communication? As someone speaks to you, are you merely the receiver? Aren't you sending at the same time? Isn't it possible that, as he delivers the message, he is taking your gestures into account? As you listen, do you simply record what is being said, or do you interpret what you hear and at least partly create the meaning of what is being said? And doesn't the meaning of the conversation change for both of you as the conversation continues?

There ought to be a way of conceiving of the communication process that would take into account this dynamic transaction. Also you should be able to study the process in such a way that you can account for the many changes that occur in communicating relationships and can deal with ideas on how meaning is created. To view communication as transaction meets these needs and more.

Our Framework: Communication as Transaction

By means of a *transaction* framework, we hope to eliminate the weaknesses and inaccuracies of describing communication either as one-way action or as on-and-off interaction. We want to show that communicating is essentially a dynamic interchange between communicators, with no periods of passive receptivity on the part of any communicator. Each communicator is always both sending and receiving actively: each is a source and a receiver at the same time. At all times the participants are actively exchanging either verbal responses (words, sentences) or nonverbal responses (gestures, glances, shrugs or other cues of their reaction to the ongoing conversation). To deal with any one element of communication—say merely to analyze the verbal message—to the exclusion of all the others falsifies the true picture of communication as a continuous interchange—a dynamic mutuality, something we call transaction. In fact, if we had to describe what communication is and how it works all in one word, that word would be "transaction."

What do we mean by the term *transaction?* We mean that the communicators are interrelated, that we can't consider one of them without considering the other or others. We mean that one perception of a communicator can't be considered apart from all his other perceptions. We mean that the external environment and the internal state of each person in

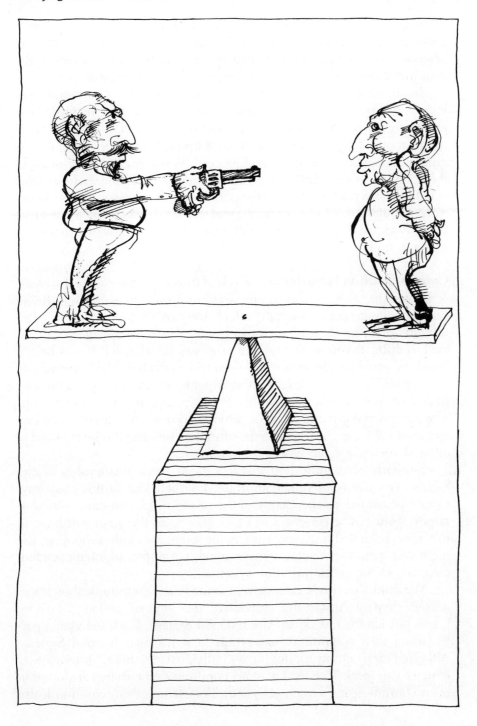

the communication are interrelated. And finally we are saying that a communicator cannot be considered apart from the world he knows and perceives. By a transactional approach we mean that all elements in the communication process are interrelated and interdependent.

In our transaction framework we intend to show how communication is explained by and composed of four components and that we need to use all these components to explain the essential nature of any type of communication. The components of communication as transaction are: system, perception, meaning, and process. As you read our discussion of these, think about them in relation to your own experiences—of what you think takes place during a conversation in which you participate. Don't worry about the exact word or occasional technical description we use; particularly at first deal with the overall concept or mental picture that we're trying to outline.

Communication Is Systemic   Each of us is a system—a living system. A problem breathing, for example, isn't just limited to your lungs. If you can't breathe properly, it usually affects your ability to function in other ways. It influences the way you move around; it affects your ability to digest food; it distracts you so that mental processes are affected. If you have a breathing problem, those around you may be affected. Furthermore you may be told to live in certain environments, to take certain respiratory treatments, to avoid certain stresses, to stay away from others, and so on. The point is that this one problem, which may deal most directly with one element, the lungs, in your system, cannot be isolated; it is interrelated to other elements and the system they compose.

Similarly communication involves the systemic relationship of elements. The nature of your communicating behavior in this class, say, cannot be treated independently of the relationships you have with your family, your past experiences in other classes, or the goals you have in mind for yourself. The temperature in the room, the clothes you wear, the night you spend before class—these are also examples of interdependent elements in the communication system.

We think that two basic systems operate in any communication transaction: elements inside the individual, the Internal System, and elements outside the individual, the External System. Each individual participating in a communication brings to it his own Internal System. Although each communicator has an individual and unique Internal System, we can speak in general of many common elements that are found in every communicator's Internal System. For example every communicator has what we can identify generally as preconceived attitudes and as personality traits in his Internal System. Thus to work with systems simplifies some of the inherent complexity of studying human communication.

The Internal System is composed of all those elements that taken together make up a unique individual. Examples of elements making up the Internal System are an individual's personal traits, his attitudes, his motives, his knowledge, his intelligence, and his past experiences—the whole inner psychological and intellectual complex. In any communication transaction each individual is thought of as an Internal System; there are exactly as many Internal Systems as there are communicators. Elements making up the Internal System are what we call *private* or internal stimuli. You can't see them; you can only infer them from the individual's words or behavior. How much of your own Internal System are you conscious of?

The External System is composed of those elements that exist in the environment outside the individual. Examples of elements in the External System are such things as the particular words used in a message, the physical gestures of the communicators, the sounds and scents surrounding the communicators, even the temperature of the room. These elements are the *public* or external stimuli of the communication transaction and are potentially accessible to every participant.

For our purposes we say that there is only one External System, which is generally shared by all participants in any given communication transaction. Of course we recognize that no two individuals will have exactly identical perceptual fields: although you may be sharing a small living room with someone, he will not have access to the identical gestures and facial expressions that you are perceiving. You are seeing him; you are not seeing yourself. Conversely you will not read the identical gestures and facial expressions he is seeing. He is seeing you, not himself. But *in general* both of you are seeing and sharing the same basic environment: the same small room, the same comfortable sofa, the same dim lamp, low ceiling. For our purposes the External System is the same for both of you.

To think of communication as systemic enables you to identify and study systems within an overall system. As an example of a "system within a system," your communication class is a system within the speech communication department; the speech communication department is a system within your college. An undergraduate school, a medical school, and a law school are systems within a university. In the transaction framework the External System and the Internal System or Systems are parts of the overall communication system.

The systemic component of our framework allows us to divide into two basic systems all the otherwise complex and unwieldy elements affecting communication—the system within the individual and the system outside the individual. Can you think of anything omitted from our systems?

Communication Is Perceptual   An understanding of the process of perception is fundamental to an understanding of communication. Very briefly, perception is the process in which a person selects stimuli (or information) from the external world and at the same time mixes and blends them with internal stimuli, which are within him. When a person tries to make sense out of the world (and people have a deep psychological need to make sense out of the world), he has basically two sources of information available to him: the elements he brings with him—all his past, his attitudes, his personality—and those elements presently existing in the external world—all other people, their words and messages, their gestures, the surroundings. *Perception is the individual's blending of internal and external stimuli.*

For example imagine you are walking through a pine woods by yourself. You see the evening sunlight slanting through the trees. As you take this in, you suddenly connect it with your fear of the dark, something already inside you from the time you were a child. You decide to pick up speed in order to get home by nightfall. You have blended external stimuli from the present environment—the coming of darkness—with internal stimuli from your past.

Perceptions are the means individuals use to make sense of the world around them. Since people have a psychological need to make sense out of those things they observe around them, they are continuously and actively engaged in organizing and interpreting relevant stimuli into a meaningful view of the world. Rather than being passively bombarded by experiences, they actively participate in and try to arrange and interpret their world —even when just sitting still in a chair and quietly looking out the window. This attempt to make sense and order out of the world is a creative activity. Perceptions are what we individually blend—and are entirely subjective. Since in perceiving we combine stimuli from outside of us with stimuli inside us—and that particular combination of stimuli within us is unlike anyone else's Internal System—our perceptions are uniquely our own and shared by no one else. So perceiving is active, creative, and subjective; much like a painter, we create our own visions of the world.

Communication Is Creating Meaning   When people perceive—or blend internal and external elements—they are engaged in the creation of meaning. The consequence or outcome of perceptual blending is the assignment of meaning to the stimuli. In our transactional approach, we assume that this *creation of meaning* is an essential component of human communication. The meaning that a person assigns to stimuli is uniquely his own. No two people can have the same meaning for any particular event, object, or message. For example, to one young individual, who has just been disappointed by a favorite girlfriend, the lyrics at a folk concert may have had much appeal and meaning; to his complacent friend in the next seat, the same lyrics may have appeared unmoving and even trivial. The individual meaning each person assigns is based on his own unique perceptual blending of the internal and external stimuli.

Although people perceive differently and assign individual meanings to stimuli, they do, nevertheless, attempt to share meaning with one another. When our friends discuss their reactions after the concert, each may have assigned very different personal meanings to the lyrics, to the music, and to the concert—but they will attempt to *share meaning* about the event.

In abstract terms, meaning evolves when a perceiving individual mixes certain internal elements he brings with him with those external elements existing in the environment. The outcome of the perceptual mix is the assignment of significance or the *creation of meaning*. The result of blending stimuli and assigning meaning is often some behavior or verbal message; that is, the individual may translate the meaning he has worked out into an act, a behavior, or a verbal message. Thus if when you're hungry (hunger is an internal element) you enter a friend's apartment and pick up a pleasant scent of food cooking (scents are external elements), you determine that your hunger can be satisfied here. This assignment of significance —blending and giving meaning to the external scent and the internal hunger state—is translated into some message or behavior. You might say, "How about something to eat?" or "I like the smell of whatever's cooking." Your precise choice of words would depend on other elements in the transaction—how well you know your friend, your own personality and self-esteem, and your attitudes about good form and acceptable social behavior.

Not all communicating transactions are as neat as this one. As you'll see in later chapters, meaning depends on some not so easily determined, complex relationships of internal and external stimuli. This component, the creation of meaning, is central to our concept of communication; we will develop it, therefore, throughout this book.

Communication Is Processual   A well-established assumption of communicating behavior, emphasized by most writers in the area, is the idea that communication is a process. The term *process* describes the ongoing, flowing, ever-changing nature of human communication. Communication has no beginning, has no ending, and analogous to perception, is continuously moving forward. The best we can do is to snap a still picture of the process—arrest the process—for the purpose of examining and analyzing its complexity.

In a moment, stop reading this page and think about your attitude toward the lovesick person at the folk concert, mentioned earlier, who has lost his best girlfriend to a rival. Should he feel sorry for himself and sulk for a few weeks? Should he try to urge her to reconsider? Should he completely avoid her? Should he try to establish any further contact? Have you ever been in a similar situation of losing the person or goal you thought you wanted the most? Are you tough-minded and think he should pull himself together? Or sympathetic and think he should indulge his blues for a few weeks?

Now think about these last few minutes. Has your attitude—toward taking disappointment—been changed or refined? Maybe not in a gross or obvious way, but probably your perceptions and attitudes have altered slightly while you were considering his plight and what his recourses were. And what you would do in his shoes. Chances are that the brief pause to think about his plight has affected your attitude toward us, this class, your girlfriend or boyfriend, yourself. Can you detect any of these changes?

In this little exercise, you've engaged in a communicating process with yourself: you've selected internal stimuli from your own past experience and external stimuli from your surroundings—the book before you with its story of the sad concert-goer. You've arrived at some meaning, and you then translated the meaning into a message or behavior of sorts: "He should forget her." Or a frown. Or a scowl—at the thought of one of your own serious disappointments. Throughout all this mental exercise, thoughts were swirling around in your mind. It is simply impossible to stop perceiving or thinking or communicating.

It's incorrect to think of communication as static; it's like time and existence, a continuous process. When we speak of communication as having "taken place" or "occurred," we're speaking figuratively of the arbitrary, fictional freezing of the process. So remember that when we say "communication has occurred," it's always a fictional expression to assist in our study. Since we cannot study all the elements swarming about continuously in communicators' minds, we're forced to separate the whole complex, ongoing process into static components that we can handle conveniently.

Outline and Review of Components   No doubt it has become clear to you that the components of communicating are very closely interrelated. They were presented in no special order; nor is one of them more important than any other. The absence of one of the components we've discussed means that not all the conditions necessary for communication to take place have been met.

That communication involves *system, perception, creation of meaning,* and *process* is, we hope, beginning to make sense. Although so far we have presented each component separately, we will eventually show how all these components are interrelated and interdependent; in our transaction framework of communication, all these components function together. At this stage, the following outline might help you review and remember the salient features of our framework.

TRANSACTION FRAMEWORK OF COMMUNICATION

Component	*Description*
1. System	(a) Elements of communication are interrelated and interdependent, both part to part and part to whole
	(b) Two major systems exist within overall communication system: External System, Internal System
	(c) External System is composed of external elements or public stimuli
	(d) Internal System is composed of internal elements or private stimuli
2. Perception	(a) Blending of internal and external stimuli
	(b) Creative, active, subjective
	(c) Means by which we learn about world

3. Creating Meaning   (a) Individual's assignment of mean-
                               ing from outcome of perceptual
                               blending
                           (b) Individual's sharing of meaning
                               with others
4. Process   (a) Ongoing
                           (b) Always changing

Contexts of Communication as Transaction   There is often the mistaken notion that several different kinds of communication exist, as for
example, intrapersonal communication, interpersonal communication,
group communication, organizational communication. We think that the
process of communication is basically similar from one context to another.

The transactional approach to communication allows us to take into
account all the various contexts or situations of communication—using
the same components and the same type of analysis. We will treat intrapersonal, interpersonal, group, and organizational communication as
basically the same transactional process. We must, however, account for
additional Internal Systems as we add communicators. And we must determine which internal and external elements are predominant in the various contexts. We will devote individual chapters to detailed discussion of
the four contexts we have mentioned.

Additional Readings

Barnlund, D. "A Transactional Model of Communication." In *Foundations of
    Communication Theory*, edited by K. Sereno and C. D. Mortensen, pp.
    83–102. New York: Harper & Row, 1970.

Basically consistent with our approach to communication, Barnlund's
model is perhaps the most influential transactional conception of communication
published thus far. Barnlund's treatment of postulates (what we call components)
of communication is well worth examining.

Berlo, David. *The Process of Communication*. New York: Holt, Rinehart and
    Winston, 1960.

Although this book does not specify a transactional approach, it is clear
from Chapters 1 and 2 that Berlo's notions of communication are close to our own.
You'll find of interest his discussion of the purposes and dimensions of communication in Chapter 1. In addition everyone should have some familiarity with the
S-M-C-R model in Chapter 2. The author's "Suggestions for Thought and Discussion," at the ends of Chapters 1 and 2, contain some very useful activities to
help you begin your study of the communication process.

Giffin, K., and Patton, B. *Fundamentals of Interpersonal Communication.* New
York: Harper & Row, 1971.

One of the most popular interpersonal texts, this book will point out some of
the barriers that may exist when individuals seek to communicate. In addition the
authors offer some "guidelines" for effective communication. Although we think
guidelines for effectiveness are somewhat idealistic, we believe that the perspective
presented in Chapters 1 and 2 is relevant to our treatment of communication. We
particularly want to call your attention to Chapter 1, "Basic Characteristics of Interpersonal Communication."

Mortensen, C. D. *Communication: The Study of Human Interaction.* New York:
McGraw-Hill, 1972.

You'll find Chapter 1 will add to and extend your understanding of the transactional approach to human communication. We particularly like the statement
of communication postulates, which flows from his definition of communication:
"Communication occurs whenever persons attribute significance to message-
related behavior." This book, which includes an excellent bibliography, is certainly one of the most comprehensive of the past decade.

Stewart, J., ed. *Bridges Not Walls.* Reading, Mass.: Addison-Wesley, 1973.

Stewart's Introduction offers an excellent analysis of the differences between
various approaches to human communicating behavior. Specifically, his comments illustrating differences between interaction and transaction will be particularly useful to further your understanding of the ideas presented so far. Stewart also
takes up interpersonal communication. The examples, illustrations, and suggestions covered in the Introduction are required reading for anyone seriously interested in the field.

Wenburg, J., and Wilmot, W. *The Personal Communication Process,* New York:
John Wiley, 1973.

An attempt is made here to take a transactional approach to the study of
human communication. The authors' thesis, presented in Chapter 1, that communication is a personal, unique behavior and that all people send and receive
communications simultaneously, deserves some thoughtful study and comparison with personal experience.

Applications

Exercise 1

What makes human beings human? Speculation about this question has engaged
philosophers and scientists for thousands of years. Think carefully yourself about
this question and try to agree as a class upon a short phrase that expresses a human
being's most distinguishing characteristic: "Human beings are the ____animal."

Exercise 2

The creation of meaning is a unique and individual activity. What is the personal meaning you assign to each of the following words?

school	fear
love	chauvinist
person	family
marijuana	hip
communication	professor

Are your subjective meanings different from others in the class? What part does past experience play in your creation of meaning? Can you attempt to share the meaning you have for one of these words with another member of the class?

Exercise 3

Do you agree with the statement, "It is impossible *not* to communicate"? Support your answer by providing a short example illustrating your position. Present your example to the class for reaction and discussion.

Exercise 4

Arrange to meet for one class discussion somewhere other than your usual class-room: outside on a nice day, in a much larger room such as a lecture hall, in a much smaller room such as someone's house or apartment, or another convenient location. When you return to the classroom, discuss the effects of the new environment on the communication process.

Exercise 5

Here is a model of communication similar to ones used by other researchers interested in communication. Evaluate it in terms of the three frameworks for studying communication: action, interaction, and transaction.

Exercise 6

Rank the following definitions of "communication" in order of your preferences (most liked = 1).

_____ Communication is a cosmic force that bonds people together in a social group.

_____ Communication is an emotional experience through which human relations exist and develop.

_____ Communication is any discriminatory response to a stimulus.

_____ Communication is the transmission of information from one person to another.

_____ Communication is all the procedures by which one comes to know oneself.

_____ Communication is a continuing realization that the world is a complex pattern, not a group of indistinguishable parts.

_____ Communication is the stimulation of a source-selected meaning in the mind of a receiver.

_____ Communication is symbolic inducement to attitude and action.

_____ Communication is identification between people.

_____ Communication is the evolution of meaning.

_____ Communication is the selection, organization, and interpretation of verbal and nonverbal cues within and outside of the individual.

_____ Communication is psychic communion.

_____ Communication is what makes humans different from animals.

What values underlie your preferences?

CHAPTER • 2

Understanding Perception

"Communication" and "perception"—words so closely related that we have difficulty discussing one without the other. An understanding of human communication is impossible without an introduction into the basic nature of perception.

Take the following glimpses of conversation.

WALTER: I only see three squares of yellow paint.

ROGER: Are you blind or what? That is a painting of a woman lying on a sofa.

JANE: Things really started falling into place today.

BOB: Not for me. The course just doesn't make any sense.

LIZ: They put out a nice sound, but the drummer's terrible.

MARGARET: Say, you do have things backwards. Without him the guitarist would be out of a job.

Dialogues like these are the stuff of daily experience. And they show very clearly that perceptions vary from one person to another. What is perception anyway?

By our perceptions we acquire a meaningful picture of our world. Perceptions are the means by which we gain an awareness of our surroundings and environment. Most of the time we engage in the process without paying much attention to how we do it. Although pretty much an automatic behavior, it's a complex activity. A lot goes into it. Many proposals have been offered to explain the process of perception, one of which we call the Common Sense View.

The Common Sense View of Perception: A Deficient View

This view of perception suggests that—similar to a movie camera—you grind away passively recording the sights and sounds of the external world.

21

Three assumptions underlie this view. First, perception is a passive affair. Sights, sounds, and smells in the environment are sent to your senses and you record them. You have little and sometimes no control over what reaches you. Like a movie camera, you record or receive whatever is put in front of you. Second, perception is an objective business. As a camera, you do not add or take away from the stimuli you're exposed to. You more or less accurately register whatever the external world presents to you. And third, this view states that the meaning of any object in your environment is inherent in the object, not in how you feel about it: a camera doesn't evaluate or interpret the things it films.

But these assumptions are oversimplified misconceptions. A person is not like a movie camera; he is neither a passive nor objective witness of the external world. However, a supporter of the Common Sense View counters, "After all, when we have a conversation, do we make up what the other person said? When we see something, isn't it there?" The answer to these questions is a firm *maybe*. The person may or may not have said what you claimed. You may or may not have seen what was there. In suggesting that perception is neither passive nor objective, we're implying the opposite: that perception is subjective, creative, and active. In the next section we'll examine the active and creative aspects of perceptual activity.

Perception Is Subjective, Creative, and Active

Anything and everything we know about the world is a result of our perceptual activities. For all practical purposes, the world doesn't exist for us except as we perceive it. Objects, sounds, sights, events, subjects—or any of the detailed array of data we know—do not exist for us as individuals unless we personally perceive them. As an illustration, atrocities committed by the Stalinist regime did not exist for most Americans until we were made aware of them by the writings of Alexsandr Solzhenitsyn, who spent eleven years in Stalin's camps and prison—or in exile. Therefore the world and all the things and events in it don't exist for us unless we know about them through some form of our perceptual activity. We each subjectively create our own view of the world—or of external reality—by means of our perceptions. Perception is subjective and personal in our transaction framework.

In addition perception isn't the passive, objective, camera-like recording of what's "out there," as assumed in the Common Sense View. Our senses don't transmit objective, impartial copies of the external world to our brain. Rather our perception of the world is an active, creative blend of what's "out there" and what's in us. Perception represents our inseparable involvement with the world. Thus we don't have different reactions to the same "thing"—for the "thing" isn't the same for each of us.

Although we might speak of you and your classmates as having differing attitudes toward this class, we would not be speaking quite accurately. For the class isn't quite the same thing to all of you: each of you *sees* the class as slightly different—filtered through your own Internal System. Whether the class exists as an objective entity "out there" is not important: in our transactional approach, it exists only as each of you individually perceives it to exist. And what you perceive reflects a blending of stimuli "out there" and things inside you that are unique to you and your own experiences. Each of you differs from your classmates in your feelings toward the word "mother" depending on your positive, neutral, or negative feelings toward your own particular mother. Therefore each of you in the class will have a different picture or perception of "mother." The daughter of a wealthy American movie actress and the son of a Mexican-American woman living in the barrio each have different perceptions of mother; mother just isn't the same for those two. Quite literally, when you perceive, you're doing your own thing. You're actively creating your own idea of the world.

The Three Activities of Perception

Perception is the complex process by which we *select, organize,* and *interpret* stimuli or sensory stimulation into a meaningful view of the world. Take another look at the conversations of Walter, Roger, and the others. Can you recognize the process of selection operating in Walter's and Roger's comments? Walter has selectively focused on the shapes and colors. Roger hasn't noticed shapes or colors but apparently has noticed a human form he finds in the painting. The comments of Jane reveal the presence, and those of Bob the absence, of perceptual organization: Jane has made sense of the subject matter of the course while Bob is still confused. Liz and Margaret clearly have formed different interpretations of the two musicians. While Liz perceives the drummer to be the worse performer, Margaret perceives just the opposite: "Without him, the guitarist would be out of a job." Notice that these conversations not only illustrate the three separate activities of perception but also show that each of our participants has dissimilar perceptions. Observe finally that our participants were in the same environment but "saw" things quite differently. Clearly the Common Sense View does not account for these differences in perceptual selection, organization, and interpretation—since according to it, we all should objectively register the same external world. Although you might find it convenient to think about these activities as occurring in stages, selection, organization, and interpretation often are taking place simultaneously. Selecting, organizing, and interpreting stimuli describe more completely what we mean by the individual's *blending* of internal and external elements. Remember how we described perception, in Chapter 1, as the process of blending stimuli. Let's take a closer look at each of these perceptual activities.

Selection

Right now, as you're reading this chapter, become aware of the sounds around you. Listen. Can you hear people's voices? Are birds singing? Is the air conditioner humming? Is the TV on? Is an airplane passing overhead? Can you hear traffic? Look around more carefully than usual. What about the room you're in? What color are the walls? What pieces of furniture are around you? How about smells? A musty odor? Flowers? What about your sense of touch? Are you aware of your shoes, tight underwear, or the watch on your wrist? We'll assume that you weren't sensitive to all of these stimuli until we called them to your attention. Only a small portion of the stimuli reaching our senses are converted to consciousness.

Perceptual *selection* is the process of neglecting some of the stimuli of the environment and focusing on a chosen few. At a dance some women may only see handsome men while others may only be conscious of what clothes and jewelry other women are wearing. Men may only notice vivacious women, or they might notice a particularly slovenly or well-dressed person in the group. When we're rushing to keep an appointment, we're likely to glance often at our watches. After a long day on the highway, we seek out Vacancy signs in front of motels. When the gauge is running low, we keep our eyes peeled for gasoline stations. Thus, perceptual selection is the process of focusing on a few relevant dimensions of stimulation from the vast array of potential stimuli. But selection is merely one activity of the perceptual process. What do we do with stimuli when we're *aware* of them?

Organization

We tend to organize what we've selected in two basic ways. One means of organizing is to distinguish between *figure* and *ground*. When we focus on certain elements, we're concentrating on what's called *figure*. The setting in which the figure is located or embedded is *ground*. Look at Figure 2.1. Notice how we can switch from the center vase to the two profiles, but we

FIGURE 2.1 How many figures do you see? Can you see the vase? Can you see the two faces?

can't focus on both at the same time. While we pay attention to one element, it becomes figure and the other becomes ground.

Think about the most recent conversation you've had. Do you remember how your attention shifted back and forth between the words (or verbal cues) and the physical characteristics (or nonverbal cues) of the other person? Recall how you would listen to the words for a moment—but then would notice that his hair was well cut or that her bracelets were silver. In time you would shift back to the words—only to become once again conscious of nonverbal cues, of how her eyes are an unusual shade of blue or how pleasant his voice sounds. Whenever we focus on one element, the other elements fall into the background. At the moment of our noticing the muscles under someone's tennis shirt, the person's words are just a droning blur. This common manner of perceiving typifies our continuous shifting between figure and ground.

A second way we organize is to perceive simplified figures—that is, our predisposition toward the *simplification* of forms. Figure 2.2 is a perceptual three-ring circus, a confusion of unbalanced and unrelated items. It's so complex and busy that the only way we can make sense of the design is by eliminating details and simplifying.

When listening to directions from the gas station attendant on how to reach an unfamiliar restaurant, we tend to throw out most of the information he's giving us and repeat in our minds only those few details that we will need: "Two rights, then two lefts, past a river." We try to make sense of many unsorted pieces of information by ordering them into a simplified, sequential pattern.

We also organize stimuli into simplified figures through the process of *perceptual closure*—which is our tendency to perceive in unified wholes.

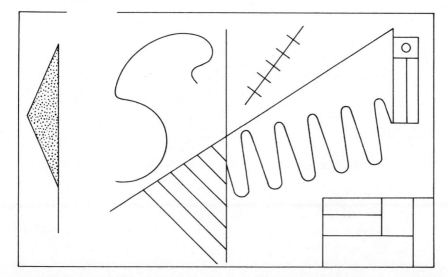

FIGURE 2.2 *An Example of an Unorganized, Complex Figure.* If you were to describe the essential aspects of this figure, what aspects would you focus on and what aspects would you omit?

For example we don't see Figure 2.3 as four separate lines, but as a square.

In the same way we experience Figure 2.4 as a circle and not as a series of dashes.

In talking with a friend, have you ever completed his sentence in your own mind before he did? This phenomenon is another example of closure. Have you ever overheard a few snatches of conversation and then filled in the rest for yourself? This again illustrates the operation of perceptual closure.

Thus perceptual *organization* is the activity of arranging stimuli into simplified, unified wholes. We've seen that perceptual organization involves distinguishing between figure and ground. We also organize stimuli into understandable patterns by simplification and closure.

FIGURE 2.3 *An Example of Perceptual Closure.* Do you perceive a square or four separate lines?

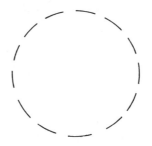

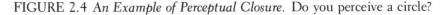

FIGURE 2.4 *An Example of Perceptual Closure*. Do you perceive a circle?

Interpretation

When we perceive, we not only select and organize but also interpret—and all in such quick succession that we might as well consider that these three activities happen at once. Interpretation is the process by which we form judgments or inferences about stimuli. Generally these judgments or inferences are of two basic types, identification and evaluation.

A person is continuously identifying the nature of the stimuli in his environment (or External System). When we hear a startling, sharp noise on a quiet summer night, we want to identify its probable source. Was it a firecracker, a backfiring car, or less likely, a gunshot in the neighborhood? Someone cleaning a rifle that accidentally discharged? Once we have established the identity of the sound as a firecracker and not a gunshot, we may then evaluate the stimuli as disruptive and startling, but not harmful. If we identified certain other stimuli, such as the sound of car wheels crunching on gravel and announcing the arrival of friends from a great distance, we would evaluate these stimuli as positive and pleasant.

In these examples you can readily see how the three activities of perception take place in such quick succession that for all practical purposes they can be considered simultaneous. We select the particular sound out of all the other auditory stimuli; we mentally engage in organizing it among all other stimuli; and we are rapidly absorbed in identifying its source and evaluating it as positive or negative, harmless or harmful. All these perceptual activities are the means by which we blend internal and external stimuli.

In the line drawing of Figure 2.5, can you identify what is shown? Were you able to identify the back view of a washerwoman? In Figure 2.6, do you evaluate the person shown as helpful or harmful?

We make these identifications and evaluations almost continuously in the course of our day-to-day experiences; we are subject both to routine and unusual or unfamiliar stimuli and also to favorable and unfavorable stimuli. Try to make a catalog of all the sounds you hear where you are

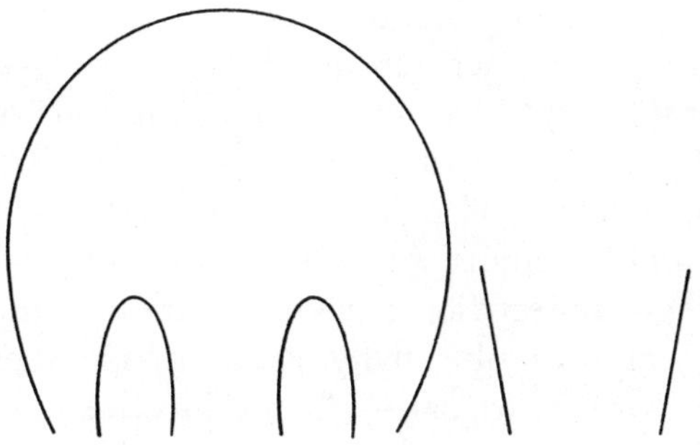

FIGURE 2.5 *An Example of Interpretation.* What do you identify these five lines to be?

right now, and try to make positive identifications. We will assume the sounds you pick up are harmless and routine.

How does an individual use interpretation—perceptual interpretation—in judging a typical communication, say a lecture or speech that he hears in a college auditorium? How does he evaluate the position of a politician coming to the campus to speak on a complex, controversial issue—perhaps the need for the government to develop new energy sources while protecting the environment from exploitation? The listener wants to identify the speaker's stand on the issue and then make evaluations about the fairness and validity of his general position and his supporting arguments. Does the speaker clearly present both sides of the issue or does he present only one side, speaking from a detectable bias? Does he attempt to be objective, fair, and impartial or is he subjective, unfair, and opinionated, neglecting all considerations that might detract from his one-sided approach or strategy?

FIGURE 2.6 *An Example of Interpretation.* How do you evaluate this person's attitude toward you?

No matter how you interpret or evaluate a speaker's position or stand on any given issue—whether you decide he is being fair or not in his approach—your interpretation of his approach reflects your own bias and is subjective. There is no way of getting around the subjectivity of perceptions, or one of its activities, interpretation. No matter how "objective" you attempt to be—and historians are aware of this in their attempts to write objective histories—subjectivity creeps in. Your evaluation of the speaker's position reflects your own subjectivity, just as the speaker's position reflects his subjectivity. However we can—albeit subjectively—attempt to distinguish between a subjective and objective approach to the topic on the part of the speaker. In other words we can evaluate his attempts to be "impartial." We may also make evaluations about what we consider the rightness or wrongness of a speaker's position, as we may decide that his position was unclear: "I can't get straight in my mind what he's talking about." In any case we make evaluations both of the impartiality of the speaker and of the rightness of his position.

When we listen to someone giving a speech, we take in the whole person. We observe physical appearance, gestures, body, poise, fluency, and other expressive external cues, as well as taking in what the person is saying. And very importantly we note how they all fit together. We form a certain impression of a student standing in front of the class saying how pleased he is to have the chance to speak on his topic—while sounding and behaving like a nervous witness ready to crack under cross-examination. We form a different impression of another student delivering his talk with the suavity of a Walter Cronkite. In the first case the speaker's appearance and behavior contradicted what he was saying. We didn't quite believe what he said. In the latter case all the cues we observed fitted together, and our perception of the speaker was quite different: we believed him. From the stimuli available, we made a subjective evaluation of the speaker.

The total setting in which the external stimuli are embedded has an impact on perception. Our perceptions of the person in Figure 2.7 are dramatically influenced by the particular situation or circumstances. Although his expression is constant, we make different interpretations about him as the setting changed. In each situation we inferred his attitudes, values, and personal traits; each setting affected our perceptions of him.

Notice, however, that it is not setting per se that determines our judgments. Our own internal experiences, attitudes, and values are superimposed upon the external stimuli in a given situation. The *blend* of these external and internal cues produces our perception. We must caution again that whatever interpretations we make are our own subjective creations. They may or may not be valid.

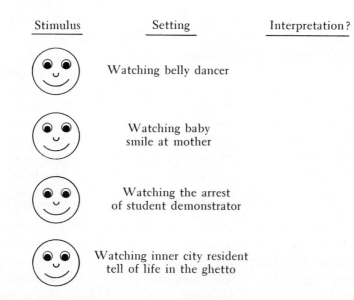

Stimulus	Setting	Interpretation?

Watching belly dancer

Watching baby
smile at mother

Watching the arrest
of student demonstrator

Watching inner city resident
tell of life in the ghetto

FIGURE 2.7 *Person Smiling.* Discuss the attitudes and feelings of the person in the varied settings. What are the implications concerning how and what we perceive?

When we observe someone praising or critizing another, our judgments about the appropriateness of the behavior are strongly influenced by the setting in which the communication occurred. Take the statement "You did that extremely poorly." When uttered by a child to a parent, a secretary to a supervisor, or a private to a captain, we tend as observers to be surprised or shocked by the person making the statement. We expect people in subordinate positions to "hold their tongues" toward people in superior positions. On the other hand, we would probably not be taken aback by the parent making the statement to the child, the supervisor blaming the secretary, or the captain upbraiding the private. Although the words were identical in all cases, the circumstances changed in each case and cast a different light on the behavior exhibited. We form different judgments about attitudes and personalities of individuals based not only upon what they say but also upon what their status or position is. Put simply, the total setting must be taken into account, not isolated stimuli.

Since stimuli we receive through our senses do not exist in a vacuum—but within an environment—the total setting is a major consideration. The nature of the environment is significant because we form *inferences* and *judgments* not upon separate stimuli but upon stimuli as they interact with one another.

Thus interpretation is the perceptual activity of making judgments or inferences about stimuli. We interpret when we reach decisions about the identity or nature of the stimulus. We also interpret when we make evaluations of what the cues imply or suggest.

We have thus far discussed the three fundamental perceptual activities. We've seen how people select—or tune in and tune out—certain stimuli and don't automatically perceive everything around them. We've also observed how people organize those things they do perceive—by arbitrarily switching between figure and ground and by tending to perceive simple and complete figures (though they in fact may not be simple and complete). Finally we've seen that we may make a variety of interpretations—or identifications and evaluations—of stimuli. These perceptual activities cannot be adequately accounted for by an isolated analysis of either internal or external stimuli alone, for these activities represent a blending of both kinds of stimuli. We want to stress the notion that our perceptions are the blend of internal and external stimuli. Yet we might confuse you if we try to deal with both internal and external stimuli at the same time. So as a convenience and for now, we'll arbitrarily separate and classify elements; however you must keep in mind that perception is not the result of any single element that we identify—but a blend of many contributing elements.

The Perceiver

Things we see, hear, smell, and feel do not enter an empty organism. Our present internal state or condition—that we bring with us to any situation—influences the perceptual blending of external stimuli in any given situation.

The perceiver's physical state existing at the time of the perception influences what he perceives; particularly *states of the organism that are necessary for the maintenance of physical life* must be taken into account. For instance the need for air, food, water, rest, elimination of body waste, and protection from extremes of temperature influence perceptions. A hungry person will be much more sensitive to sights and smells of food. And when one is looking for them, restroom signs take on high priority. An exhausted person will absorb far fewer stimuli than someone feeling fresh, vigorous, and well rested.

The perceiver's past experiences with the stimuli also bear on perceptions. A person tends to perceive what he's familiar with. Have you noticed that in the midst of the buzz and confusion of a party you can easily hear your name mentioned in a conversation? Studies have shown that

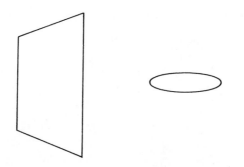

FIGURE 2.8 *Two Shapes: a Trapezoid and an Ellipse.*

Spaniards tend to notice a picture of a bullfight amidst an assortment of scenes whereas Americans are inclined to pick out a familiar hot dog or a baseball game. Policemen are sensitive to behavior suggesting possible criminal activity; teenagers loitering outside a drugstore may look suspicious to a police officer. Our training also affects what we perceive: speech therapists are especially conscious of articulation errors.

To illustrate how past experience influences perceptions, we offer the following demonstration. Here are two familiar shapes—a trapezoid and an ellipse (see Figure 2.8). We have no problem identifying these shapes properly. But notice what happens in Figure 2.9. We recognize these same shapes as doors and dishes. Notice that their shapes are identical to the original figures, yet we perceive them as rectangles and circles. Our experiences with these objects are such that we usually see them from foreshortened, perspective views; we almost never see them "head on" as rectangles and circles. Yet we know from previous experience that they have these shapes. Thus, when exposed to objects producing trapezoidal and elliptical retinal images, we automatically adjust and see them as rectangles and circles. This phenomenon is described as *perceptual constancy*. Past experiences not only affect our tendency to be sensitive to particular stimuli but also influence our ability to recognize stimuli even under "inaccurate conditions."

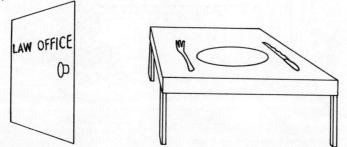

FIGURE 2.9   *Two Shapes: a Rectangle and a Circle.* What led to these shapes?

The perceiver's psychological state influences his perceptions significantly. His attitudes, motives, desires, and emotions affect his experiences of perceiving. We tend to perceive that which we want to see. If we have a positive psychological attitude toward a particular film director, one of our favorites, we bring with us a favorable predisposition when we attend his most recent film—which we have probably looked forward to seeing. Whether we are fans of Alfred Hitchcock or Ingmar Bergman, our favorable attitude makes us more attuned to the quality, artistry, and style of the new film than others in the audience, who are not perhaps as receptive to the director's methods and who do not share our initial favorable predisposition. They will not pick up the same cues in the film that we will.

Our strong desire to have our favorite team win affects the way we perceive a game. When watching a football game or other athletic contest, we tend to see more infractions of a questionable nature committed by the other side. Our team has played good aggressive football when we take out their dominating quarterback; the other team has taken underhanded or possibly illegal means to injure our star halfback.

Your emotions of exhilaration and joy, when your favorite girlfriend announces that she loves you as much as you love her, makes you see the whole world as pleasant and comfortable—the best possible place—even when you're the last car in a four-mile-long traffic jam.

During a political campaign—if we're partisan—we're likely to listen only to candidates of our choice and avoid speeches of opposition candidates. If we somehow find ourselves unable to avoid listening to an opposition candidate, we tend to focus selectively on certain parts of his speech —the bad or weak points. As for his good points—were there any?

The internal stimuli we have mentioned are just a very few of those making up a communicator's Internal System: all perceptions are influenced by a person's Internal System. We have now seen that the relationship between external stimuli and perceptions is much more complex than is assumed in the Common Sense View discussed earlier. We are not movie cameras recording what is before us; we are closer to painters —creating our own canvases. And you know how no two painters paint alike. Matisse doesn't paint like Picasso.

Summary

So we can see the perceptual process is indeed a complex one. The three activities of perception—selection, organization, and interpretation—are affected by the simultaneous blending together of internal stimuli of the individual and external stimuli from the environment. Taken together, all internal and external elements of perception operate within an interrelated system. Thus changes in any one element of the system will affect the total process. Perception is an active, creative, and subjective process in which everyone creates his own unique meanings.

Although we've referred to communication, relationships between perception and communication were, for the most part, only implied. In Chapter 3, we will thoroughly examine the direct relationships between *perception* and communication. At that time we will present a communication model based upon the perceptual process. For now, we only wish to recall our basic premise: perception is a fundamental component of communication as transaction.

Additional Readings

Mortensen, C. D. *Communication: The Study of Human Interaction.* New York: McGraw-Hill, 1972.

  Chapter 3, dealing with the nature of perception, presents a thorough review of theories, variables, and research on the processing of information.

Myers, G., and Myers, M. *The Dynamics of Human Communication.* New York: McGraw-Hill, 1973.

  In the chapter "Perception—The Eye of the Beholder," the authors discuss the perceptual component of the communication process, treating the perceptual activities of selection, organization, and interpretation. In the laboratory manual, they present a chapter devoted to perception exercises designed to illustrate concepts previously discussed. We should note that, although their treatment of perception appears similar to ours, these authors insist that perceptions are communicated. As you recall, our position is that meaning is the outcome of perception.

Editorial Staff of Communications Research Machines, Inc. *Psychology Today.* Del Mar, California: CRM, 1970.

  Containing numerous interesting and colorful optical illusions, Chapters 11 and 17 are exceptionally readable discussions of perceptual learning and problems in perception.

Tagiuri, R., and Petrullo, L. *Person Perception and Interpersonal Behavior.* Stanford: Stanford University Press, 1965.

  In this collection of somewhat advanced, in-depth essays, prominent theorists discuss theory and research on person perception. Some of the topics covered include person perception and problem solving, interpersonal perception and group effectiveness, interpersonal perception based on facial features, and the perception of traits in isolation and in combination. Although first published in 1957 and somewhat outdated, it does convey the depth and scope of the area.

Toch, H., and MacLean, M. "Perception and Communication: A Transactional View." *Audio Visual Communication Review* 10 (1967): 55–77. Also in *Foundations of Communication Theory*, edited by K. Sereno and C. D. Mortensen, pp. 125–136. New York: Harper & Row, 1970.

In this essay the authors fully develop the transactional view of perception and compare it to other explanations of perception. The essay also discusses some implications of the transactional view for explaining nonverbal communication.

Applications

Exercise 1

Have each member of the class make a separate list of everything in the room that he or she can perceive in a given time. Take about two minutes to do this; everyone should start and stop at the same time. Now compare the lists. Did you all perceive the same things?

Exercise 2

Rank in order the following occupations according to your perception of their status.

Occupation	Rank
politician	_____
clergyman	_____
professor	_____
actor	_____
used-car dealer	_____
police officer	_____
undertaker	_____
housewife	_____
student	_____
physician	_____

Compute the class average for each occupation. Compare your rankings with the class average. Discuss past experiences or psychological reasons leading to your rankings. Discuss the implications for communication.

Exercise 3

Occupation	Rank
politician	_____
clergyman	_____
professor	_____

actor   _____
used-car dealer   _____
police officer   _____
undertaker   _____
housewife   _____
student   _____
physician   _____

Now rank the occupations above in the order of your desire to engage in conversation with them. Compute the class average for each occupation. Was the class average the same as before for each occupation? Compare your rankings with the class average? Discuss some typical characteristics of each occupation which led to the rankings.

Exercise 4

Divide up into groups of four people. Discuss a topic you're all interested in for about twenty-five minutes. Then fill out the following chart for each person in the group, including yourself. When everyone has finished the charts (you may have to finish them outside of class if you run out of time), share your results with the other group members.

*Name*_____   *Name*_____
          (of describer)   (of described)

A. *Personal characteristics*
    1. Describe his/her physical characteristics.
    2. What do you think are his/her previous experiences with the topic we discussed?
    3. What are his/her attitudes toward this topic?
B. *How he/she communicates*
    1. Describe his/her manner of *verbal* communication.
        a. Level of formality and grammatical usage.
        b. Is he/she fluent or halting?
    2. Describe his/her manner of *vocal* communication.
        a. Variation in pitch or monotone.
        b. Volume of his/her voice.
        c. Quality of his/her voice (pleasing, harsh, strident, musical, other).
    3. Describe his/her manner of *nonverbal* communication.
        a. Facial expressions.
        b. Hand and arm gestures.
        c. Relaxation/tension.
        d. Body posture.

Now discuss the implications of this exercise for the study of: (1) selection, organization, and interpretation of external stimuli; (2) importance of perceiver characteristics in the perception process.

Exercise 5

Mister A: Picture a man who is warmhearted and honest. He has a good sense of humor and is intelligent and unbiased in his opinions. He is responsible and self-confident, with an air of refinement.

Mister B: Picture another man who is ruthless and brutal. He is extremely hostile, quick-tempered, and overbearing. Known for his boorish and vulgar manner, he is an unsympathetic person.

Rate the facial features of Mr. A and Mr. B on the following traits. Place an "X" at that point on the scale that best registers your feeling.

Trait		Mr. A	
waviness of hair	straight ___ ___ ___ ___ ___	very curly
grooming of hair	slicked down ___ ___ ___ ___ ___	disheveled
heaviness of eyebrow	light ___ ___ ___ ___ ___	heavy
directness of gaze	direct ___ ___ ___ ___ ___	averted
distance between eyes	close ___ ___ ___ ___ ___	far apart
width of nose	narrow ___ ___ ___ ___ ___	wide
mouth curvature	corners up ___ ___ ___ ___ ___	corners down
nostrils	relaxed ___ ___ ___ ___ ___	distended
fullness of lips	thin ___ ___ ___ ___ ___	thick
complexion	pale ___ ___ ___ ___ ___	dark

Trait		Mr. B	
waviness of hair	straight ___ ___ ___ ___ ___	very curly
grooming of hair	slicked down ___ ___ ___ ___ ___	disheveled
heaviness of eyebrow	light ___ ___ ___ ___ ___	heavy
directness of gaze	direct ___ ___ ___ ___ ___	averted
distance between eyes	close ___ ___ ___ ___ ___	far apart
width of nose	narrow ___ ___ ___ ___ ___	wide
mouth curvature	corners up ___ ___ ___ ___ ___	corners down
nostrils	relaxed ___ ___ ___ ___ ___	distended
fullness of lips	thin ___ ___ ___ ___ ___	thick
complexion	pale ___ ___ ___ ___ ___	dark

Compute average scores for Mr. A and Mr. B on each trait. Use the following key in assigning score values:

straight 1   2   3   4   5 very curly

Compare the averages for Mr. A and Mr. B on each trait. Were they identical? Discuss the elements leading to the ratings.

CHAPTER • 3

Trans-Per: A Model of Communication

Our communication framework, transaction, involves the components of perception, creating meaning, systems within a system, and ongoing process. With these components we are able to explain what takes place in any communicating context, no matter how many communicators are involved. With these terms we are able to analyze the whole range of communicating transactions from the simplest—the person communicating with himself—to the most complex—group and organizational communication. At the risk of being repetitious, we will take a brief backward look at some key points about these components. That you maintain a firm understanding of these ideas is necessary because all the material that follows builds upon these introductory concepts.

When we talked about perception, we observed that an individual knows only what he himself perceives with his senses. If a person knows nothing about the field of quantum mechanics—he has never even heard of it—it might as well not exist as far as he is concerned. In fact for all practical purposes, it does not exist for him. Therefore we can only know, and are limited to, the data of our own senses—those persons, objects, ideas, and so forth, that we individually perceive. Thus each individual will have a different idea of what the world is like, based on his own subjective perceptions of it. If we do not perceive an object, it might as well not exist and is not real for us. At any given moment, the world and its contents are what we subjectively perceive them to be through our own past experiences and accumulated perceptions. If we agree that we can only know what we perceive subjectively, then we do not know an external, objective reality out there. Instead we *create* what we believe to be external reality; by perceiving, we actively participate in the creation of our subjective reality. We have concluded that perception is creative, subjective, and active.

We wish to focus even more clearly on the perceptual process itself: perception is the *active* blending or mixing of internal and external stimuli. This blending consists of three interrelated activities of perception: selection, organization, and interpretation of stimuli. These activities take place almost simultaneously—we select, organize, and interpret in very quick succession. For all practical purposes we may consider that they take place all at once.

The outcome of these perceptual activities is the *assignment of meaning* to the stimuli. As we said in Chapter 1, *creating meaning* refers to the individual's creation of meaning out of his perceptions. Very important to an understanding of our framework, this activity of assigning or creating meaning is one of the essential components of the communicating transaction. It is one of the distinguishing features that tells us whether or not what we are analyzing is communication. If meaning is not generated, communication has not taken place. In conclusion, perception is the processing of external and internal stimuli; the outcome of the process is the individual's personal creation of meaning.

Next we want you to recall that communication has a systemic component. Communication must be looked at as a whole—an entire *system*. We can't, for example, understand communication by looking at any single element—either the words, the gestures, the situation, or the preconceived attitudes of the communicators—to the exclusion of other elements of the system; we have to consider all communication components as they operate together. Although communication is characterized by complex relationships among its parts, our framework allows us to account for all the diversity by means of two simple systems: the Internal System and the External System. These two major systems operate within the overall communication system. We are speaking of systems within a system—that is, the External and Internal Systems within our overall communication system, Trans-Per.

Thinking of communication as a system means: (1) no element of the system exists independently of the others; (2) a change in the system will affect all the elements within it; (3) a change in any element will be reflected by changes in the entire system; (4) no single element can be fully understood in isolation; (5) an understanding of each element as it relates to all other elements is necessary to the understanding of the whole system.

Finally we wish to repeat that communication is an ongoing process. The following components can be considered essentially as processes: perception is an ongoing process; the creation of meaning is an ongoing process; our two major systems, the Internal and the External, can be considered as ever-changing processes. Communication itself is an ongoing process. So the concept of process underlies our whole analysis. Process implies the idea of continuous change, flow, and forward motion. For our analysis, we have stopped or frozen the ongoing process—by dividing communication into components. However remember that the components work together in a close relationship: our attempts to analyze them separately is a fictional convenience.

In Chapter 3 we will focus on the two major systems of the communication process and the elements composing these systems. Our intention is to construct for you a model of the communication process from the components we have developed previously in our framework of communication as transaction. Our model is an elaboration, a refinement, and an objectification of our framework for studying communication.

Why Use a Model?

Meanwhile we'd like to raise a question you may be asking: "Why do we need models at all?" Aren't we just adding to our difficulties—with one more thing to study? Can't we study communication without going through the business of using a model? Put simply, why bother? Well we believe there are sound reasons for approaching communication through a model. We think that, once you see what models are, you'll agree that they offer distinct advantages in studying the communication process.

First let's make clear what models are *not* or, more precisely, how we're not using the term. When we speak of a model, we're not referring to an *ideal worthy of imitation*. For example Michelangelo's statue *David* is held out as a worthy model for aspiring sculptors. We're not using model in this sense. For one thing, communication is not a physical object like Michelangelo's marble; communication is an ongoing process. Another sense in which the word "model" is often used refers to the photographic, fashion, or artist's model. Nor are we using model in this sense. So now let's move on to what we do mean.

A *model is a means for showing what is fundamental to the process under study*. In the case of communication, models are typically symbolic diagrams with verbal explanations that indicate relationships of elements and that describe the essence of the event under study. Since communication is a process and not a physical object, communication models are not of a physical sort—such as miniature replicas of boats, planes, or rockets. The key notion here is that models identify significant features of the event being modeled. They're a means of our pointing out the critical elements of a process so that they can be readily grasped—and at the same time a means of our disregarding insignificant distractions.

One characteristic of a model is that it describes the thing or event being modeled only in specific ways—and not in a complete way. Thus several models of the same event or process may be constructed, each with its own emphasis. A model of a building emphasizing structural engineering illustrates a series of structural girders, concrete columns, joists, steel plates, elevator shafts, and so forth. On the other hand, a model of the same building emphasizing architectural design illustrates symmetry of exterior form, surface materials, placement of windows, and other exterior features. A model that emphasizes the engineering of the engine and suspension system of a sports car looks radically different from a model of the same sports car emphasizing body styling. The point is that *no single model can include every factor.* The fundamental elements of each model reflect the modelmaker's perceptions of what is basic to the process—what needs to be shown and what can be shown. One man's crucial component may be another's trivial irrelevancy.

Let's return to the question raised before: why have models? Our goal is to try to convey a clear, practical, and sound conception of the communication process. As you undoubtedly realize by now, the process of communication is extremely complex. How can we reduce such a complex event to a manageable form? How can we convey what is fundamental to the process? How can we describe relationships between components in the communication process?

Trans-Per is an elaboration of those fundamental components explaining the process of communication that we have already outlined. In addition its greatest advantage is that it's a simple model, with a small number of elements. And it is easily grasped. Despite all the complexity of any single communication transaction, our model simplifies and organizes the complexity. Furthermore the same analysis can be applied to the whole range of communicating contexts—intrapersonal, interpersonal, group, and organizational. Other researchers have thought of these four contexts as separate and unrelated forms of communication; we feel that they are all related and that the interrelationship is explained and clarified by our model.

We believe that Trans-Per provides the means of understanding the continuous interchange between all the elements of the communication process. We hope you will attempt to work with it and apply it to your own experience of communication. See if it does what we say it will do.

Trans-Per: Our Model

We call our model *Trans-Per*. The word is a combination of the first syllables of the words "transaction" and "perception." Ours is a transactional-
perceptual model. *Transactional* stresses that communication is more
than a one-way action or on-and-off interaction. It means that all the
components—perception, meaning creation, system, and process—are interrelated and operate simultaneously in every communication situation.
Perceptual suggests that the perceiver actively blends all internal stimuli
(that which he brings with him to a communicating situation) with all the
external stimuli of the present (that which is "out there" in the surrounding
environment) to create meaning. Our selection of these two terms is admittedly arbitrary; however, we feel that they concisely embody the components of communication that we feel are dominant. Transaction is our
overall approach to the study of human communication; it stresses the
individual's inseparable *involvement with the world*. Perception emphasizes the means by which we attempt to create a meaningful world.

Trans-Per consists of two interrelated, interdependent systems—the
Internal System and the External System. For now we'll describe the nature of each system and briefly introduce major elements within each of
these systems.

Internal System

The Internal System of Trans-Per contains all those elements or stimuli
that are within the individual. These internal elements are what someone
brings with him to a communicating situation. It's impossible to list all internal elements that an individual brings to a communicating situation.
Every person brings his memories, hopes, attitudes, fears, values, hates
—indeed, a lifetime of experiences. Those identified in Figure 3.1 are

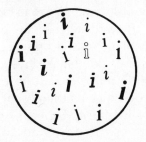

FIGURE 3.1 *Internal System*. The *i*'s represent internal stimuli that show up as
attitude, personality, sex, IQ, information, needs, and so forth.

among those that theory and research have stressed are the crucial elements in the communication process.

Elements of this system can also be called private cues or internal stimuli. These are mental processes or past perceptions or in-the-head factors that can't be observed directly. Their existence can only be inferred or assumed by observing an individual's behavior.

We tend to assume that overt behavior is related to certain internal states. We may be mistaken in this inference, as in the case of kindly old Mr. Knox who befriends widow Rutledge. He seems to have her best interests at heart—as far as we can tell from his solicitous behavior. But we later learn he's run off with her $15,000 of insurance benefits, money he assured her he would "invest for her in apartment complexes." Clearly his overtly helpful behavior did not reflect his true intentions toward Mrs. Rutledge. The point we're making is that we make judgments about an individual's internal states on the basis of observing his outward actions.

Attitude Element   A person's attitudes are perhaps the *most* significant internal element. Attitudes are a person's favorable or unfavorable evaluations of objects, issues, people, ideas, events, and so forth. A person has positive and negative attitudes both toward other communicators and toward the issues or topics being discussed in a communicating situation. We can look at *attitude* from three approaches. For now we only wish to introduce you to the major features of these three approaches, since we'll develop them fully in Chapter 4.

One way we can approach the attitude element is to analyze the *functions* it serves: attitudes are held for four primary reasons or functions, first described by Katz in his study "The Functional Approach to the Study of Attitudes" (1960).

First, someone may hold a particular attitude because it helps him gain rewards and avoid punishment. We're using the words rewards and punishment very loosely. Rewards refer to any physical or psychological gain or pleasure; punishment includes any physical or psychological loss or pain. Thus many businessmen develop positive attitudes toward Republican politics because Republican politicians have tended to have the best interests of corporate business high on their list of priorities. This function of an attitude has been called the *adjustment* or utilitarian function.

Second, attitudes also serve as *defense* mechanisms that help people avoid facing up to their distasteful, nasty sides. A poor, racially bigoted white may find it necessary to hold negative attitudes toward racial minorities in order to avoid facing up to his own inadequacies. He says to himself that he may not be financially successful, but he's "certainly better than those damn _____." He retains his own sense of self-esteem by being able to look down upon ethnic minorities. The function of this type of attitude is one of ego-defense.

Third, attitudes express the higher values or better side of our nature. A white may have a positive attitude toward racially integrated neighborhoods because he thinks of himself as a fair and humane individual. This attitude serves as a means of expressing the humanitarian and positive side of his nature. We will refer to this as the *value-expression* function of attitude.

Fourth, an attitude may be held because it helps us understand the complexity of events occurring in the world; this attitude serves a *knowledge* function. A person seeking to make sense of the extremely complex problem of the shootings and assassinations of political leaders may develop the attitude that "People are by nature aggressive, and most are basically evil." This helps him put all events connected with increases in crime into a neat little compartment in his mind.

In many cases we are concerned with *changing attitudes* by means of our communication: knowing the function served by an attitude enables us to find effective methods of changing attitudes—by means of appropriate communication. Unless we realize why people hold the attitudes they do, we may be totally ineffectual in effecting change. Two students, for example, may both have positive attitudes toward pass-fail systems of grading, but they may also differ in the reasons why they hold these attitudes. One feels that if he earns a D, it's just as useful as an A—for the purpose of getting through a course with the least amount of effort. He holds his attitude for a utilitarian reason: he wishes to avoid the work necessary to earn an A and to avoid the punishment or harm that would result from a D on his record. Our other student holds a positive attitude to the pass-fail system because she objects philosophically to the current grading system—with its emphasis on working for grades rather than on acquiring knowledge for its own sake. Her attitude expresses *values* she holds and wishes to communicate to others. Any attempt to change the attitude of these two people would have to be geared to the different functions served by the attitudes. A communication geared to changing an attitude held for value-expression may be totally ineffective in changing the attitude held for a utilitarian function. Persuasive strategies that are effective for changing attitudes held to serve one function may not work at all for changing attitudes held to serve some other function.

In describing the attitude element of the Internal System, we have first discussed the possible reasons a person may have for holding a particular attitude, that is, the function each attitude may serve. A second approach to understanding the attitude element is what we will call the *balancing of attitudes*. Although we have just talked about individual attitudes and the function each serves, the truth is we hold our attitudes in related clusters. We have an inner need or psychological drive to maintain these clusters of attitudes in a consistent and harmonious relationship. In other words we attempt to achieve a balance of attitudes, which—when achieved —provides us with a feeling of well-being.

For example people tend to like the styles of music and musicians their friends like—and dislike those they dislike. To have a positive attitude toward a friend, only to find that he dislikes Bach, your favorite composer, creates psychological discomfort. The striving for balance among attitudes may produce several possible reactions: you may, for instance, change your attitude toward Bach to achieve balance. Or you may attempt to create balance by persuading your friend to listen to Glenn Gould play one Bach Prelude—hoping to convert him. Or, if your attitude toward Bach's music is very strong and deeply felt, you might achieve balance by changing your attitude toward your friend: if he's no longer your friend, you have no need to like the same things he does. The balance approach to attitude has generated extremely interesting and useful findings for communication analysis and practice, which we'll explore in depth in future chapters.

The third approach to viewing the attitude element deals with ego-involvement, that is, how strongly or intensely a person holds his attitudes. *Ego-involvement* refers to the strength of an individual's feelings about the relevance or significance of a particular issue. For example you may have positive attitudes both toward a course in communication and toward a course in biology. Yet if you are a pre-med major, your level of involvement in the biology course would probably be higher than your involvement in a communication course. This attitude also serves to illustrate an adjustment function—serving a long-range goal. As we'll describe later on—although it's probably self-evident now—people respond more to things or people they're involved with compared to those they aren't.

Personality Element   Personality traits make up another major element of the Internal System. Whereas *our attitudes vary with the topic*—we like some things and don't care about others—*personality traits are more or less enduring and fairly constant across varying situations and topics.* Two personality traits demonstrated to have major consequences for communicating behavior are *dogmatism* and *self-esteem*. The highly dogmatic or closed-minded person exhibits consistent communicating behavior across

various settings and issues. For example he is highly susceptible to persua-sive appeals from an authoritative source. No matter what the topic is—as long as an authoritative source says so—he tends to accept it. On the other hand, people who are weakly dogmatic or open-minded exhibit less pre-dictable or less consistent communicating behavior. We will expand upon these ideas of dogmatism later.

Self-esteem refers to our underlying sense of self-worth or self-respect. Our self-esteem springs from our own and others' evaluations of our intel-ligence, appearance, physical abilities, talents, or any of our physical or mental characteristics. Persons with low self-esteem tend to be much more susceptible to persuasive appeals than persons with high self-esteem.

As we've learned in the previous chapter, internal elements have much to do with what we ultimately perceive. Those we've identified, at-titude and personality, are particularly crucial in influencing outcomes of communicating transactions: the particular attitude and personality ele-ments that make up an individual's Internal System strongly affect the meanings he creates.

External System

As depicted in Figure 3.2, the External System of Trans-Per contains all those external elements existing outside the individual's Internal System: all the things "out there" are elements of this system. They also may be called external stimuli or public cues because they are stimuli potentially available to all persons in a given communication setting. The phrase *potentially available* serves to stress the point that a stimulus in the envi-

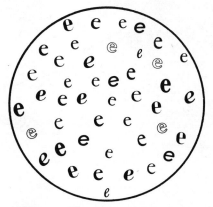

FIGURE 3.2 *External System.* The *e*'s represent external stimuli potentially available to a perceiver: verbal cues (words, content, arrangement, style), nonver-bal cues (body motion, characteristics of appearance and voice, use of personal space and distancing).

ronment may or may not be perceived by someone else in that same setting. We've seen, in Chapter 2, that we perceive selectively, focusing on a
relatively small number of all the cues that make up our environment.
Elements of the External System may be divided into two classes: verbal
and nonverbal.

Verbal Cues   Verbal cues are the words used in communication,
whether spoken or written. Words are elements of language: language is a
set of words or symbols used according to some meaningful pattern. Since
languages were developed to enable people to communicate with one
another, people speaking or using a language agree on which symbol is
linked with a certain idea, object, or event. In English-speaking countries,
we use the word "horse" to identify the animal the French call *cheval*. The
word is merely an arbitrarily agreed-upon symbol for, in this case, the animal we perceive. The muscle strain a person feels when he plays tennis
after a long layoff is not identical to his saying, "My body aches." The pain
he feels is inside; the words he utters are outward symbols of his pain.

Words, languages, and symbols are external stimuli. When we think
of words, it's helpful to distinguish between two aspects of meaning: denotation and connotation. We all recognize objects belonging to the category
called chairs, though there may be many variations: large, small, wooden,
metal, and so forth. What leads us to identify objects we call chairs are the
criterial attributes of chairs: seats, legs, and backrests seem to be essential
features; other parts such as armrests seem to be optional. *Denotation* refers
to those aspects of an association between a symbol and a category involving criterial attributes. *Criterial attributes* are features that must be present
for the object to be a part of the category referred to by the word. Typically
there is fair agreement among language-users on the relationship between
the category and criterial attributes associated with words like "tree,"
"dog," "bird," and "fish."

Connotation refers to those aspects of an association between a symbol and a category involving attributes unique to the person. We're referring here to *all* attributes, not just criterial ones. Connotation involves
attitudes, feelings, and emotions we associate with a particular word or
symbol. "Mother," "equality," and "love" are all words having varied individual connotations, depending upon the person's past experience. Each
of these words has associated with it—in addition to criterial attributes—a
variety of emotions and feelings. A child whose father is an alcoholic will
have feelings associated with the word "father" that are unique.

The content expressed through spoken or written words is a basic external cue. Topics of discussion, judgments, speeches, conversation, and

evidence used in support of arguments are a few illustrations of verbal content.

The form in which the verbal content is arranged is also a relevant external stimulus. For example, is a speech organized in such a manner that the main points are clearly emphasized, or are they hidden among a confusion of minor details? Do the strongest ideas come first, in the middle, or last? And finally the style of language is a prominent external cue in the communicating transaction. For instance can the vocabulary be easily understood? Is profanity being used? Humor? Figurative devices such as metaphors and similes? We recognize a big difference in style between "he's an egotistical person" and "he gets up in the morning, looks in the mirror, smiles, and says, 'Don't ever die!' " They both express the same basic content but the difference in style between the two expressions can make greatly different impressions on the listener.

Nonverbal Cues   Nonverbal cues include all external stimuli other than spoken or written words. Such cues include all bodily actions exhibited by a communicator: gross movement, posture, gesture, and facial response. Most students, for instance, don't realize how they appear to their teachers. Instructors are accustomed to looking at classes with students exhibiting various degrees of enthusiasm. About 10 percent are alert and already interested in the instructor's lecture. About 80 percent convey through their posture and facial responses: "Okay, I'm here. Now entertain me." And finally, about 10 percent suggest through their bored expressions, "I wish I were anywhere but here."

The distance between communicators is considered a significant external nonverbal cue. How close to one another do the participants in a conversation group themselves? Vocal qualities—such as the shrillness, quietness, exuberance, or monotone of a person's voice—can be analyzed for their contribution to the communication. We can detect a difference between the tone of "It's a nice day, isn't it?," expressed as a question, and "It *is* a nice day, isn't it?"—almost demanding that the listener agree. Other external cues that we take into account in the course of a conversation are clothing—and what the clothing expresses about the wearer. Is the person we are talking to aware of, or indifferent to, current styles? Is he well groomed or not? Does he prefer to be informal and casual in his dress or is he formal and "studied"?

All these nonverbal cues affect one's emotional, conscious, or subconscious feelings about what he is saying, how he reacts to the person he's talking to, and how he values himself. A person might speak in a consider-

ate voice and stand quite close to a friend toward whom he feels great admiration and affection.

And not to be overlooked are physical factors of the environment. Is the location comfortable where the communication is taking place? Is there enough room around the table, or are people crowded? Can everyone see everyone else clearly? Is the room too hot? Are the window shades flapping? Is the door slamming? Is it a familiar environment or a new and unfamiliar one? Intimidating or comfortable?

So far we have mentioned the two major systems of the communication process, the Internal and External, and have introduced some significant elements of each system. But we have not specifically delved into what communication is like—what the evolution of meaning is like. We will now focus on the nature of communication by means of the *Trans-Per* model, beginning with the most basic context, intrapersonal communication.

Trans-Per and Intrapersonal Communication

What is intrapersonal communication? "Intrapersonal" means *within the person*. Thus *intrapersonal communication is the individual process of creating meaning*. Figure 3.3 shows the intrapersonal communication system. Meaning occurs when perceptions for elements of both Internal and External Systems blend and overlap in the Trans-Per model. That area where the circles of the Internal and External Systems overlap represents the individual's creation or assignment of meaning. This portion of the

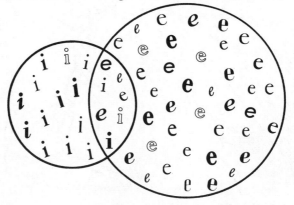

FIGURE 3.3 *Intrapersonal Communication System.* Meaning occurs when perceptions for elements of both Internal and External Systems (*i*'s and *e*'s) are within the overlap of Trans-Per. The overlapping circles represent the creation or assignment of meaning.

diagram also represents the outcome of the perceptual blending of internal and external cues. The communicator essentially uses those internal and external cues that are significant to him in assigning meaning at the time. We say "at the time" because at another time other internal and external cues may influence his assignment of meaning.

We mentioned that intrapersonal communication involves the creation of meaning within a single individual. *This does not mean that the person must be alone: other people may be present.* The communication taking place is considered intrapersonal because *no perceptual recognition or engagement occurs* between the persons who are present. Since no direct engagement takes place between them, they are operating in psychological isolation. For example you may be sitting alone in the campus coffee shop. Unnoticed by others, you may observe fellow-students as they walk, eat, talk with friends, and so on. Your observations may trigger all manner of meanings within your own mind about the students you're watching. Although from a physical point of view several persons are present, the development of meaning in this case is of an intrapersonal nature for no person-to-person contact or active perceptual engagement has occurred.

We will now look at some examples of intrapersonal communication in operation. While reading these examples, we want you to observe how the two systems of Trans-Per, Internal and External, come into play and how specific internal and external cues combine to influence the assignment of meaning. Notice how meanings change over time within the same person. Also notice how different people—because they have different Internal Systems—assign different meanings by utilizing different cues, although they may be in the same physical situations. These examples will illustrate the creative, personal nature of the development of meaning in intrapersonal communication.

Picture John Straight, a freshman, carefully groomed, sitting in a typical university coffee shop. This is his first exposure to a major metropolitan university—his first exposure to a big city in fact. He was raised by parents who instilled in him the fear of God, love of "clean living," and suspicion of drinking, smoking, and good times. He has been influenced by their ideas and dogmatism. Into the coffee shop walks a beautiful girl with flowing blond hair, a deep tan, a long dress, bare feet—arm in arm with her bearded boyfriend. They sit in a booth directly opposite John Straight and are busily engaged in conversation. Straight is immediately preoccupied by their easy affection and smoking and casual dress. In his mind, their clothes, gestures, and public display of affection are deeply disturbing. John says to himself: "They must be promiscuous types. I wish

he'd stop putting his arm around her in public. She should know better."
Our purpose is not to question the validity of Straight's intolerant judgment. The point is that certain internal elements—rigid attitudes—when
combined with certain external elements—dress style, gestures—produced the meanings he created.

In the booth next to Straight we find James Urban. Since his father
manages large hotels, he's lived all his life in various cosmopolitan
cities—New York City, London, Los Angeles, and Chicago. He is used to
the diversity found among city dwellers. When he notices our affectionate
couple sitting so close, he can't help overhearing their lively conversation.
He hears the girl describe a sports car race she has attended over the
weekend—the speed, the sounds, the danger, the crowd. And James says to
himself: "Now she's the kind of girl I could like. How can I get to know
her?"

Four years later, at the same coffee shop, John Straight notices
another blond, tanned girl in a long dress and bare feet talking excitedly
with her boyfriend and occasionally giving him a good-natured hug. This
time, however, Straight doesn't respond in quite the same way he did four
years ago. Since then he's become accustomed to the diversity among students, so much so that his roommate is a native of India studying Far East-
ern religions. If we would read Straight's mind this time, we would note
that the kinds of meanings he creates are now closer to those of James
Urban—more tolerant of diversity. Times have changed; Straight has
changed; his meanings have changed.

Although the examples we've presented are on the simplistic side,
they illustrate the operation of intrapersonal communication—how meaning is a personal, unique, active, creative affair. They demonstrate how
particular internal cues that we bring with us to a communicating
situation—our total background and experience—combine with selected
external cues to affect the particular meaning that evolves. They illustrate
how internal and external cues affect selectivity, organization, and
interpretation—and how meaning is assigned. They stress how meanings
vary among different people in the same setting, and they show how meanings can vary and evolve within the same individual over a period of time.

Let's now consider what happens when two or more people begin
communicating—interpersonal communication.

Trans-Per and Interpersonal Communication

Figure 3.4 shows the interpersonal communication process in operation,
according to the Trans-Per model. Here we have two persons engaged in

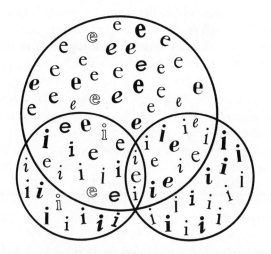

FIGURE 3.4 *Interpersonal Communication System.* Two people engaged in conversation; notice the two Internal Systems. Observe that there is only one External System of public cues. Notice too that both individuals have evolved some meaning unique to themselves, designated by the overlap of two circles, as well as some shared, common meaning, designated by the overlap of the three circles.

conversation. In comparing this diagram with the intrapersonal diagram, observe the following features. First, components of transactional communication—perception, system, meaning, and process—apply here as well as to the intrapersonal context. The major change is that things are a little more complicated. Second, interpersonal communication includes additional communicators: notice in our example the additional Internal System. Although we've shown only two communicators in the diagram, the number of additional communicators (added Internal Systems) is limited only by the number of circles representing Internal Systems that could be conveniently illustrated. We very well might have shown five people engaged in discussion—the diagram would have been very complicated and busy. Although for simplicity we've limited the number to two, the same principles apply to any number of communicators.

Third, notice that, regardless of the number of communicators and Internal Systems, we can say that there is just one External System—since it is for the most part and most of the time considered one External System by the participants. Recall that the External System is made up of public cues, consisting of all verbal and nonverbal stimuli. All cues "out there," including the public cues produced by the two communicators, belong to this External System. All communicators within the setting have access to these stimuli, which are potentially available.

Fourth, observe in addition that each communicator's meaning results from a blend of internal and external stimuli: see how each communicator has evolved a certain area of meaning that's unique to him and that isn't shared with the other communicator.

Fifth, we can see that the two communicators share some common meaning, that is, meanings they've each evolved independently have some shared, common aspects. This shared meaning is shown in that portion of the diagram where the three circles overlap.

Finally we might point out that the overlapping area isn't fixed—it has the ability to expand or contract as the communicators achieve greater or lesser amounts of shared, common meaning.

Let's show interpersonal communication in action through an example that illuminates essential points about its nature. Our drama consists of two players: Walter, who is from a conservative upper New York State family, and Thomas, who is an indulged mother's boy from Los Angeles. Here's the situation. Both are members of a class in communication and are a little puzzled about the nature of the homework assignment. So arranging to talk about the assignment after class, they meet in the hallway outside the classroom. Let's now bring in the pertinent internal stimuli that each participant brings to the situation—the ones that specifically apply to our example. Thomas, with a permissive upbringing, has a tendency to show warmth and express emotion, while Walter, from a conservative background, tends to withhold any demonstration of emotion and affection.

Walter begins the conversation at a psychologically comfortable distance for him—a little beyond three feet from Thomas. Thomas notes this distance and feels slightly upset. He begins to think, "Walter seems cold, unfriendly, and distant. Maybe Walter doesn't like something about me." To overcome his uncomfortable feeling resulting from the physical distance, he steps in closer. Walter notices this movement and feels uncomfortable. He thinks to himself, "God, I wonder why certain people are so confident and aggressive?" Meanwhile they are talking about the homework assignment, which they straighten out after a while. They part with a "see you on Tuesday." Let's analyze this brief encounter in terms of Trans-Per.

Did you notice that there was only one External System? All public cues sent out by each of the participants were external stimuli. Thus everything they said and did, and of particular importance in this instance the distances they took in relation to one another, became relevant external stimuli. In addition you should have observed how the meanings each evolved reflected a combination of external and internal stimuli. Each communicator brought his own set of internal stimuli to the situation; of special relevance in this instance are internal cues of Walter's rigid and Thomas's permissive backgrounds. Finally, although Thomas and Walter shared some limited meaning—denotative understanding of the nature of the homework assignment—they also evolved individual meanings unique to each of them—their personal reactions to one another.

Summary

We have now introduced the Trans-Per model of communication and have illustrated the operation of the major systems and their elements in both intrapersonal and interpersonal contexts. We believe Trans-Per is a sound, simple, yet comprehensive means of looking at the complex process of communication. But before we get too one-sided, too partisan, we will put up for consideration some possible weaknesses of Trans-Per—although we believe Trans-Per is fairly free of major weaknesses. You should also give Trans-Per a rigorous examination—to see if it is a consistent, useful model for understanding human communication. See if you can uncover any possible flaws in the model—other than those we mention.

We've admitted that we haven't considered all possible elements making up the Internal and External Systems of Trans-Per. Basing our study on existing theory and research, we've selected from current thinking in this field only those components that are consistently discussed by theorists and regularly used by researchers in communication. But the fact remains that variables probably exist which bear upon communication processes that neither we nor others have yet identified. So, as students of communication, you should keep your minds open to additional variables or possible adjustments that might add to the usefulness of the model. We certainly will. As future theory and research shed more light on the nature of communication, we will modify our views on the elements making up the two systems of Trans-Per, perhaps by dropping certain questionable variables in favor of other more promising alternatives.

We want you to avoid the pitfall of thinking of Trans-Per as *the* model of communication. We want you to avoid hardening your thinking so that you are limited to the terms of the systems and elements already described in our approach. Trans-Per is only a model—it's only a conception of the communicating process.

Perhaps the most important strength of Trans-Per is that it makes manageable the complexity of human communication. Although communication is an extremely complex process, Trans-Per contains only two basic systems: the Internal and External. Any element or variable a person can name fits into these two systems; any number of internal and external elements can be easily accommodated. Thus the model is simple to understand and easy to apply.

Additional Readings

Kaplan, Abraham. *The Conduct of Inquiry*. San Francisco: Chandler, 1964.

Chapters 30 to 33, on the structure, functions, and shortcomings of models in behavioral science, are excellent discussions on an advanced level. These chapters should be tackled only after more fundamental materials have been successfully mastered.

Mortensen, C. D. *Communication: The Study of Human Interaction*. New York: McGraw-Hill, 1972.

Chapter 2 on "Communication Models" is a good survey of the nature, strengths, weaknesses, and types of models used in communication theory and research.

Smith, Ronald. "Theories and Models of Communication Processes." In *Speech Communication Behavior*, edited by Larry L. Barker and Robert J. Kibler. Englewood Cliffs, N.J.: Prentice-Hall, 1972.

In Chapter 2, Professor Smith presents a good introductory survey of major types of communication models.

Applications

Exercise 1

Describe for the class different models with which you are familar: a model car or airplane, a model city, a fashion model, a grammatical diagram of a sentence, a plastic model of the internal system of the human body, or a blueprint of a building. What is the relationship of each model to the thing described? Discuss ways in which the function of each model is similar or dissimilar to Trans-Per.

Exercise 2

At any point during a class discussion, briefly interrupt the ongoing class to analyze what kinds of communicating transactions are taking place. After discussing these questions, try to reach a consensus.

a. Is the communication occurring in a system? If so, describe this system.

b. What kinds of external cues exist?
c. Have several class members attempt to describe the internal cues they are generating within themselves.
d. What kinds of problems, if any, did you have in answering these questions? Are the problems that you faced relevant to an understanding of the communication process?

Exercise 3

Divide the class into pairs for this activity. With your partner, agree to discuss a topic for ten to fifteen minutes. You may talk about yourselves and your relationship to each other, or you may prefer to discuss some controversial topic that you both find of interest. After this discussion, each person should individually write out answers to the following questions, if applicable:

a. My attitudes toward the topic we discussed are:

b. The reasons I hold these attitudes are:

c. My general feelings toward my partner are:

d. I feel that in this discussion I was: (check traits)
____ dogmatic
____ knowledgeable
____ understanding
____ ignorant
____ ego-involved

a. My partner's attitudes toward the topic we discussed are:

b. The reasons he holds these attitudes are:

c. My partner's general feelings toward me are:

d. I feel that in this discussion my partner was: (check traits)
____ dogmatic
____ knowledgeable
____ understanding
____ ignorant
____ ego-involved

After you have finished answering the questions, compare and discuss your answers. What does this exercise teach you about Trans-Per?

CHAPTER • 4

The Internal
System

As we've said so many times, communication is ongoing—it's dynamic. Therefore any time we talk about the process, we do so with the understanding that we are freezing the process and looking at it as we imagine it occurs. In Chapters 4 and 5, you must be particularly aware of this fictional stopping of an ongoing process. Otherwise you run the risk of oversimplifying the complexity of human communication.

In the last chapter we presented a model of the communication process, Trans-Per. We tried to introduce the two major systems of Trans-Per and to show how meaning—the substance of communication—is created. Now we want to examine each of these major systems in detail. As we discuss the Internal System, you'll become acquainted with the private cues or internal elements that each individual brings to any situation. In the next chapter we will focus on the public cues or external elements—those outside the person.

A word of caution: we have subjectively created and classified every element that we will present through our own perceptual blending of internal and external cues—but *no cues are exclusively or purely internal or external.* That point is so important that we'll repeat it. When we call your attention to an internal or external element, remember that the element was previously created by our own subjective blending of internal and external cues. We must strongly emphasize the arbitrariness of our decisions in classifying elements as external or internal. For example we'll discuss at length in this chapter the term *attitude* as an internal element. Obviously a person's attitude toward a topic represents things he brings with him in combination with those things that exist outside him. The attitude has evolved over his lifetime and is not purely internal or external. However, we will arbitrarily assume that it is an internal element at this stage of our analysis. The fundamental idea of Trans-Per is the perceptual blending

63

that occurs and not the specific assignment of elements to either Internal or External System. We want you to think beyond specific elements to the general process we're trying to describe.

Since we obviously cannot discuss *all* internal elements, we've chosen those we think form an adequate representation—attitude elements and personality elements. As we move through Chapters 7 to 10, we'll be adding more, but you might want to keep your own list of internal elements. We've provided exercises at the end of this chapter that should help you think about other internal elements.

As we've said many times, elements in the Internal System are those private cues *within the individual.* When we speak of internal elements or the Internal System, we are referring to the person and the in-the-head things he brings with him. Now let's move to a more thorough analysis of some representative internal elements, previously introduced in Chapter 3.

Attitude Element

Very simply we can think of an attitude as a *tendency to evaluate any object or issue or person in a favorable or unfavorable manner.* Can you think of one person, place, symbol, object, idea, or behavior toward whom or which you have no feeling or opinion? Probably not, for people tend to form evaluations of anything or anyone that they perceive. In fact the formation of attitude is directly tied up with our perceptions. Whenever we perceive anything, we attach meaning to it. An essential part of the meaning we form is our attitude, or our favorable or unfavorable evaluation of the object or issue.

Think for a moment about your experiences concerning this book. You may have looked at its cover or been attracted to the graphic design or typography. You may have been interested in puzzling out the diagrams of the Trans-Per model, while you were browsing through it. These visual qualities might have led you to form an attitude toward it—favorable or not. Or you may have had an attitude toward the book based on the remarks of a friend who was explaining Trans-Per to you. All of us have inclinations to evaluate or make judgments, continuously, about things we perceive.

Attitude and Attitude Object

Just as an arbitrary distinction is made by us between internal and external elements, so attitudes are created partly by what the person brings with him (his internal cues) and formed partly by the external object itself (or the thing being evaluated). We call the object toward which the attitude is directed *attitude object*. We call the element that the individual brings with him his *attitude*. And for the moment, we will treat attitude element exclusively in the domain of an internal element—to get a better feel for its operation.

An individual's attitude, like any other internal element, cannot be directly observed. We can only infer it from a person's behavior and responses. In their research, communication theorists have attempted to investigate attitudes by having individuals press buttons or mark questionnaires to indicate a specific attitude toward a given object. They have used numerous other experimental techniques to try to determine an individual's attitude toward a given topic or issue. By the way, the attitude element has been the most popular research variable studied by communication scholars. At the end of this chapter we'll suggest some additional readings which summarize the research on the attitude element; we'll say more about the results of that research later.

We have noted that we can't directly observe an individual's attitude and that we can only observe some response that might be related to it. In order to increase our insights into this complex and elusive element, we will now look at two interrelated areas of the attitude element: the *functions* an attitude can serve and the extent of a person's *involvement* with the attitude. (In Chapter 7 we'll introduce attitude as an element useful in helping a person maintain a balanced psychological state.) Although once again we find close relationships and overlapping in these areas, we will make some artificial distinctions and attempt to treat them separately.

Four Functions of Attitude

Of what use are attitudes? What do they do? How can we determine the influence of something we can't directly observe? And whose existence must be inferred? Talking about an attitude in terms of the function it serves is a useful starting place for understanding it. When we speak of an attitude serving some function, we are saying that we hold an attitude to serve some need—to satisfy some requirement. In other words, holding a specific attitude serves to satisfy some psychological drive. Keep in mind that a person's conscious or unconscious psychological motivation underlies the forming or holding of an attitude.

All of us are motivated or driven in one way or another to behave in certain ways. As you sit in a classroom, a bus, a class meeting, an employment office, or an unemployment office, you can see that your behavior has something behind it—a motivating force. In the case of this class, you may be taking it to fulfill a requirement for a degree or to prepare for a certain career you wish to pursue. The same general pattern underlies the other acts or behaviors you perform. A major difference between sitting in the classroom and holding an attitude is that the former can be seen; the latter must be inferred from some behavior. And the motivation for taking the class is obvious—you want credit for what you are learning. The motivation for holding an attitude is complex and not easily explained.

In 1960, Daniel Katz presented one of the more popular approaches to the attitude element; he attempted to explain why individuals hold certain attitudes by identifying the function their attitudes served. We'd like to use his basic model in describing one facet—the functions—of the attitude element. Katz found that people acquire attitudes for a number of reasons—that people have deep-seated psychological motivations for forming attitudes (or favorable or unfavorable evaluations). Katz describes four functions that attitude serves: (1) an adjustment or utilitarian function, (2) an ego-defense function, (3) a value-expression function, and (4) a knowledge function.

Adjustment   Perhaps the most common attitudes are those that serve adjustment or utilitarian functions. These attitudes are explained by our basic psychological motivation to like those things which satisfy our needs both to attain new goals and to maintain present circumstances that are consistent with past favorable experiences. Conversely attitudes serving this function lead us to dislike those things which fail to help us attain goals or maintain favorable circumstances.

If the motivation exists to satisfy some particular long-range objective, a person who has a desire to help people in a personal, concrete way will probably favorably evaluate—or have a positive attitude toward—the specific work involved in being, for example, a paramedic. However that same person will probably dislike jobs that require isolation or consist entirely of paperwork. We can see, from another perspective, that an attitude serves a utilitarian function if we consider the particular group that an individual chooses to join. An individual joins a group, such as a labor union, because it serves his own best economic interests: the labor union works for legislation, bargaining procedures, and working conditions that are beneficial to its members. Thus attitudes serve a utilitarian or adjustment function when they are consistent with the attainment of some future goal or objective.

In addition, an attitude may serve an adjustment or utilitarian function when it satisfies our need to maximize past pleasurable experiences associated with an attitude object, or to minimize past unpleasurable experiences associated with an attitude object. Thus your present unfavorable attitude toward the chemistry department may be the result of an earlier experience in a strenuous course in organic chemistry. On the other hand, you may have a favorable attitude toward lasagna because of your past pleasurable experiences with it.

In summary an attitude that serves the adjustment function helps us maximize rewards and minimize punishments. Or, stated another way, we all are psychologically motivated to like those things which we consider good for us and to dislike those which we consider harmful. Attitudes that allow us to do this serve an adjustment function.

Ego-defense   We often hold attitudes as a way of covering up or disguising the kind of internal insecurities or external threats we perceive. An attitude that serves this ego-defense function acts as a *defense mechanism*, allowing a person to distract attention from his perceptions of his own questionable self-esteem. It allows an individual to hide any undesirable feelings he may have about his own inadequacies. A girl turned down for the swimming team might make the following statements on her attitude toward sports: "Going to school and being on a team—you don't have any time left over for yourself," or "I hate the workouts and other stupid nonsense that coaches make you go through." Of course we're speculating now, but it appears that everyone holds some attitudes that are defensive in nature. They serve the purpose of allowing a person to balance his internal conflicts or rationalize his disappointments. In essence attitudes that serve an ego-defense function give the individual a "safety valve" by allowing him to express an attitude that protects his own self-esteem.

Value-expression   This function can be best approached by saying that it is just the opposite of the ego-defense function. Attitudes that serve ego-defense *hide* an individual's internal values or beliefs; attitudes that serve the value-expression function *express* an individual's cherished values or beliefs.

We gain satisfaction from expressing ourselves. And our satisfaction from expressing ourselves is greater if the conditions are such that we may express our deeply held feelings. We join groups so that we can reveal certain values without threat: religious, social action, and political groups provide us with the ideal environment in which to express very personal and cherished attitudes. But the key to this function still exists in the psychological motivation that causes us to want to express a personal or cherished attitude.

Consider the attitude implied in this statement: "Homosexuality is abnormal." In serving an adjustment function, this attitude may be expressed by a person who knows he may lose his job or friends if he were to say otherwise. In serving an ego-defense function, this statement might be made by a person who is married but notices and feels threatened by certain homosexual tendencies within himself; the attitude gives him a way of masking his internal conflict. But a person who honestly feels that homosexuality is abnormal may make the statement to affirm a strong belief that he maintains and acknowledges openly and honestly. The point is that three different motives may underlie the same attitude statement.

Knowledge   One of our strongest motivations is the need to *organize and structure* our world. Many of our attitudes serve this need. These attitudes provide us with standards for understanding our environment. One person may respect science because science gives a stable structure to his knowledge of the world. Another may respect a political ideology because it gives a stable structure to his knowledge of the world.

Perhaps the most common example of attitudes serving the knowledge function is the use of *stereotypes*. A stereotype is a generalization people make about a class or group of objects, ideas, other people, and so forth. It gives them a neat and simple way of meeting the drive to organize a lot of varied information. For example, to consider a painting, say *The Guitar* by Georges Braque, in terms of the school of painters known as cubists immediately helps a person view the particular painting with understanding. From the stereotype cubism, a person knows that this school of painters typically reduced natural forms such as a guitar or the human body toward geometric forms such as cubes; and he knows that the artists did this in order to present their paintings more as works relating to color, shape, and design than as works showing actual physical objects. When he looks at *The Guitar,* the stereotype cubism directs him away from the painting's flaws as a "likeness" of a guitar and toward the musical way the colors green and gray relate to each other on the surface of the painting; the stereotype helps him learn what the painting has to say about color and surface instead of what it has to say about the look of guitars.

Attitudes that serve the knowledge function give us focus and order, but they also give us a simplified view of the world. If a person looks at the painting *The Guitar* only to see how it fulfills the stereotype cubism, he will miss the unique value of a particular painting. Nevertheless we can't deny that we all have this need to simplify things; this drive leads to attitudes that serve the knowledge function.

Review and Outline   We began our discussion by saying that the attitude element has many different dimensions. Up to this point we have been talking only about the functions that attitudes serve—the reasons that

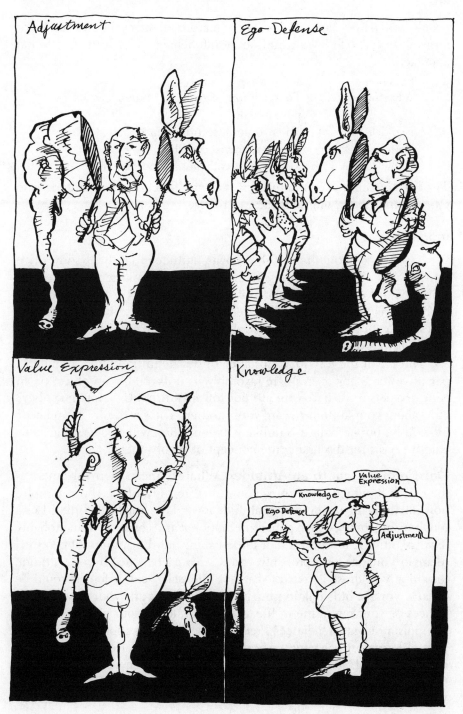

people hold particular attitudes. These reasons all satisfy different drives or motivations. The following outline should help you review the functional approach.

Function	Motivation
Adjustment	To maximize rewards, to minimize punishments
Ego-defense	To cover up insecurities and external threat
Value-expression	To assert cherished beliefs
Knowledge	To organize and classify information

The key concept to keep in mind is this: the function of an attitude is to satisfy some underlying motivation or drive.

Involvement

We have talked about the usefulness of an attitude in satisfying some drive or need. Now we shall investigate the levels of commitment that an individual holds toward a particular attitude. How strongly do we hold our attitudes? How involved in issues are we? How significant are they to us? These questions are fundamental to an understanding of *attitude involvement*—another facet of the internal element of attitude.

You recall the essential substance of our definition of an attitude: a pervasive tendency to evaluate favorably or unfavorably an object or an issue or a person. What's your attitude toward current U.S. foreign policy? How about your attitude toward your mother? You say they're not related? Obviously, but perhaps this unlikely juxtaposition will give us some comparative basis for discussing the concept of involvement.

Our Commitment to an Attitude What we mean by involvement is the extent to which a person is committed to his attitude. For example, how intensely do you hold your attitude toward free medical clinics? Low-rent housing for the urban poor? International arms control? You probably have an attitude toward each of these issues, but the amount of commitment to your attitude probably varies with each issue. If your attitude toward any of those issues listed is not intensely held or felt, it could be because you see little relationship between the issue and your own circumstances or your own time of life. Now what about your attitudes toward compulsory class attendance? Premarital sex? Legalization of marijuana? Pass-fail grading systems? Abortion on demand? Requirements for graduate school? The point is not whether you can effect any solution to these problems; the question is how closely related is the issue to you and your life and interests. Involvement is measured by how much you care.

The concept of involvement—ego-involvement—refers to the individual's perception of the significance of the attitude object to him. We can think of people as either strongly or weakly committed to an issue. Some conclusions from research that has been conducted on involvement are of interest here. For example researchers are in general agreement that a highly involved individual is not very susceptible to persuasive influences; furthermore, such a person tends to reject any position which differs from his own. Thus when a person brings a highly involved attitude to a communication transaction, it is unlikely that his attitude will be changed. Conversely individuals only weakly involved in a certain issue are quite susceptible to persuasive attempts and will yield more easily to persuasion.

Latitudes   In identifying levels of involvement, we need to distinguish between latitudes of acceptance, rejection, and noncommitment. These refer to possible responses that an individual may have to a particular attitude issue. The *latitude of acceptance* identifies the range of responses or stands that a person will accept, one of which is his *most acceptable* position. The *latitude of rejection* identifies those stands which are outside the range of acceptance. And the *latitude of noncommitment* refers to those positions on which the person has no strong feelings one way or the other.

The point is that involvement is not identified simply as a single evaluation of an attitude object. Rather it takes in the most acceptable position and some combination of the three latitudes. A strongly involved person is one who finds almost any positions other than his most acceptable position unacceptable. We would say that he has a wide latitude of rejection—he rejects nearly all stands but his own. Correspondingly he has a small latitude of acceptance and noncommitment. A weakly involved person, on the other hand, finds many positions acceptable—he has wide latitudes of acceptance and noncommitment. In addition he sees few positions as unacceptable: he has a narrow latitude of rejection.

In determining an individual's susceptibility to persuasion and argument, we must consider the degree of his involvement on the specific issue. If we perceive that a person is highly involved, we realize that he is unlikely to be persuaded by arguments for or against a specific topic. On the other hand, if we can say with confidence that he is only weakly involved on some topic, the chances of persuading him are fairly good.

Remember that involvement is a measure of the significance and relevance of an attitude to an individual. Moreover it can be thought of as a useful concept in predicting a person's persuasibility—or how open he is to persuasion. Although we wanted to use the concept to extend our development of the attitude element, our purpose in this section has not been to give you all the available or interesting research on involvement; instead we have listed some material at the end of this chapter that will give you more detailed information.

Personality Element

It is clear to us that the communicator's personality—what we call *personality element*—must be studied to understand the process of communication. Although all personality elements affect transactions, we have chosen to look at two we think most significant, self-esteem and dogmatism. In later chapters we'll introduce other personality elements—all of which are directly or indirectly related to those we discuss here.

Self-esteem

In this section we will use the term *self-esteem* to refer to an individual's perception of his own self-worth.

Although we've always been concerned with our self-esteem or the good or bad feelings we have about ourselves, recent trends in sensitivity and encounter groups have started many of us thinking about ourselves even more closely. Recently we've been hearing the question "how does that make you feel?" much more than we used to. How do you feel about yourself? What do you think about yourself? Are you worth worrying about? A person's answers to such questions will give us hints of how he perceives himself—or reveal his self-esteem.

The meanings that we assign to certain stimuli are directly related to the self-esteem we have. Ask someone to describe those qualities he respects or admires in a friend or wife or companion. Then ask him to give you an objective description of his own personality characteristics. It's almost a certainty that the two lists will have many similarities. Test this for yourself. We come to an understanding of our "self" through our past experience, and it is through experience that our perceptions of self are modified.

For example the person from a slum or ghetto may learn, through his experience and years of living there, that he is "disadvantaged" compared to those living in more affluent areas of the city. He knows, either directly or through the media, that he dresses differently from, and "not as well as," others. He may hear his ethnic group referred to in derogatory terms or in distasteful jokes. He may know that his parents can't get housing in certain places. He knows that for comparable work, he may get less pay than others. Naturally all these and other factors lead him to be unsure of himself and to lack self-confidence. In other words he may develop low self-esteem. In the manner of the "self-fulfilling prophecy," his future experiences reinforce this concept. Of course we may trace this same pattern in an individual with strong self-esteem. He may come from the finest neighborhood, attend quality schools, have a summer home in the mountains, frequently travel to Europe—and he may see himself as "advantaged." However self-esteem may vary with additional and cumulative experience; the individual's concept of himself evolves over time.

In the earlier section of this chapter, we discussed at length the attitude element. In our comments about the functions that an attitude serves and about the concept of involvement, we were referring indirectly to self-esteem and its effect on the formation of attitudes.

Regardless of where you are reading this, look around the room or library or wherever we catch you. Can you make estimates about the level of self-esteem of the people whom you see around you—those whom you know? You may say that you are in a library and don't know anyone. Yet you can still make estimates about the level of self-esteem of even people you don't know; people often make estimates of the level of self-esteem of strangers by analyzing their walk, posture, gestures, expression, and appearance. Our point is that by using all our past experience, we make judgments about people—both those we know and those we don't—and continuously make evaluations of their levels of self-esteem. In the library, taking a pause from a puzzling paragraph, we may observe a stranger walk into our perceptual range; we study his behavior and make conscious or subconscious judgments about how he regards himself—by the decisive way he walks, by a confident swagger, by flip behavior, or by his biting his lips. Valid or not, we make assessments of the individual's self-esteem by observing his whole range of mannerisms. Often we hear the comment that someone has a "high opinion of himself" or that "he thinks he's God's gift to the world." Such statements are correct or incorrect estimates about levels of self-esteem that only by knowing the individual in question could we possibly verify as true or false. And even then these estimates are subjective: we are apt to be very wrong in our assessments. A person who initially strikes you as self-effacing, timid, and withdrawn when you meet him at a party may turn out from later conversations with him to be a highly respected scientist holding a powerful position in the scientific community.

If you were all alone when we asked you to observe the level of self-esteem of others in the room with you, consider your own self-esteem.

How highly do you regard yourself? Your own assessment of your self-esteem strongly affects all your communicating behavior. The assurance with which you clarify or defend your stand on a certain topic both influences and persuades the other communicators in the transaction.

Normally we can think of self-esteem as existing on a continuum in which people are ranged from very high to very low levels in their perceptions of themselves. Individuals high in self-esteem are more confident of their behavior, perceive themselves to be more competent, and are more hopeful of obtaining favorable results from their efforts than individuals low in self-esteem.

Individuals low in self-esteem appear to be unsure of themselves and exhibit little or no confidence in ambiguous or in uncertain situations. For example the person low in self-esteem is often reticent about entering into unfamiliar communicating situations: he may be afraid to ask strangers for directions when lost in a strange city. Those low in self-esteem follow the crowd and tend to conform to known group norms. In addition those low in self-esteem are more persuasible than those who regard themselves highly. Individuals high in self-esteem question norms and are much less afraid of an independent position.

We are attempting to show that, first, we all perceive ourselves as a result of our past experiences. Second, we continually test these accumulated perceptions against present experience. Third, we make judgments about the self-esteem of others on the basis of our own self-esteem. Finally, we've shown you some of the differences that can be observed when we compare people of high and low self-esteem. We cannot overstate the impact of self-esteem on the way we assign meaning to stimuli.

Dogmatism

Dogmatism is a general personality characteristic: the popular terms *open-minded* and *close-minded* are used to describe less dogmatic and more dogmatic individuals. Professors who accept different points of view from students are open-minded; those who do not are close-minded.

The notions of open- and close-minded personalities are related to the concept of dogmatism developed by Rokeach in 1960. Highly dogmatic people tend to take a narrow perspective of the way the world operates, tend to be rigid in their thinking, and tend to believe only those people who are in strong positions of authority. Generally they are responsive to other highly dogmatic persons.

On the other hand, less dogmatic or open-minded people are more flexible in the way they view the world. Rather than seeing concepts in

absolute terms as highly dogmatic people do, they are willing to look at or tolerate other sides. The less dogmatic or open-minded person is more receptive to new ideas. He generally spends more time paying attention to the logic of a message than to the source of it.

Since dogmatism is a general personality characteristic, people who are close-minded on one issue are probably that same way on other issues. That a person is generally either strongly or weakly dogmatic has significant implications for our communication model. If a person is dogmatic on the issue of integration and thinks that "those people are in too much of a hurry," he is predictably dogmatic on other complex issues.

Dogmatism is not to be confused with the notion of involvement that we discussed earlier. Ego-involvement refers to a strong interest in specific topics or issues—it is not the general personality trait that dogmatism is.

Generally the person's high or low level of dogmatism will affect the way he processes information. If a person is highly dogmatic, he'll be less inclined to pay attention to the message itself; instead, he'll be more interested in the source or authority of the message.

A highly dogmatic or close-minded person enters each situation with a very simple mental map of the options: his way and the wrong way. The close-minded person's Internal System is so bound by past experiences that he is not affected by present information or by future implications—unless the source of the information is another highly dogmatic person.

Self-esteem and dogmatism have served to introduce the discussion of personality elements in the Internal System.

Summary

Throughout this chapter we've called your attention to attitude and personality elements that serve as examples of stimuli in the Internal System. After defining the term attitude, we looked at four of the functions that attitudes serve; we examined the individual's involvement and commitment as part of the attitude element; and we looked at the significant personality elements of self-esteem and dogmatism.

Although we temporarily looked at the Internal System as if it were a separate entity, internal elements should never be considered as operating independent of external cues. But, of course, you recall that our fiction of freezing the process is not the way it works in practice.

In Chapter 5 we'll carry out a similar analysis of the External System, looking at verbal and nonverbal cues and their related elements. To recapitulate, we can only understand communication when we consider the perceptual blending which occurs between the Internal and External Systems.

Additional Readings

Bettinghaus, E. P. *Persuasive Communication*, 2d ed. pp. 57–76. New York: Holt, Rinehart & Winston, 1973.

In this chapter, the author presents a good overview of various personality characteristics of communication. These elements, all of the Internal System, enable the reader to get a "feel" for internal elements in communication transactions.

Katz, D. "The Functional Approach to the Study of Attitudes." In *Foundations of Communication Theory*, edited by K. Sereno and D. Mortensen, pp. 234–259.

Katz defines attitude as "the predisposition of the individual to evaluate some symbol or object or aspect of his world in a favorable or unfavorable manner." He then describes the four functions which attitudes perform for the individual. Very simply, "the functional approach is the attempt to understand the reasons people hold the attitudes they do." Katz argues that it is difficult to change an attitude unless one knows the psychological need which a particular attitude meets.

McCroskey, J.; Larson, C.; & Knapp, M. *An Introduction to Interpersonal Communication*, pp. 54–76. Englewood Cliffs, N.J.: Prentice-Hall, 1972.

These pages represent a significant extension of the material we have called internal elements. Essentially these authors suggest that attitude can be discussed in more complex terms when one is dealing with attitude change. These pages, and the later discussion of dogmatism, should provide the reader with practical implications of what we've been discussing in this chapter.

Rokeach, M. *The Open and Closed Mind*. New York: Basic Books, 1960.

The definitive treatment of dogmatism, this book contains reports of research conducted by the author and his associates on the behavior of dogmatic people. Particularly interesting is his discussion, in Chapter 2, of the organization of belief-disbelief systems. The study of dogmatism has preoccupied many communication researchers; if you are interested in the element, Rokeach's book is a required source.

Wenburg, J., & Wilmot, W. *The Personal Communication Process*, pp. 171–175. New York: John Wiley, 1973.

Taking a transactional view, Wenburg and Wilmot discuss the many internal elements as important factors in the decoding of a message. Their discussion of dogmatism is excellent—if somewhat different than ours.

Applications

Exercise 1

Think of the two or three most basic attitudes you hold toward the following subjects:

Republicans	your mother
religion	marriage
sex	vacuum cleaner salesmen
graduate school	drugs
Women's Liberation	communism

Phrasing these attitudes as specifically as you can, make a written list of them. Next to each attitude, write, as honestly as you can, what kind of function you think it fulfills for you. Now consider these questions. Are the attitudes you hold beneficial or harmful to your personal growth? What effects does the holding of these attitudes have on your communicating? How personally involved are you with each attitude? How resistant would you be to attempts by others to change these attitudes?

Exercise 2

Think of two or three circumstances in which your behavior was not consistent with the attitudes you then held about that behavior. Without telling the class the reasons for the inconsistencies, see if they can guess them. Then ask them to explain the reason behind these inconsistencies. Every class member should have a chance to do this.

Exercise 3

Choose one or two classmates with whom you agree on most topics and one or two with whom you don't agree. From discussions in or outside of class, observe for a time your and your classmates' attitudes about the same attitude objects: this class, the school you attend, or some controversial topic. Observe your feelings about the relationships. Whenever there is a disagreement, observe what happens and write down the outcome.

Exercise 4

Marie H. Nichols, in *Rhetoric and Criticism* (Louisiana State University Press, 1967), cites a situation in which a U.S. Senator completely changed his stance on American foreign policy—unintentionally. The senator happened to read in public a speech in which his ghostwriter had changed the major thrust of the senator's known opinions. Noting the favorable public reaction to his speech, the senator gradually changed his stance, and eventually became a leading proponent of the views he had originally opposed.

Why do you think the senator changed his stance? Do you think he changed his basic attitudes or only his behavior? Can you think of other instances in which a politician either changed his mind or became more committed to his original position on some issue as the result of a public act.

Exercise 5

Think of the way you feel in these different situations: when you are with a group of peers drinking beer, with a group of all males, with a group of all females, with a group of faculty members and administrators; when you are in front of a large audience giving a speech; and when you are alone. Does the amount of self-esteem you have vary in these different circumstances? If so, why? Specifically, how does variation in your level of self-esteem affect your verbal and nonverbal communication?

CHAPTER • 5

Verbal Cues
The Nature of Words
The Word Is Not the Thing
Words Mean Different Things to Different People
Verbal Content
Logical Content
Emotional Content
Sequential Arrangement
Internal Arrangement
Primacy or Recency
Style
Dialect
Jargon
Figurative Language
Opinionated Language
Nonfluencies
Nonverbal Cues
Body Motion
Characteristics of Appearance
Characteristics of Voice
Use of Space and Distancing
Summary
Additional Readings
Applications

The External
System

In the last chapter we looked at the Internal System of Trans-Per and paid particular attention to attitude and personality elements. We discussed the functions of attitude, ego-involvement, and the personality traits of self-esteem and dogmatism as they make up the communicator's Internal System.

In this chapter we will outline the other major system of Trans-Per, the External System, and examine its major elements. In describing what's happening "out there," we will illustrate the nature of the public cues outside ourselves that influence communication transactions.

In both Chapters 4 and 5, these systems are discussed *as if* they exist independently of one another. They don't, of course. Although our eventual aim is to describe how communication is the result of the perceptual mix of both Internal and External Systems, it's impossible to explain how these two systems combine and integrate before you have a firm grasp of each system independently. We are allowing ourselves to separate the inseparable, temporarily. So for now, let's consider the External System of Trans-Per as if it could exist independently of the Internal System. And in focusing on the External System—just as in studying the Internal System—we will freeze what happens in the communication process. Rather than analyzing a complex moving picture—which would show elements in action, in transaction—we are presenting a still picture.

What we intend to do in this chapter is offer our classification of—our way to categorize—the contents of the "out there," the elements of the External System. We're not going to attempt to make a comprehensive survey. For one thing, we can't; there's too much to cover. So we'll be selective. We do believe, however, that the external elements that we point out will give you a substantive foundation for a later, detailed consideration of how the two systems combine.

The categories we present are meant to help you visualize things as they exist "out there." But keep the following caution in mind. Since any classification system we might set up is determined by our accumulated perceptions, the categories we present are the results of our minds and those of other theorists and researchers in this field. Using our own ideas and those of other researchers, we created these categories. They don't exist except as we have perceived and created them to exist—as conveniences for helping us in this study. We're asking you to assume for the time being that the classifications we describe *are* descriptions of things "out there"—while warning you that they are creations or conveniences.

We have conceived of the External System of Trans-Per as comprised of two major parts: verbal and nonverbal. We will begin with an examination of the verbal.

Verbal Cues

As noted previously, verbal cues are the words we use, whether spoken or written. Let's begin by looking at the nature of words.

The Nature of Words

The first thing to note is that words are *symbols.* A symbol is something standing for or taking the place of something else, whether it be an object, a behavior, or a feeling. Thus we have words like "diploma," "promotion," and "satisfaction." There are two points about words or symbols that we'd like to stress: (1) the word is only a representation of the thing and not the thing itself, and (2) words mean different things to different people.

The Word Is Not the Thing   Since this is an obvious point, you reply, "Come on now, anyone can tell the difference between the word 'flag' and the physical object flag. So what's your point?"

The point is that we often confuse words with the things they represent or stand for. How? By reacting at times to the word rather than to the thing represented by the word. The most obvious examples can be seen in responses people make to food. We all know people—maybe you're among them—who enjoy the taste and texture of a new food, until they're told it's liver, or rabbit, or snails. And then they turn pale and ask to be excused. Some people look much more appreciatively at a woman's dress once they find out it's an original by Halston. Certain people act quite differently once they find out someone's an ex-convict or a radical or a cop.

Words Mean Different Things to Different People   "Sure," you say, "I know that I sometimes have trouble communicating with someone —because one of us probably misunderstood the other. But why precisely do words mean different things to different people?" To understand why, we're going to have to grapple with two related ideas: (1) no necessary connection exists between a word and what it represents, and (2) words are abstractions having both denotative and connotative meanings that vary.

First, no necessary connection exists between a symbol or word and what it represents. We could rename "horse" and call it "goat"—as long as we agreed. The term "horse" is an arbitrary naming. We gradually learn the specific meaning of words in our particular language. Otherwise you'd know automatically what we meant when we used the words "systemic," "processual," and "transactional." But you probably didn't know what these words meant until you studied their meanings. You are familiar with words which have multiple meanings or definitions in the dictionary. The word "fly" can refer to an insect, to the act of piloting a plane, and to a baseball hit in a high arc, usually caught. To sum up, the fact that the meanings of words are in practice agreed upon by tradition and consensus does not mean that everyone agrees or has to agree to a particular meaning. The fact that the same word can have several seemingly unrelated meanings can create unintended and involuntary disagreement. People only transmit words; they don't transmit meanings.

Second, words frequently mean different things to different people because they're abstractions. What do we mean by that? A *single word is very limited*: it doesn't describe completely or include full details about an object, an idea, an experience, or anything else for that matter.

The problem is that whenever we begin to use words, we may have one picture in mind when we use a word, but someone else may have a completely different notion in mind. When you hear the word "dog" what do you picture? We happen to think of dachshunds; both of us own dachshunds. But we're sure many of you immediately had other breeds in mind, of different size, appearance, and color combinations.

When we are asked to read an abstract, say, of a novel, play, or speech, we see that the abstract contains only essential plot details, main characters, and major points, but leaves out all the minor plot developments, supporting characters, and minor details. Essentially an abstraction is an omission of details. We'll be better able to see what we're getting at by looking at what semanticists, scholars concerned with symbols and their meanings, call the abstraction ladder or levels of abstraction.

The lowest level, level one, of the abstraction ladder is what's actually going on. We mean what's going on "out there"—what's actually happening. Everything that you are experiencing as you turn the pages of this book. We can't describe what's *actually* going on because the moment we use words, we omit details and thus fail. Not even the novelist James Joyce could get so refined in his description and so sensual in his wording that his description of turning pages would be equal to the live experience. Level two is the next level of abstraction. It's what you *see*. Right off you probably all recognize that you don't see everything. For one thing, you can't see everything. Where you happen to be located in relation to the object or event limits what you are able to see. You all know how little you can see if you're seated on the thirtieth row of the ten yard line. For another thing, as you've seen in Chapter 2, you're selective about what you observe in the environment. You may see only the other team's illegal procedures, while rooters for the other team may see only the unfair players on your team. At level three, you begin to describe what you see. At this point you use words; you haven't until this point. At this level you attempt to describe what you see. At level four, you *generalize* from what you've described at level three. In other words, the relation between the words you use and the thing you are attempting to describe becomes more vague. At level five, we generalize beyond level four. And so on. At each succeeding level, we leave off more details. We are in essence attempting to describe more and more by using less and less detail. But we, ourselves, are somewhat vague and abstract at this point. Let's try to clear things up by *adding detail*.

Let's play a guessing game. Your task is to identify the thing we're referring to as soon as you know what it is. Okay? We'll begin with a very high level of abstraction and work our way down the abstraction ladder. Here we go. Physical object. This leaves out an idea, a ghost, or a dream, but it could still could be almost anything, right? Okay, let's become more specific. Utilitarian device. Better? Not much. It still could be many things: a shovel, a computer, or a bandage. Here's another clue: mode of transportation. Are you closing in on it? Is it a plane, a ship, a car, or a horse? All right, we'll give you a more specific clue: car. How's that? This still isn't very specific, is it? Is the car American, Japanese, German, Italian, or Swedish? Is it a family sedan, a convertible, or a sports car? Let's say it's a Porsche. Does that do it? Not quite. Is it a 911, a 914? What color is it? What engine does it have? What kind of upholstery? To know precisely what car we mean, you'd have to see the car—have the opportunity to examine it. At that point we would be at level one, the level without words, without abstraction.

As soon as you use words, abstraction starts; and when abstraction starts, room for differences in meaning starts. For example maybe the clue "physical object" did not exlude the word "idea" for you because you believe ideas always and only exist in the physical biochemistry of the brain. Or perhaps "transportation" meant to you "carrying devices that are not self-propelled" so you thought of a wagon. And so on. Abstracting always leaves room for different meanings.

In addition, words mean different things to different people through differences in denotation and connotation. As we've seen in Chapter 3, denotation refers to those aspects of an association between a symbol and a category involving criterial or essential attributes. Criterial attributes are those features that must be present for the object to be a part of the category referred to by the word. For example we all know what cars are. They have four wheels, an engine, and a place for a driver and perhaps a passenger or passengers. However, as we've seen in the previous paragraph, the word "car" is not specific. It could be any one of a hundred different automobiles. What we've identified are the criterial attributes of the word car—the denotation of the word car. To identify the precise, specific car we have in mind, we'd have to be much more specific, adding many more words to furnish precise details.

In general, denotation doesn't give us as much trouble as connotation. Typically people agree about the denotative or criterial attributes of words. We all know what others mean by cow, sheep, buffalo, sports car, bikini, and marijuana; however, as we will see, the connotative association between a symbol and a category is far more problematic.

Connotation involves those attributes that are unique to the individual and to his or her own past experiences with the object, behavior, or symbol. To David money may mean luxury—the ability to buy whatever he wants. To Karyl it may mean independence. To Jim it may mean power and prestige. A De Tomaso Pantera sports car may mean speed to one and maneuverability to another. Connotative associations are unique or peculiar to each person. When we communicate with one another, the symbol or word automatically triggers different connotative responses. We all generally agree on the denotative or criterial attributes of school, professor, father, mother, senator, Chicano, and acid. But we probably have widely divergent connotations for each of them. If you've had good experiences in school, your connotative associations about the word "school" will be quite different from those people who have had unpleasant experiences in school.

In conclusion keep in mind that words are external cues—elements of the External System of Trans-Per. Although words or symbols are being treated here as external elements, the ways in which they're interpreted, the ways in which they come to have meaning, involve the blending of both Internal and External Systems. For example an attitude we hold is an internal element; the verbal expression of that attitude is an external element. Remember that as processual elements, these stimuli don't actually reside in the External or Internal System. We arbitrarily assign them to be external or internal elements depending on the particular transaction under analysis.

Verbal Content

In discussing *verbal content*, we will distinguish between the *logical* and *emotional* content of the message.

Logical Content   Courses in communication have often stressed the advantages of logical argument for a communicator who is attempting to establish the credibility of his message. We include, as part of the logical content, the *evidence* an individual uses to bolster a claim or assertion he may make—all the well-founded facts and statistics that support a claim. The evidence may also include various opinions of experts. Evidence is the means a communicator uses to support his position.

Evidence *by itself* will not have any definitive influence: the communicator will not *necessarily* be more effective if he uses evidence than if he does not. The outcome seems to hinge upon the other elements that are blending at the time. For example, if a communicator has high personal credibility, he doesn't need to rely upon the use of evidence as much as he would if he had low credibility. The point is that the meaning we assign after listening to a message or speech is not the result of any single variable such as evidence: the development of meaning is the result of a blending of many relevant external and internal cues operating together. It makes little sense to speak of effects due to any single variable. In later chapters we will expand upon the transactional blend of various external and internal cues in various communication contexts.

In addition to evidence, we will include under logical content the amount of information the communicator provides on an issue. Let's say your task is to persuade someone to accept a particular point of view on, say, the legalization of marijuana or the lowering of the legal drinking age. In your communication, how much information on the topic should you provide? Should you present only those points supporting your point of view? This approach is known as the *one-sided message*. Or should you also present evidence in support of the opposite point of view? In other words, should you also present weaknesses in your own position? This second approach is known as the *two-sided message*. Just as the influence of evidence is not fully understood, no clear-cut conclusion has emerged on the question of whether a one-sided is preferable to a two-sided message in effective communication. Again the effect of a one-sided or two-sided message depends upon what other cues are operating at the same time. A one-sided message may be adequate for a listener of low or average intelligence; highly intelligent listeners, however, may be more suspicious of one-sided messages.

But logical content makes up only half of verbal content; the other half involves emotional content of the message.

Emotional Content   Threat is one of the common emotional appeals used in communication. A threatening message announces that, if the stated recommendations are not followed, dire consequences will come to the person listening to the message, or to someone he loves. For example, the original cancer commercials on television stressed the possible dangers of persisting in harmful cigarette smoking. They were effective, but only to a point. Too many people said to themselves, "I can't give up smoking. It's not worth it. If I go, I go smoking." Consequently later commercials tended to focus on the message that loved ones should not start to smoke. An often-used commercial showed a father and son walking and playing together, with the narrator emphasizing how the son tried to do everything his father did—how he tried to model himself after his father. With every scene of shared activity, the narrator would intone, "Like father, like son." At the end of the commercial, the father lights a cigarette, the son watches the father smoking, and the narrator says again, "Like father, like son?" in a very gloomy voice. We've all been exposed to threats used in numerous televised campaigns; those showing us car accidents and urging us to drive with care are a good example of threat.

As you can probably guess, the effect of threat depends upon what other internal and external stimuli are present. Threat, for instance, is more effective used against individuals low in self-esteem than against those high in self-esteem. Similarly threat is taken more seriously by the listener when uttered by someone known to be highly credible than when uttered by someone of lesser reputation.

Emotional content, however, isn't restricted to threat appeals. Humor may be a relevant stimulus: the overall meaning of a speech or message may be radically changed depending on the presence or absence of humor. Speakers and instructors often use humor either to help illustrate a point or to relieve the tedium of an otherwise unrelieved presentation. Love, as an emotional appeal, has been used in television commercials to encourage people to use seat belts: "Show someone you love them; have them buckle up." The appeal of love has been used to encourage people to make long-distance phone calls to friends and family far away. In addition, the emotional appeals of anger and revenge may be employed as stimuli. Hitler used hate appeals against the Jews in his messages to the German people. Orators of various racial groups, whites and blacks, Chicanos and Anglos, American Indians and whites, have used hate appeals against their opponents. Of course you can probably think of other emotional appeals typically used in political speeches, in fund-raising, and in other controversial causes.

Sequential Arrangement

Although what is said is obviously pertinent, we mustn't overlook how a message is presented, or to be more precise, how the ideas of a message are arranged sequentially. We've all heard the saying, "It's not what you say, it's *how* you say it."

Internal Arrangement   Internal arrangement refers to the organization of content by the individual communicator. Let's say you have three points to make in a speech you wish to be persuasive: you have one strong argument, one moderately strong argument, and one relatively weak argument. The question is how do you arrange these three arguments for effective presentation? Where do you place your strongest argument—first, last, or in the middle? When a speaker arranges his arguments with the strongest placed first, he's using what is called the *anticlimax order*. When he arranges arguments with the strongest argument put last, he's using the *climax order*. Researchers seeking definitive answers to this question have failed in their attempts: studies have conflicted—sometimes supporting the effectiveness of climax order and sometimes of anticlimax order. Once again the reason is almost certainly due to the contribution of other variables that happen to be blending at the time.

Primacy or Recency   These two terms refer to a situation in which two speakers are debating—each advocating an opposite point of view. In a situation like this, is a speaker more effective speaking first or speaking last? In communication research, this question is known as the primacy versus recency issue. You might feel intuitively that in speaking first (primacy) you can capture the attention of the listeners and have your message impressed upon their clear, fresh minds. Speaking at the end (recency), however, has the advantage of imprinting your message last on the listeners' minds. Will the listeners forget your ideas if you speak first? If you speak last, will the listeners not listen to your speech because they have already accepted the point of view of the first speaker? Early research seemed to favor primacy; later research tended to contradict these early findings. The best we can say about primacy and recency is—that it depends; very frankly, we don't know. As is true of all of our other external variables, the effect of the message upon the listener depends upon what other cues are also in operation—and not simply upon whether the message came first or last.

Style

Whether a person speaks or writes in a simple or complex manner is part of his verbal style. There's a clear stylistic difference between these statements: "The less the attraction between A and B, the more nearly strain toward symmetry is limited to those particular X's co-orientation toward which is required by the conditions of association" (Newcomb, 1953) and "If two people don't like each other, they'll talk only about what's necessary." Some people prefer to express themselves simply and directly; others use more convoluted syntax and more complex vocabulary.

In this final section on verbal cues, we will discuss verbal style—*how* things are said rather than what is said. Verbal style is an extremely elusive term to define or describe. We can speak of many types of verbal style: an individual speaker may be casual or formal, friendly or distant, argumentative or seemingly reasonable, grammatically correct or incorrect, imaginative or pedestrian, fluent or hesitant, figurative or literal, biased or fair, and so forth. Style refers to that combination of the above-mentioned qualities that is unique to the individual.

In this section we will examine various aspects of style: (1) dialect, including pronunciation and syntax, (2) jargon, (3) figurative language, (4) opinionated language, and (5) nonfluencies.

Dialect Dialect is an immediately identifying characteristic of one's spoken style. We all recognize Southern or New England accents and Bronx, Italian, or Black dialects. In the Southwest, the Mexican-American dialect is familiar. These dialects frequently produce stereotypic responses among listeners. In other words some people have set attitudes toward people who speak various dialects. Although these may be positive—many

Americans admire a British accent—they are more typically negative, particularly toward people who speak dialects from unfamiliar cultures.

Principal dialectal variations involve the presence, absence, or distortion of the following sounds:

1. The presence or absence of the *r* sound in final positions just after a vowel, as in "beer," "mother," and "Watergate."
2. The sound of *a* in such words as "aunt," "ask," and "rash."
3. Pronunciation of the vowel in such words as "dog," "talk," and "all."
4. The substitution of *d* for *th* in words like "this" and "that."
5. The substitution of *t* for *th* in such words as "three" and "thing."

In dialects, standard syntax—or the way a speaker puts words together to form sentences—is frequently altered. For example speakers of certain regional dialects may exhibit some or all of the following characteristics (Hopper and Naremore, 1973):

1. Generally accepted use of the possessive case is not observed. Standard English: "Joe's pencil."
   Dialect: "Joe pencil."
2. Negation is expressed by double negatives (often with "ain't"). Standard English: "I don't have a pencil."
   Dialect: "I ain't got no pencil."
3. Subject-verb agreement differs. Standard English: "We were there" or "They are here."
   Dialect: "We was there" or "They is here."
4. *S* is omitted from third-person singular verbs. Standard English: "He sings."
   Dialect: "He sing."
5. The use of "is" is omitted in the present tense. Standard English: "I am going" or "He is here."
   Dialect: "I going" or "He here."

Research shows that dialect and syntax may be among the most critical factors affecting our attitudes toward speakers. Dialect and syntax have a strong bearing upon our perceptions of a speaker's credibility. Perceptions of competence, intelligence, honesty, trustworthiness, and even of ambition are closely linked with dialect. For instance some white Americans of low intelligence perceive speakers of Black or Spanish dialects to have lower intelligence, lower ethical standards, and lower ambition than they have. Dialect is a critical external cue which feeds into the transactional blend.

Jargon   Scientists, engineers, mathematicians, and physicians are especially prone to using technical language—*jargon*. Unless you're knowledgeable in the use of these terms, you're lost. "Proximal and distal stimuli," "monotonic functions," and "sum of squares" are typical terms from psychology and statistics. Every technical field has its own vocabulary or jargon. But jargon isn't necessarily bad; it's sometimes even beneficial since, for those initiated into it, it may be precise, convenient, and time-saving. One word may stand for a whole series of words or even sentences. The technical phrase "sum of squares," for example, is commonly used in statistics and refers to the sum of the squared deviations about the mean score. To understand this phrase one must know, in turn, what's meant by "sum," "squared deviations," and "mean score." The phrase "sum of squares" is very handy, short, and accurate. The only problem with jargon is that it's precise and economical only for those who are familiar with the terms. For all others it's confusing. In certain circumstances, a speaker using jargon may confuse, intimidate, and antagonize. Many professionals are unaware of the technical nature of their specialized vocabulary and easily forget that the layman is confused and baffled by it.

Figurative Language   The use of *figurative language*—metaphors, similes, and other literary devices—is also an aspect of style. A metaphor establishes a likeness or analogy between two unrelated objects—usually not connected. For example Robert Frost wrote, "The day the sun lets go ten million lizards out of snow."

Similes also relate two previously unrelated characteristics but use the words "like" or "as" to make the relationship or connection. For instance Gerard Manley Hopkins wrote that the grandeur of God would show itself "like shining from shook foil." Both of these lines are obviously very rich in emotional expression. What's the effect of metaphors and similes on listeners? Poets seem to know that it engages the senses and emotions as well as the intellect and therefore increases the range of the appeal. The impact of metaphors and similes as external stimuli, however, is not well established at this point.

Opinionated Language   In using *opinionated language,* a person not only states his position but also overstates it. A user of opinionated language supports those who agree with him and rejects and attacks those who oppose him. Whereas a nonopinionated stance might be "marijuana should be legalized," an opinionated statement on the same issue might be "only a fool would oppose the legalization of marijuana." Opinionated statements are heavily slanted, much stronger statements than nonopinionated ones. A highly dogmatic listener is inclined to accept opinionated statements when uttered by a speaker he considers authoritative. Notice the complex blending of external and internal cues in this case: opinionated language (external), the personality trait of dogmatism (internal), and authoritativeness of the source (external).

Nonfluencies Disruptions exhibited in a person's speech are the final stylistic characteristic we will discuss. These are typical nonfluencies (Sereno and Hawkins, 1967):

1. "*Ah.*" The sound inserted between two words of the speech. For example, "The Women's Liberation 'ah' movement is . . . ."
2. *Sentence correction.* A correction in the choice of a word or words while the sentence content remains basically unchanged. For example, "Religions benefit students by insisting on high morality . . . moral standards."
3. *Stutter.* The serial, superfluous repetition of sounds. For example, "William Faulkner was an American novelist who won the N-N-Nobel Prize. . . ."
4. *Repetition.* The serial, superfluous repetition of a word. For example, "To him all . . . all Democrats were. . . ."
5. *Tongue-slip correction.* A correction of an unintended sound. For example, "We shall realize that the Black Mos . . . Muslim Movement. . . ."

Observations of nonfluencies may cause the listener to question a speaker's competence. However nonfluencies don't necessarily affect perceptions of character or trustworthiness, nor do they necessarily lessen persuasive impact. Under certain conditions the listener's low assessment of a speaker's competence may not be the crucial persuasive factor in changing the listener's attitude toward a topic under discussion; rather, the speaker's trustworthiness seems to be a more critical factor. You can readily see that the relationship between nonfluencies, credibility, and persuasibility may be complex.

Thus far our effort has been to present an overall picture of verbal cues, a major portion of the External System of Trans-Per, and to present the influence of words, logical and emotional content, sequential arrangement, and style on the listener's perceptions. And as we've seen, verbal cues are a vital part of communication. Verbal cues, however, are only one part of the External System of Trans-Per. The other cues belonging to the External System are *nonverbal cues*.

Nonverbal Cues

Nonverbal elements of Trans-Per include all external stimuli other than spoken or written words. They range from characteristics of body motion to patterns of voice to effects of the physical setting. We've broken down these public stimuli into four subcategories: (1) body motion, (2) characteristics of appearance, (3) characteristics of voice, and (4) use of space and distancing.

Body Motion

All forms of body movement are included here. Typical body motions or kinesic behaviors are facial responses, including eye and eyebrow behavior, posture, movement of the torso, hands, head, feet, legs, and an infinite range of gestures. Grouped under facial responses are such expressions as smiling and frowning as well as looks of boredom, amazement, disgust, and so forth. Observations of eye behavior might include: whom people look at, how long they look, whether the look is returned and for how long, and even dilation of the pupils. We all know that the more positively two people feel toward one another, the more frequent and longer will be the eye contact between them. People exhibit postures that are relaxed or uncomfortable, authoritative or submissive, and friendly or unfriendly. Examples of body movements might include: the way a flirting woman tilts her head when she establishes eye contact with an attractive man; the shaky knees of an inexperienced speaker; the shrugging of the shoulders, shaking of the head, and furrowed brow of the student who can't answer a question.

Gestures are, of course, telling behavioral, nonverbal cues; think of how speakers use their hands and arms in expressing themselves. Research to date indicates that body position in the direction of the person addressed becomes closer with increase in attraction or increase in positive attitude. A leaning forward is interpreted as showing a positive attitude; a leaning backward indicates the opposite. Open arm positions are presently thought to indicate relaxation.

Interestingly studies show that the relationship between a communicator's degree of relaxation and his attitude toward the other person is not easily interpreted. Despite extreme disdain for his listener, a speaker may be very relaxed. With increases in attraction or positive attitude, the individual may become more alert and less relaxed. But at the highest level of attraction or positive attitude, the speaker may again exhibit a very relaxed posture.

Characteristics of Appearance

All other things being equal, good-looking women and men are somewhat better off than their plainer friends in their relationships with the opposite sex. And the advantage extends beyond sexual relationships. Think of the

movie actors who have become successful politicians and of the successful politicians who look like movie stars. What physical characteristics do we notice about people? Let's describe the head. Is the hair straight, slicked down, wild and frizzy, or soft and slightly wavy? Is the nose straight or hooked? Narrow or broad? Are the eyebrows thick or thin? Heavy or light? Are the eyes close together or set apart? Narrow or open? Are the lips thick or thin? Is the mouth curved up or down? Is the complexion smooth or rough? Are the ears big or small? Do they protrude? Are the teeth straight or crooked? White or yellow? We should also include wigs, moustaches, lipstick, pimples, eye makeup, moles, and glasses. Appearance is more than superficial—because we associate certain personality, intellectual, and moral traits with individuals possessing certain physical characteristics.

Characteristics of Voice

What are the basic qualities of a person's voice? Is it high or low? Rich or thin? Smooth, raspy, or hoarse? Loud or soft? In addition to a person's vocal quality, the control an individual has over his voice is worth studying. What kind of pitch variation does he exhibit? What variation in tempo of speech does he exhibit? Does he use his voice to emphasize his meaning? Does the person use silence as an integral part of his regular speech? Don't you associate certain personality, intellectual, and moral traits with vocal characteristics? We have noticed that heroes have rich, deep, resonant voices and that villains have harsh, strident, and cold voices.

Use of Space and Distancing

The term *territoriality* is used to express the tendency we all have to claim a personal space or territory that is ours alone, that we do not wish others to intrude upon. Some people require larger personal spaces than others. The invasion of personal space without invitation produces negative attitudes on the part of the person intruded upon. The distance people place between them when they talk is included under this subcategory. We've seen, in Chapter 3, how Thomas and his friend preferred different distances when communicating—and how this led to some unfortunate consequences in a communicating transaction. In general close distances between communicators indicate that they have positive attitudes toward one another. Even here, however, the conclusions are not straightforward. When one of the persons is an authority, distance between parties is primarily a result of the attitude of the person of higher status toward the person of lower status.

Also included under this classification are the effects of inanimate objects and physical surroundings. Size of the room, for example, has its known influence: if a group of people are having a discussion, the room must be neither too large nor too small. It's as difficult to have a productive discussion in the middle of a gymnasium as in an oversized broom closet, which is sometimes passed off as a conference room. The style and comfort of the furniture also contributes to one's impression of the External System, as does the interior decoration, which serves to create mood or atmosphere.

In a communication setting, is the table being used one at which each person can see the others? Is everyone in an equal position or do some people have the head or leadership positions? When a rectangular table is used, the leadership positions are typically on the shorter sides; the person in a corner position almost never achieves a leadership position. We might finally note that the temperature, ventilation, and scents of a room can affect the communicators. Some people, for example, can't tolerate being in a room with someone who smokes. In the same communication environment, some people are in favor of opening the windows to let in light and fresh breezes; other people prefer to draw the shades and block out the sunlight. So people sometimes do not agree on what type of atmosphere or ambience they will share.

Physical surroundings contribute innumerable stimuli or public cues that are potentially available to the communicators within it. Which particular stimuli they select or focus on is an individual matter. Certain people seem much more observant, more aware of external stimuli: they recall many of the details of color and furniture and architectural features of a new restaurant they visit; others are more oblivious to their surroundings and observe far fewer of the stimuli that are available. When a person's attention is called to his present surroundings, he is immediately aware of many more sounds, smells, and sights than he had previously observed.

Summary

In this chapter we've looked at major elements of the External System of Trans-Per. We've seen how external stimuli don't exist "out there" except as we subjectively perceive them to exist; the cues that we discussed were created by us and are merely our way of helping you to classify the elements making up the communication system. We also observed that, in concentrating our attention upon external stimuli, we have distorted the process of communication by attempting to freeze what actually is in constant change and transition. By concentrating on only one system, we have temporarily put aside the total process—with its dynamic interplay between external and internal cues.

External stimuli of Trans-Per were viewed as falling into two classes: verbal and nonverbal. Verbal cues include symbols or words, logical and emotional content, sequential arrangement, and style. Nonverbal cues refer to all stimuli other than spoken or written words and include facial expression, posture, characteristics of voice and appearance, any effects of the physical setting, and so forth. Perhaps the most important point about the External System is the futility of seeking absolute conclusions about the effect of any external cue operating by itself, since external cues achieve their effect in combination with other external and internal stimuli. Communication is a transactional process and can only be explained by taking into account the blending of specific external and internal cues.

Additional Readings

Hopper, Robert, and Naremore, Rita C. *Children's Speech*. New York: Harper & Row, 1973.

Chapter 10, "School, Communication, and Minority-Group Children," is a straightforward presentation of the nature of dialectal speech patterns —especially the Black English dialect.

Knapp, Mark. *Nonverbal Communication in Human Interaction*. New York: Holt, Rinehart and Winston, 1972.

Chapter 1 is a good survey of the nature of nonverbal communicative behavior. This chapter deals with definitions of nonverbal communication, the place of nonverbal communication in the total communication process, the prevalence and importance of nonverbal communication, and the origins and universality of nonverbal behavior.

Leary, William G., and Smith, James Steel. *Thought and Statement*. 2d ed. New York: Harcourt, Brace, 1969.

A good collection of essays by prominent scholars on the nature of language. Lionel Ruby's "Words, Words, Words," Anatol Rapoport's "What Do You Mean?," and S.I. Hayakawa's "The Discussion of Reports" expand upon ideas we introduced in our discussion of the nature of words.

Martin, Howard H. "Communication Settings." In *Speech Communication: Analysis and Readings*, edited by H. Martin and Kenneth E. Andersen. Boston: Allyn and Bacon, 1968.

A different perspective on the advantages and disadvantages associated with the variables and situations that are covered in the chapter.

Williams, Frederick. "Analysis of Verbal Behavior." In *Methods of Research in Communication*, edited by Philip Emmert and William D. Brooks, pp. 237–290, Boston: Houghton Mifflin, 1970.

An advanced, thorough survey of verbal cues as they are categorized and employed in communication research.

Applications

Exercise 1

What emotions other than fear and love are often used as appeals in communication? Find several messages containing emotional appeals and analyze the content for the type of appeal used. What are their probable effects on the audience? Here are some suggestions*:

a. John F. Kennedy's "Inaugural Address," January 20, 1961.
b. Richard Nixon's "Checkers" speech, September 23, 1952.
c. Martin Luther King's "I Have a Dream," August 28, 1963.
d. The magazine and billboard commercials for Marlboro cigarettes.
e. Mick Jagger and Keith Richard, "The Salt of the Earth," *Beggar's Banquet* on London (C2 30110); Joan Baez, *Joan Baez*, on Vanguard (VSD 79330) "Blessed Are . . ."
f. Kendrew Lascelles, "When All the Laughter Dies in Sorrow," *Chicago III* on Mediarts Music, Inc. (PS 539).

Did you have a hard time distinguishing between emotional and logical appeals?

Exercise 2

Discuss which pattern of organization would be the best for the following topics. (You may think of patterns other than those we mentioned.)

a. How to pack a backpack for a five-day trip.
b. "What's Ahead for the American Economy—Regression or Progression?"
c. How acupuncture is performed.
d. The advantages of acupuncture in curing diseases.
e. Legalization of psychedelic drugs.

Exercise 3

Listen to samples of the speaking style of these public figures or others you may wish to use:

Barbara Walters	Margaret Mead
Jane Fonda	George Wallace

*The addresses by Kennedy, Nixon, and King are all found in the Appendix to James C. McCroskey, *An Introduction to Rhetorical Communication* (Englewood Cliffs, N.J.: Prentice-Hall 1968).

> Gloria Steinem   Cesar Chavez
> Mohammed Ali   Walter Cronkite

Now answer these questions:

a.   Do these people exhibit any dialect differences?
b.   What kinds of grammatical, syntactic, and vocabulary differences do you find in these samples?
c.   What kinds of figurative language are used?
d.   Do any of these speakers characteristically use opinionated language?
e.   Do any of these speakers exhibit excessive nonfluencies in their speech?
f.   How do these differences in style affect your attitudes toward each speaker as a person? How do they affect your opinions about what they say?

Exercise 4

Choose a TV personality who plays him or herself on a program, for example, a talk or quiz show host. Turn the picture on and the sound off; merely watch for a few moments. What does this person communicate through body motion and physical characteristics? Now turn the sound back on. What else can you now add about this person's communicating style? Are his body motions and physical characteristics consistent with his vocal characteristics and verbal style? Discuss your findings with the class.

Exercise 5

Try this experiment just for fun. Walk into the school library carrying books—as if you plan to study. Find a person sitting alone at a large table or on a long couch. Instead of sitting across or a few seats away from him, sit directly beside him and begin to study. Note what happens and report your findings to the class.

Exercise 6

Write one-sentence, objective definitions for the following words. Then give an association or personal meaning for each word.

> birth   faith
> happiness   mine
> apology   conservative
> poetry   learning
> success   politician

religion   community
fool   friendship

Now discuss your definitions with the class. If there is disagreement, what is the cause of it? Discuss the personal associations. What degree of agreement is there for these? What is the cause of it?

CHAPTER • 6

Contexts of Communication

Up to this point we've been developing the Trans-Per model and its two major systems and discussing examples of elements that make up the Internal and External Systems. You will recall that, in our transactional approach, meaning occurs when elements of these systems are blended by means of the perceptual process. We have said that through perception the individual assigns meaning to stimuli and that this creation of meaning is one of the essential components of our transactional framework—without which communication does not occur. In order to demonstrate the usefulness of the Trans-Per model, we want to show you how the perceptual blending of certain internal and external elements and the creation of meaning takes place in every communication context.

It is necessary, as we move through the present chapter, for you to keep in mind that a basic component of every communication transaction is always the creation of meaning. At times in this chapter we may appear to be talking about different and unrelated kinds of communication. We aren't. Rather we are describing four related *communicating contexts*—to all of which we can apply our basic transactional framework and our basic components. Contexts do not change the nature of the communication process; common to every communication context is still the creation of meaning. Although researchers agree that classification is fairly arbitrary, in our case we've chosen to deal with four contexts that are frequently discussed in many books and articles in the communication field: *intrapersonal, interpersonal, group,* and *organizational* communication.

If you were to think back over an average day and to write down the different communication transactions that you experienced and where they took place, we think you'd be surprised at just how active you were. Just getting through each day can be an amazing effort! On one particular day, as you dressed, you might have thought about the exam you had to take that afternoon—and how much reading you still needed to finish. You decided that you would have to cut your morning class to finish studying for the exam; the exam had a higher priority for you than the morning lecture. As you prepared to leave your apartment or room, you probably talked with one of your roommates, and you told him your plans to spend the morning studying in the library instead of going to class. In the library you talked with some fellow students who had also cut classes to study for the exam. Several of you then decided to work together in the library lounge so that you could toss questions and answers back and forth and think up possible questions you might be asked on the exam. Later, heading for the classroom, you were relieved that you didn't have to study anymore. You spoke briefly to the instructor and to some classmates before the exams were distributed. You took the exam and were pleased that some of the questions were ones you had anticipated while others were "losers." After the exam you went out for a cup of coffee to celebrate with some friends and then headed back, in your car, to home and dinner. Later that evening you watched TV—to find out how things were going in the outside world. And these reports caused you to do some more communicating with yourself. Finally you end the day by flopping into bed and, even in bed, once again, you perceptually arrange your world.

No wonder you're worn out at the end of the day, but that's just about the way you move through each waking day—constantly engaged in communicating with yourself or with others. What makes communicating an ever-interesting and sometimes exhausting activity is that you must constantly adapt to each change of environment and to the change of people within it.

In your average day described above, the communication process was basically the same for all the circumstances—you were continuously creating meaning. From all the things going on around you, you selected certain stimuli, organized and arranged them, interpreted them—making judgments or evaluations about them—and then assigned significance or meaning to them. And in each situation—by yourself, with your roommate, with the study group, in the classroom—this process of creating meaning continued.

Of course there is a common tendency to think about these different transactions as representing different kinds of communication. We certainly don't deny that there are some characteristics of one context —communicating alone with yourself—that differ from those of other contexts—communicating with your best friend or communicating at a meeting of the officers of the student government. Although we will describe typical characteristics of each of these four contexts, the process of communication remains essentially the same. We will continue to point out that contexts do not change the basic nature of communication; common to any context is still the creation of meaning.

Intrapersonal Context

Communication in intrapersonal contexts is the most basic and the most common of all communicating experiences. Communication in this context takes place when we communicate with ourselves. Since people must first create meaning *within* themselves before they can attempt to *share* meaning with others, we say it is the most basic form of communication. Even as we communicate with others, we are simultaneously communicating with and within ourselves. We say that intrapersonal communication is the most common form of communication because it goes on within us continuously—regardless of the presence or absence of other people. We spend more time with ourselves, fortunately or unfortunately, than with any other human being. And we spend more time communicating with ourselves than with any other human being.

In terms of the Trans-Per model, the intrapersonal context contains an Internal System and an External System. The environment of intrapersonal communication can be as varied as the number and type of places in which you find yourself. You can carry on intrapersonal communication in your room or in your car or in an elevator or in a bathtub. More surprisingly, if you haven't thought about it, you can communicate intrapersonally while sitting in a football stadium with thousands of other cheering people.

Have you even been sitting alone when a friend comes up and asks what you're doing? And you reply, "Just thinking." What you were doing was probably a bit more complex than your answer suggested. You were engaged in the process of intrapersonal communication—making some part of your world more meaningful than it had been. Perhaps you were trying to make sense out of some problem troubling your mind. Or organizing your thoughts about a friend. Or remembering a past experience. This *thinking*—as some people call intrapersonal communication—occupies a great portion of our time. In fact many scholars, philosophers, poets, recluses, dreamers, thinkers, gurus, as well as some ordinary people prefer the intrapersonal context to any other communicating context. As we have said, intrapersonal communication is the *individual's* perceptual blending of stimuli and his ongoing assignment of meaning.

Let's assume that, as you read this book, you are in the library. You

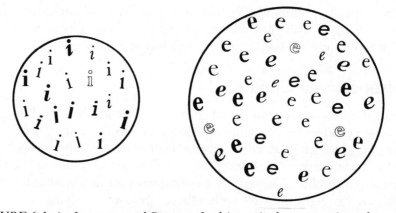

FIGURE 6.1 *An Intrapersonal Context*. In this particular transaction, elements of the Internal System are attitudes, past experience, self-esteem, knowledge, and so forth. Elements of the External System are written words of the book, its logical or emotional content, its style, and so forth.

are sitting alone with these pages serving as the major external stimuli or the stimulation for your thinking. You are reading these words (external elements) and perceptually blending the words with your attitudes, past experiences, self-esteem, and previously acquired knowledge (internal elements). In Trans-Per terms, the systems are illustrated in Figure 6.1.

As you perceptually mix these internal and external elements, you at-

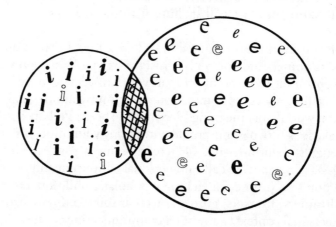

FIGURE 6.2 *Communication in an Intrapersonal Context*. Internal elements such as reading skill and attitude are perceptually mixed with external elements of words and content. The shading represents that area in which meaning is assigned.

tach significance—you create meaning. As illustrated by Trans-Per, such a communication experience would look like Figure 6.2.

Quite clearly you are engaging in a communication transaction with yourself. Although we, as authors, are the "source" of these written words, we can't react to your questions, arguments, suggestions, and so forth. You're on your own.

People can also communicate in the intrapersonal context when other people are present. Returning to the example of the library, let's assume that sitting at the table with you is another person—a stranger to you. In addition to the elements of the External System—already mentioned —the library, the book, its contents—we now add another person. As you sit and read, your concentration breaks, your eyes wander, and you notice the clothing that the stranger is wearing. You begin to think of his clothing—colorful and pleasant to look at. You make judgments about this person's self-concept—he must be fairly self-confident to wear such an eye-catching combination of plaids and colors. Or you think "his shirt's something like one I used to have." And so forth. This perceptual process and this creation of new meanings suggest the Trans-Per illustration shown in Figure 6.3. We have created additional meanings to those shown in Figure 6.2, and therefore the overlap is greater. You are still communicating with yourself, but you are now blending new and additional external stimuli with your internal stimuli.

The stranger across the table should be considered an *additional element in the External System and not an Internal System* in this context.

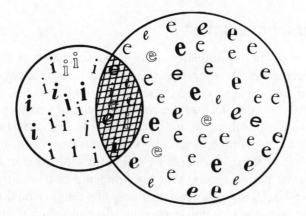

FIGURE 6.3 *Increase in Intrapersonal Communication.* Larger area of overlap indicates increase in meaning.

As long as no perceptual recognition and no engagement take place with the other person, the context is still considered intrapersonal. (Even a glance or a nod is considered a form of perceptual recognition and would change the analysis: the other person would become an additional Internal System in an interpersonal context.) From a physical point of view, other people may be in the same room, on the same bench, or in the same car with you. But if you do not attempt to communicate with one another, your personal creation of meaning takes place in an intrapersonal setting. Although the meanings created in this context are constantly changing, they change independent of transactions with anyone else. When one person is involved in intrapersonal communication, he must be responsive to and depend upon his own internal cues, for no one else provides verbal cues or external stimuli; he has no one with whom to test out or share his meanings. Intrapersonal communication is a deeply personal experience: we share perceptual outcomes or meaning with ourselves that we share with no one else.

In summary intrapersonal contexts are those contexts in which one person communicates with himself; it is an individual creation of meaning. Other Internal Systems are not perceptually recognized or engaged. The manner in which an individual perceives stimuli and creates meanings in the intrapersonal context will determine to a large extent the way he will do so in other communicating contexts. The ability to cope with troublesome problems, new sources of information, and different physical settings—to name just a few possibilities—is determined *within* the individual.

Interpersonal Context

In interpersonal communication contexts, people attempt to *share meaning with each other.* At a very basic level we can say that any time at least two individuals engage in face-to-face conversation we find some type of interpersonal communication. Several major characteristics of this context distinguish it from others; we will not be able to describe or classify all of them here. For example, a telephone conversation you may have with your best friend would involve a type of communicating in the interpersonal context. Keep in mind that the following characteristics represent only *major* characteristics distinguishing the interpersonal setting from others; they are not a complete or exhaustive mapping of this context.

First, communication in the interpersonal setting requires at least two individuals who must recognize and acknowledge the presence of one another. In other words they must be aware of each other; they must be perceptually engaged. Of course the most obvious example of this characteristic takes place when two people are engaged in intimate conversation and self-disclosure. But there is the opposite situation in which two people sit next to each other on an airplane for a long period of time and barely acknowledge each other's presence—except for a few polite and cursory remarks. The point is that at least two individuals are necessary, and even more important than that, they must take each other into account. Our two people sitting on the airplane are probably engaged much more frequently in intrapersonal than in interpersonal communication. The jovial person who tries to strike up a conversation with a stranger in a bar, only to be politely snubbed with brief, cold answers, has certainly not engaged in interpersonal communication of any but the most perfunctory and minimal type.

A second general characteristic requires, with certain exceptions, that the people be close enough, physically, to make transaction possible. As we said earlier, a telephone conversation may certainly serve as an example of an exception to this rule; but for the most part communicating in an interpersonal context is a face-to-face experience.

Third, communication transactions in interpersonal contexts are generally *informal* and contain *little structure* or planning. The persons communicate freely and spontaneously—even with frequent pauses or discontinuities. The participants may typically deal with a wide variety of topics or issues. Each one may introduce a new topic, suggested or triggered by an internal cue or by an external stimulus. They may not work through the topic to a mutually satisfactory conclusion, that is, one of them might interrupt with a new topic. They may or may not come back to the original subject under discussion. A new interruption may move them even further from the original topic. Sometimes, if a subordinate wishes to talk to a principal in a firm, he writes a list of topics he wishes to cover—in order to make good use of the few minutes he has with his boss; however this is probably as close to an organized conversation as one would find. More orderly rules or an agenda of topics are found in the group or organizational context. In this context, participants may or may not pay attention to each other's status or position. They may engage in intimate or secret disclosures ("Let's keep this between ourselves"). Or they may keep at a fairly formal level for years. They may feel a sudden surge of understanding or sympathy toward the other person's disclosure, or they may remain untouched. In other words, there is wide latitude for free expression and self-disclosure and personal style in this context that doesn't exist in the others.

In Chapter 3, we described how a typical interpersonal communication transaction is analyzed by means of Trans-Per. You recall that our two students—Walter and Thomas—were talking about the details of an assignment; they were then relatively unknown to one another. As our Trans-Per illustration showed, the two students shared a relatively small amount of meaning: their interpersonal communication was somewhat limited. We also called your attention to individual meanings they created (intrapersonal communication) during the transaction.

The overlap or intersecting area—shared meaning—is not fixed. As communicators achieve more or less common meaning, the overlap can expand or contract. Let's return to Walter and Thomas to illustrate what might happen as their shared meaning increases. What we're going to be interested in are the changes in their perceptions and assignment of meanings, which led to the increased Trans-Per overlap.

We'll pick up Walter and Thomas a little later in the term. They've had several opportunities to talk and to observe each other's behavior. After observing him for several months and talking to him, Walter decides that Thomas isn't actually aggressive or arrogant—but that he's a warm, outgoing, amusing individual. Thomas decides in turn that Walter, rather than being aloof, is probably shy and introverted. In the course of several conversations, they find that they have similar attitudes toward sports. Walter's an enthusiastic Mets fan; Thomas is a fanatical Dodger supporter. In gen-

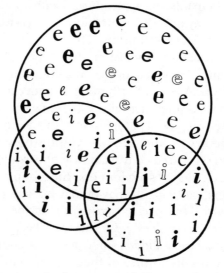

FIGURE 6.4 *Increase in Interpersonal Communication.* Compare overlap achieved now by Walter and Thomas with that shown in Figure 3.4.

eral their level of interpersonal communication has moved beyond talking about homework assignments and beyond worrying about the physical distance between them. Now they communicate about a wide range of topics; they even socialize quite a bit outside of class. According to Trans-Per, their shared meaning would now appear like the diagram in Figure 6.4. As you can see, they still create individual meanings (intrapersonal communication) but the amount of shared meaning has increased.

Not all communicating transactions in interpersonal contexts grow as neatly as this one. And you should not conclude that as meanings grow, mutual agreement increases. A husband and wife who divorce each other may have as large an overlap of meaning as two people can possibly achieve. The issue is not whether meaning creation leads to agreement; rather the issue is the extent to which meanings are shared. Your closest friend may be one who completely disagrees with your position on a number of issues. But even in discussing what you disagree about, you and your friend have shared meanings. For example Walter and Thomas may violently disagree about which is the outstanding National League team, but the fact that they perceive baseball to be a significant external element, combined with their positive attitudes (internal stimuli) toward the sport, leads them to a shared or common meaning.

For many people communication in an interpersonal environment is a pleasurable experience; it brings out their very best. For others, interpersonal communication is a painful experience and brings out their worst.

Each day is filled with communication in interpersonal contexts. Beyond the characteristics that we've been describing, the very important point to keep in mind about the interpersonal context is that one of its basic purposes is the creation of meaning.

Group Context

Everyone is a member of one group or other: a class, a family, a sorority, a political group are just a few examples of the group communication context. In the previous section we identified several characteristics associated with communicating behavior in the interpersonal context, all of which can be applied to the group context as well; in addition three other characteristics identify the group setting.

First, any group has a set of *norms*—standards of behavior. Members of a group are expected to act according to these norms or they are soon alienated from the group. Often these norms or rules are written down, but they can also be unwritten and can often be considered to be "tradition."

Teachers establish norms or rules about attendance; sororities set down standards about dress; and religions outline norms concerning holy days. When persons communicate in group contexts, one basis of their attempts tocreate meaning is their perceptions of norms.

A second characteristic that distinguishes the group context is the matter of the group's *enduring nature*. For the most part, a group is established to last for a period of time. This characteristic emphasizes the formality and the structure of group settings. Think of the groups that you belong to —your church, class, college, family, and so forth. Each one has a period of duration or permanence that distinguishes it from the others. And this enduring nature is tied into the group's task—the reason for its formation. Regardless of the group—a social group, a professional organization, or a labor union—it is a planned and lasting collection of people.

Communicating in group context is affected by the enduring nature of the group and its task. Some members of the group will perceive tradition to be very important and, in turn, attach a great deal of significance or meaning to such things as handshakes, old songs, and so forth. On the other hand other members of the group may see such tradition as meaningless; they don't attach significance to such behaviors. To some members, the group is a political power; identification with it may mean a good job. Obviously the communicating that goes on in this context—particularly at the group's regular meetings—will be affected by these different meanings.

The final characteristic of the group context concerns the expectations that members have of the part each is to play. These shared expectations of member behavior are termed *roles* and strongly influence each person's communication in the group. Freshmen are expected to behave a certain way; pledges another way; and work trainees yet another. Communicating in group contexts is affected by this role characteristic. For example the freshman who joins a campus political group is not expected to be as outspoken as the seniors or older members of the group; the freshman's role may be identified as a listener. In his specific role he perceives stimuli from a different perspective than other members of the group.

In addition to these three basic characteristics of group contexts, the group's *orientation* distinguishes it from other communication contexts. The group's *task orientation* refers to its concerns for completing its assigned task: task orientation refers to the group's preoccupation with procedures, particular jobs, and so forth. On the other hand the group also has a concern for the personal relationships of its members: the *social-emotional orientation* of a group deals with the group's concern for a cooperative at-

mosphere, a liking among members, and so forth. Every group reflects both these orientations to some extent.

A fraternity, for example, is a group which may have an orientation or a concern for some particular task. Let's say the fraternity is planning a summer camp for underprivileged children. Subcommittees are formed to locate a site, determine costs, and so on. The fraternity in this instance is task-oriented and has a concern for getting a particular job done—all the details associated with lining up the camp. But the executive council, realizing that its members will work better if their social life is also fostered, maintains an interest in the social-emotional welfare of the fraternity. Therefore committees meet comfortably in lounges; beer is provided; and weekly parties are held.

Taken together, norms, permanence, roles, and orientations typically lead to a great deal more structure and more formality than that found in interpersonal contexts. In fact notice the difference across the three communicating contexts—intrapersonal, interpersonal, and group. As we add participants (Internal Systems) and a prescribed set of rules for behavior, we impose more requirements on the communicators. What is the nature of perceptual activity in group settings? What is the nature of meaning assignment in such settings? These questions may be answered at least partially if we examine a hypothetical group with the Trans-Per model.

Keep in mind, as we move through this illustration, that the communicating behavior that we have observed in the intrapersonal and interpersonal contexts is the same in the group context: the individual's creation of meaning through the perceptual blending of internal and external stimuli continues. One more thing: keep in mind that intrapersonal and interpersonal communication is also going on at the same time as group communication. In other words communicating behavior operating in one context affects and is affected by communicating going on in other contexts. In terms of a concept we discussed earlier, these communicating contexts are systemic. Since our concern right now is communication in group contexts, for the moment we'll ignore intrapersonal and interpersonal communicating contexts.

Assume that our group is composed of three students who have been assigned by the student government to the student athletic ticket committee. (Obviously such committees are normally larger; we've used a group of three to simplify our illustration.) In the past, fraternities, sororities, and service groups had taken the best seats at the basketball games while other members of the student body had to fight for even the bleacher seats. The committee is instructed to remove this inequity by devising a plan for the fair distribution of basketball tickets. The committee is told that a final re-port will have to be submitted. Further the members are told that they are to hold their meetings in a particular room and that they are expected to meet weekly until the report is completed. In other words a number of reg-ulations or norms are established initially. Many other norms evolved throughout the group's meetings. For example members sat in certain chairs, spoke in a particular order, raised their hands to be recognized, didn't interrupt one another, and so forth.

In terms of the group's length of existence the members are told that they will have to serve just one year, since a tentative plan is to have this ticket committee become part of the permanent structure of student gov-ernment. A number of roles are assigned to members of the group. A chairperson is named and a secretary appointed. Each member is told that the group is responsible to the executive council of student government.

So with these general notions in mind, let's see what communication in the group context might look like at a meeting of our student ticket committee. Our three members—Matt, Amy, and Chris—each have unique Internal Systems composed of the elements attitude, self-esteem, knowledge, and so forth. Matt is only slightly involved in the group be-cause he uses his father's tickets rather than buying his own. So he is not personally affected by the lack of fairness in ticket distribution. Chris is highly involved because for the past few years he's been personally fighting for the establishment of such a committee. He feels a personal stake in figuring out a fair system. Our third member, Amy, a senior, can best be described as moderately involved. On the one hand she knows that the sys-tem must be changed; on the other hand the past few years haven't been all that bad as far as she is concerned.

The single External System for our group members contains a number of stimuli: the requirement that the task be completed by a certain time, the regular meeting times that are required, the limited number of tickets available as opposed to those requested, the seating arrangement during meetings. All these are cues that will go into the perceptual mix re-sulting in the shared meaning our group members will create. We might expect a Trans-Per illustration of our group to look like Figure 6.5.

What are some of the things you notice? First, pay attention to the in-dividual, interpersonal, and group communication taking place simul-taneously. During the group meetings each member individually creates meaning within himself—even as he communicates with the others. Two of the group may, in addition, transact with each other and share some common meaning, aside from the group's discussion of ticket problems.

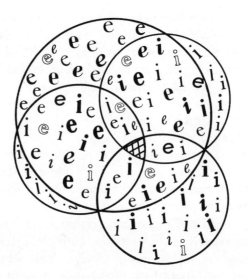

FIGURE 6.5 *Group Communication.* The group communication is represented by the overlap (shaded area) of the three Internal Systems and the External System. Note the intrapersonal and interpersonal communication which may occur simultaneously.

Second, notice that the shared meaning for the group occurs in that interaction in which *all* Internal Systems overlap with the External System. It is clear that a great deal of meaning may not be shared in any group context.

Third, as you look at the amount of overlap, consider the characteristics of the group context—norms, roles, and enduring nature. How did these affect the perception and assignment of meaning that occurred in the group context? Would more shared meaning occur if a different person were named chairperson? Or if the group were only going to exist for a couple of months instead of a year? Or if members had more freedom in establishing the norms?

Fourth, can you make any estimates about the nature of the group's orientation? Is there likely to be more concern with the task itself or with the social-emotional aspects? Would you expect the shared meaning to be greater if there were more concern with one orientation than with the other?

Communication in group contexts contains all the characteristics that we discussed in the intrapersonal and interpersonal communicating context. In addition the characteristics of norms, roles, and enduring nature distinguish the group from the interpersonal setting. When we discuss the next communicating context, you'll notice that the distinguishing characteristics of the group are carried over into it.

Organizational Context

You've noticed by now that our descriptions of the various communicating contexts are cumulative: characteristics of the intrapersonal context exist in the interpersonal setting; and features of both the intrapersonal and the interpersonal contexts are found in group settings. Similarly organizational communication contains all those characteristics found in the other contexts—and additional ones we'll discuss in this section.

It has been estimated that most of us spend about a third of our waking day dealing with organizations in some form or other. If you were to think about the organizations that you've come into contact with today alone, you might think that this estimate is conservative. If you bought groceries today, sat in a classroom, and took your car to the gas station, you had some typical experiences with organizations. Let's turn our attention to some distinguishing characteristics of organizational settings.

First, an organization is concerned with the *coordination of a number of interrelated group activities.* Any organization is made up of a number of subunits—systems within the system; these subunits are all related to and dependent on each other. For example our basketball ticket committee may have a very specific goal—to come up with a plan for ticket distribution—but its work is related to the overall purpose of the student government unit. And that unit works with others within the overall university organization. The basketball ticket committee, the interfraternity council, and the student activities committee all are interrelated. It may turn out that the members of the various committees barely know each other or that they are the best of friends. How well they know one another really doesn't matter too much. What does matter is that the university organization is responsible for coordinating all their activities. Thus the first distinguishing characteristic of an organization is its coordination of a number of interrelated group activities.

A second characteristic of organizational contexts is the pattern of predictable activities that take place within it. In other words certain units are expected to perform consistent and predictable tasks. Our ticket committee will allot basketball tickets as long as it exists. To be sure it may make recommendations that other units in the organization help out—for example it may want the football committee to give some suggestions—but its

task remains the same. What is both a strength and weakness of any formal organization is its predictability. Members in an organization can't really "do their own thing"; everything depends on their dependable performance of a specified job.

A third characteristic of organizational contexts is the general outline or structure of authority and responsibility. Our ticket committee is responsible to the executive council of the student government, the student government is responsible to the vice-president for student affairs, and so forth. The general outline of authority may vary from one organization to another. In one organization, for example, responsibility may be highly centralized; the members of a particular unit may have little or no authority, as often happens in smaller colleges in which the president is the true

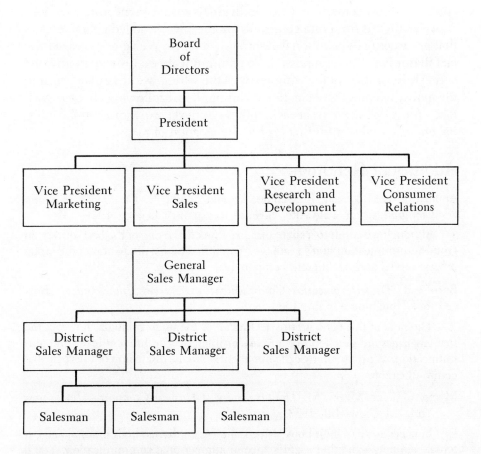

FIGURE 6.6 *Simplified Organizational Chart.*

authority-figure of the institution. In larger university organizations, authority is decentralized, with each dean of each particular college within the university having primary authority, in consultation with his department chairpersons.

As you can tell, the organizational context is distinguished from the others in terms of its *complexity*. The interrelationships between units, predictable tasks, and general outline of authority and responsibility indicate that this context has much more structure and many more rules than the others.

Summary

In this chapter we've introduced you to the four major communicating contexts—those settings in which individuals engage in meaning creation. As we've moved from one context to another, we've added characteristics that are essentially additional external elements. We've emphasized the fact that it is virtually impossible to communicate exclusively in any one context. Regardless of the complexity of the setting, we are still engaged in the individual process of creating meaning. In the following chapters we'll take a more detailed look at each of these contexts, expanding on the internal and external stimuli that lead to the creation of meaning.

Additional Readings

Applbaum, R.; Bodaken, E.; Sereno, K.; and Anatol, K. *The Process of Group Communication*. Palo Alto: Science Research Associates, 1974.

Although we admit to a slight bias, we think this is one of the best sources on group communication that's available. You'll find here a discussion of the group process model and its different components.

Barnlund, D. *Interpersonal Communication: Survey and Studies*. Boston: Houghton Mifflin, 1968.

The bulk of this book is fairly technical for the undergraduate, however the first few pages are excellent for any reader interested in different levels of communication. We particularly call your attention to the discussion of interpersonal communication.

Myers, G., and Myers, M. *The Dynamics of Human Communication*. New York: McGraw-Hill, 1973.

In pages 1–91 of their book, Myers and Myers discuss both internal and external elements—and their significance in intrapersonal communication. You'll find this section easy to read and helpful in furthering your understanding of what we have discussed in Chapter 6. Their treatment of perception and meaning is particularly good.

Redding, W. C. *Communication Within the Organization*. New York: Industrial Communication Council, 1972.

This book, one of the most comprehensive works in the area, covers everything of interest across the entire field, including a description of the major problems in researching formal organizations and a fairly thorough review of the literature. Easily read, it is very worthwhile if you're interested in communication in organizational contexts.

Applications

Exercise 1

Divide into groups of four or five people and discuss these questions for about thirty minutes.

a.   Can you identify and explain any transactional patterns that have emerged when you engage in intrapersonal communication?
b.   Do these patterns influence your interpersonal communicating behavior in any way?
c.   How does your communicating behavior when you are among people you know well differ from your behavior when you are with people you do not know at all?
d.   What kinds of opinions do you think other people have of you?
e.   What kinds of opinions would you like other people to have of you?

Now working individually, draw a Trans-Per diagram for the interpersonal communicating relationship you formed with each class member during the discussion. Indicate how much "shared meaning" you perceived in each relationship by the amount of overlap between the External and Internal Systems. When everyone has finished, share your diagrams with the group.

a.   How much do individual diagrams of the same relationship coincide?
b.   How do you feel about sharing your perceptions with the group?
c.   What are the elements in the External System in this situation?
d.   If you did this exercise again towards the end of the term, do you think your diagrams would be different? Try it and see.

Exercise 2

Bring to class two symbols that tell something about yourself: one should symbolize something about what you perceive yourself to be; another should symbolize your perceptions of what others perceive you to be. Your "symbol" may be a tangible object, a painting, a photograph, an article of clothing, or a piece of literature. (One girl who thought that others initially perceived her as cold and impersonal brought to class an ice cube; she explained that the fact that it was melting revealed something about her personality.)

The rest of the class should have a chance to try to understand your perceptions of yourself and to react to them. What functions are served by the stereotypes that we have of one another? What does this exercise suggest about your transactional communication on an intrapersonal level? On an interpersonal level?

Exercise 3

Does your communication class qualify as a group? If so, what is its task orientation? Its social-emotional orientation? Are there any clearly defined roles in the class? How about norms of behavior? Were there any conflicts among members in answering these questions?

Exercise 4

Observe closely two contexts with which you are familiar: (a) an informal group (a club, an encounter group, a family); (b) an organization (your place of employment, a standing committee at your school). After taking notes in both situations, fill out the following chart in as much detail as possible.

	Group	*Organization*
Goals		
Roles of different members		
Rules or norms		
Channels of communication		

Now think about these questions:
a.   For which environment was it easier for you to fill in the chart? Why?
b.   How do these roles, rules and channels either help or hinder the achievement of the goals of each group?
c.   In which environment do you feel most satisfied? Why?

Exercise 5

Follow these steps to play the "animal game":
a.   Take some time for everyone in the class to think about these questions: If you could be any animal other than a human, what would it be? Or, what animal best corresponds to the image you have of yourself? In deciding on your animal, keep in mind these things: its natural habitat; its natural enemies; what it looks like; its habits.
b.   Take time for everyone in the class to think about and write down an "animal image" for each other person in the class.

c.   Each person tells the class what animal he picked for himself. Then all of the other members share their animal images of that person.

Now discuss these questions: What kinds of cues were considered when you picked the animal images—verbal cues or nonverbal? Do you think you project the same image to others that you have of yourself?

CHAPTER • 7

Communication in the Intrapersonal Context

Intrapersonal communication is one of the four fundamental contexts of communication that we will describe; it's also the most basic form of communication. Although we say intrapersonal communication is the "simplest" form of communication, it is still a complicated process and not easily analyzed. We say it's the simplest form of communication, nevertheless, because the other contexts are even more complex—with the addition of other communicators.

Communication, as we have often stated, is the process by which individuals create or evolve meanings. Intrapersonal communication focuses on the development of meaning within the individual. This process is fundamental since it is carried over into all the other communication contexts: interpersonal, group, or organizational. For us to understand how two or three, or more, communicators evolve meanings when communicating with one another, we first must understand how each does so individually.

Taking Stock

We noted earlier that one of the outcomes of perception is the development of meaning. We observed that transactional communication is a perceptual process and involves External and Internal Systems. We've seen how meaning is created as a result of the blending of a variety of internal and external stimuli and how the perceptual activities of selection, organization, and interpretation are prerequisites of meaning assignment.

We've proceeded to look at the nature of models—the strengths and limitations of their use—and offered the Trans-Per model of communication to help us in our study of the process. Trans-Per consists, as you'll recall, of two basic systems, the Internal System and the External System.

125

The Internal System comprises all the cues or stimuli we as communicators bring with us to a communicating transaction. The External System consists of all verbal and nonverbal stimuli as well as all other public cues potentially available in the environment. We suggested that Trans-Per can be used to help understand communication in all of its contexts. And in the preceding chapter, we introduced four communication contexts and the identifying characteristics of each. All of this has been a preface to the final chapters of this text, in which we'll get into the heart of the study of communication as transaction—and of Trans-Per.

The Nature of Intrapersonal Communication

Our study of intrapersonal communication describes the creation of meaning within a single individual. Intrapersonal communication involves the ways in which individuals process stimuli and assign meaning to the stimuli.

Although we deal, in the intrapersonal context, with the meanings created by only one person, we do not mean that other people aren't present.

Let's deal a little further with this notion of how we can still have intrapersonal communication despite the fact that other people are present. Let's say you're driving on a deserted road—up a lonely, lovely mountain. No one else is around; it's just you, the car, and nature. As you drive, a variety of thoughts or meanings run through your head—some pleasant, some less pleasant. You probably have no trouble in thinking of this process, off by yourself, as intrapersonal communication.

But now consider this situation: you're in a doctor's waiting room, surrounded by other patients. You notice an old woman with cataracts; you say to yourself, "I'm glad I don't have what she has." As you look at the other patients, you ask yourself, "I wonder what's wrong with all of them?" In this example, although other people were present—even quite close —the process of creating meaning was still intrapersonal. Unless you enter into a transaction—even by a glance or nod—with some other patient, you are still engaged in intrapersonal communication within yourself. In the same way, when listening to another student speak in class or when watching a news report or a speech on TV—despite the fact that other people are nearby—you are engaged in an intrapersonal process. The way an individual combines the cues he observes with those he brings with him—in order to create meaning—is an intrapersonal process. The point is that it's not the presence or absence of other people that defines intrapersonal

process. Rather the intrapersonal communication process takes place whenever an individual creates meaning within himself by blending internal and external cues—including even the observed verbal and nonverbal behaviors of others nearby. Unless a person is perceptually engaged with others who are near him, they are merely parts of his External System. Intrapersonal communication occurs whenever an individual blends cues from his Internal System and his External System—in order to make meaning out of his world.

Even when two or more people communicate—in the other communication contexts—each person, in addition and simultaneously, will be creating his own intrapersonal meanings. Each individual represents a separate Internal System within the interpersonal or group context.

Now that we have some idea about the pervasiveness and importance of intrapersonal communication in relation to the other communication contexts, let's look at the nature of meanings that might evolve in an intrapersonal setting. It's obvious that the number and kinds of meanings someone could evolve are limitless. Meanings might consist of new information gained, insights into one's own nature, development of likes or dislikes, sudden illuminations, and so forth. Since we can't possibly treat all possible types of meaning that may evolve in an intrapersonal setting, we're going to be selective. We are mainly going to describe the element *attitude* —how we develop attitudes and how we change our attitudes.

Attitude is an element that seems to most researchers to be of primary importance in intrapersonal communication. An attitude, as we have said, is a tendency to evaluate an object or issue or person in a favorable or unfavorable manner. We create, maintain, or change attitudes as we process internal and external cues in the course of intrapersonal communication. As you probably remember, we described attitude, in Chapter 4, as a fundamental internal cue we bring with us to any communicating context. However that was only part of the story: attitudes may be looked at not only as internal cues—but also as external cues.

Consider this: a preconceived attitude may clearly be an internal cue that we bring with us to a communicating context. Preconceived attitudes can affect the impressions we form of another communicator—whether we accept or reject what the other person says or whether we even hear what the other person is saying. This seems clear enough.

But an attitude may also be considered an external cue. Brenda's strong Women's Liberation statements are likely to be interpreted by a listener as reflecting Brenda's positive attitude toward the ideals and practices of the Women's Liberation movement. In this case Brenda's attitude is an external cue—a cue that the listener would process in creating his own meanings or interpretations.

As a matter of fact attitude may also be a meaning that results from a communicating experience. For instance listening to someone discuss a political crisis may create, maintain, or modify attitudes we have about that situation. In this instance attitude is the *meaning* or *communication factor* that has evolved. The point we're trying to make is that *attitude may be an internal cue, an external cue, or a meaning or communication factor.*

In the same way many other elements may be looked upon as being either internal‚ cues, external cues, or meanings or communication factors—depending upon how we're looking at the specific element. A personality element—say self-esteem—may be an internal element we bring with us when we talk with someone. We may perceive the external element of self-esteem reflected in an individual's behavior. And in addition self-esteem may be a meaning that develops within us while listening to our boss describe to a visitor how well we handled a certain assignment.

In the rest of the chapter we're going to approach attitude as a meaning or communication factor that evolves during intrapersonal communication and in this sense we will call it *attitude change.* First, we'll look at some interesting theoretical approaches directly concerned with attitude and attitude change, to help in our understanding of the intrapersonal context. Second, we'll look at cues from the Internal and External Systems that seem most related to the formation and change of attitude. Finally, we'll illustrate how the blending of internal and external cues affects attitude change—by means of Trans-Per.

Theoretical Approaches to Intrapersonal Communication

The Nature of Theory

Theories can be thought of as possible or proposed general explanations for behavior. Typically many different theories are proposed to explain the same behavior. The reason for this is that a single theory usually doesn't explain all the manifestations of the behavior in question; therefore new theories are proposed to fill the gap or to account for deficiencies of earlier theories. In attempting to explain attitude behavior, researchers have formulated a great number of theories. Theories then, in general terms, are *proposed explanations of observed behavior.*

More precisely, a theory may be defined as *a number of interrelated constructs and propositions used to predict and explain a phenomenon.* Several terms of this definition require further explanation. We'll start with constructs.

Constructs are concepts, abstractions, or generalized terms. For example the terms *credibility* and *threat appeal* are constructs commonly used in communication research. Notice that these are very broad, general words that cover a wide range of specific behaviors. For instance many different communicators might be perceived to have either high or low credibility. Thus credibility is the general term standing for a great number of specific behaviors. In essence constructs are the basic elements or units of a theory.

Propositions are sentences from a theory expressing relationships between two or more constructs. In other words constructs in a theory are related or linked by means of propositions. For instance a theory exists that expresses a relationship between the constructs of frustration and aggression. The major proposition from the theory states: "The greater the frustration, the higher the aggression." What this says is that the more frustrated someone is the more aggressive he will become. Another example of a proposition is: "High ego-involvement in a topic will be associated with great difficulty in changing attitude on the topic." In all theoretical propositions, there will be a functional connection or relation between two or more constructs.

As we've just mentioned, propositions from a theory consist of two or more constructs; and constructs are general, abstract terms. It thus follows that propositions are broad and general statements. Such general statements from a theory are often used to *predict* specific behaviors. On the basis of a proposition from a theory, a researcher might foresee or foretell specific findings. For instance from the proposition "the greater the reward, the faster will be the learning," a researcher might predict a large number of specific behaviors. Although it's obvious that reward and learning can take many diverse forms, he might reasonably predict that if higher grades are given, learning of textual content will be more rapid.

When we use the word "explain," we're referring to scientific explanation. A theory, or more usually a proposition from a theory, is said to be an explanation for observed behaviors. A theory can be said to be an explanation if (1) the behaviors observed can be shown to be logical and valid forms of the constructs contained in the theoretical proposition and if (2) the behaviors are consistent with the relationship expressed in the proposition. For instance let's examine this proposition: "Individuals who are highly ego-involved on a topic are less susceptible to changing their attitude on the topic." In order to make a scientific explanation, a researcher must first demonstrate that he has valid ways of measuring high ego-involvement and attitude change on a given topic. If he does have valid means for measuring these two constructs and if the people identified as highly ego-involved demonstrate a high resistance to attitude change, then the observed behavior is said to be explained by the proposition from the theory. Thus a single theoretical statement may explain a limitless number of behaviors. Since theories represent economy of thought, the most useful theories are those that can account for the widest range of specific behaviors. By the use of theories thousands upon thousands of findings and facts may be grouped and classified according to how they are best explained. Thus our decision to deal with theories.

We called this section "Theoretical Approaches to Intrapersonal Communication" and not "Theories of Intrapersonal Communication." We made this distinction between "theoretical approaches to" and "theories of" because many theories from the other social sciences, which were not created specifically as theories of communication, may be used to explain communicating behavior. If we think of the proposition linking frustration and aggression, "the higher the frustration, the higher the aggression," this statement says nothing specifically about communication, yet it can be used to explain communicating behavior. If, when Jeremiah is explaining his view of Watergate to George, George keeps interrupting and cutting him off, Jeremiah is likely to develop a high level of frustration. One possible prediction from the theory is that Jeremiah will ultimately exhibit some kind of aggressive verbal response, shouting something like, "Will you keep quiet a moment and give me a chance to finish what I'm trying to say!" This same frustration-aggression proposition may be used to predict other communicating behaviors.

We will take a close look at three theories: (1) Heider's Balance Theory, (2) Osgood's Principle of Congruity, and (3) Festinger's Theory of Cognitive Dissonance. The choices of Heider, Osgood, and Festinger represent the most prominent theories that deal with communication in the intrapersonal context. Before getting into each of these theories individually, we will examine some of the points they have in common.

First, all three theories are concerned with attitude: they explore the ways in which attitude operates in an intrapersonal environment. Second, all three theories have similar underlying assumptions. It's assumed that people have a need for balance or consistency in their attitudes, thoughts, and actions: a staunch radical doesn't give money to conservative causes.

It's further assumed that inconsistency is uncomfortable and that a need will arise both to reduce and to avoid it. Consistency, however, doesn't necessarily mean logical consistency, especially as viewed by an outsider. A racial bigot may have no trouble maintaining consistency between his discriminatory behavior toward Blacks and his conception of himself as a good and loving Christian.

In our discussion of these theories, we will use each author's original concept and our own interpretation and examples of it.

Heider's Balance Theory

Heider (1958) proposed the first balance or consistency theory, using three components: P, O, and X (Figure 7.1). P refers to *person*. O stands for *other person*. X symbolizes the *topic* or thing talked about. Why is this balance

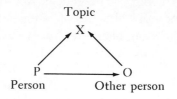

FIGURE 7.1

theory considered an intrapersonal theory? Since two people are obviously involved, P and O, how can it be intrapersonal? The reason is that we are looking at things completely from P's point of view. Imagine yourself inside P's head: you are now P. The other person and the topic are parts of P's external system. Relationships existing between P, O, and X are shown by plus and minus signs: the plus sign indicates a positive relationship and the minus sign a negative one. Through the use of plus and minus signs, one can see if P likes or dislikes O—and note how each of them feels about X, the thing talked about.

Certain relationships among the three components indicate psychological balance. The two combinations that produce psychological consistency or balance are: (1) positive relations among all three compo-

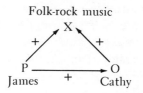

FIGURE 7.2

nents and (2) one positive and two negative relationships among the components. We will describe the four ways in which these various combinations can occur. Consider this first situation (Figure 7.2). James (P) likes Cathy (O), and they both like folk-rock music (X). Consider a second condition of balance (Figure 7.3): James (P) likes Cathy (O); they both hate opera (X). In these two cases, balance exists because James has a positive

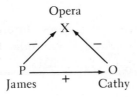

FIGURE 7.3

attitude toward Cathy, and both have identical favorable or unfavorable feelings toward the same topic.

    Now let us consider the two other ways in which balance exists: this

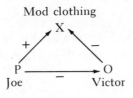

FIGURE 7.4

time Joe (P) doesn't like Victor (O). Joe likes colorful mod clothing (X) while Victor doesn't (Figure 7.4). Can you see why this is a balanced state for Joe? Observe that it conforms to the rule that two negative signs and one positive sign represent psychological balance. A fourth possible balanced condition shows Joe disliking an X, soccer, that Victor likes (Figure 7.5).

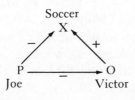

FIGURE 7.5

So these are the four basic states of psychological balance. But what about imbalance?

    Imbalance exists when we observe two positive and one negative rela-

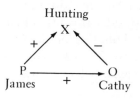

FIGURE 7.6

tionships, or three negative relationships, among *P*, *O*, and X. Again four specific combinations are possible. Consider this first situation (Figure 7.6). James (*P*) likes Cathy (*O*); James likes hunting (X) but Cathy despises

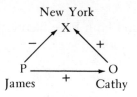

FIGURE 7.7

it. This creates tension and discomfort for James: people typically want those they care for to like the same things they do. Consider a second situa-

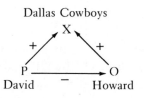

FIGURE 7.8

tion of imbalance (Figure 7.7). James (*P*) likes Cathy (*O*); James hates living in New York (X) but Cathy loves New York. James again feels an imbalance. A third situation of imbalance looks like this (Figure 7.8): David (*P*) doesn't like Howard (*O*), but they both like the same football team (X). This is clearly unsettling for David. He says to himself, "What's the matter with me? If Howard likes the same team I do, something is all wrong." A final condition of imbalance looks like this (Figure 7.9): David (*P*) doesn't like Howard (*O*), and they both dislike the same team (X). Again we have an imbalanced situation. David thinks, "Howard's stupid, and I think the Oilers are terrible. Yet Howard agrees with me. Maybe I've been

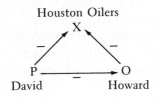

FIGURE 7.9

wrong about Howard, or I'd better take another look at my opinion of the Oilers."

With the creation of imbalance, a need arises to achieve a balanced state. Recall a balanced state is characterized by three positive relationships, or two negative and one positive relationship, among all three components. Three options are available to P to restore balance: (1) to change his attitude toward O, (2) to change his attitude toward X, or (3) to try to convince O to change his attitude toward X. Think about James and Cathy again (Figure 7.7). James hates living in New York; Cathy loves it. He can either (1) change his attitude toward New York and try to come to like it or (2) change his attitude toward Cathy. "If she likes New York so much, she's not my kind of person." If James no longer cares for Cathy, it doesn't matter to him how she feels about New York. Or (3) he can try to talk Cathy into changing her attitude about New York.

One of the advantages of this theory is that it shows clearly the elements that a person attempts to keep in psychological balance. In addition the theory specifically defines the relationships leading to balance or imbalance. Another advantage is that the theory suggests options available for restoring balance.

Three deficiencies of this theory must, however, be pointed out. (1) Attitudes are either positive or negative; gradations of attitude strength can't be indicated. (2) Options for restoring balance are all equally possible; there's no way of determining what option P will choose. (3) Balance can be obtained by changing only *one* of the three relationships among elements; there's no possibility of altering more than one element to restore balance.

Osgood's Principle of Congruity

Imagine yourself listening to someone giving a speech. The basic situation of Osgood's congruity theory (1955) is an individual listening to a communicator or speaker give a speech. Osgood sets up three components: (1) a speaker or communicator, (2) a topic, and (3) an individual who listens.

In such a situation you, as listener, form attitudes toward both the speaker and the topic. Unlike Heider's theory, Osgood's theory measures *degree* of attitude. For instance your attitude toward the speaker could be determined on a scale indicating how favorably or unfavorably you react toward the speaker (Figure 7.10). Your attitude toward the speaker might

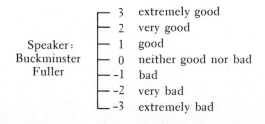

FIGURE 7.10

be a +3, which means you have an extremely positive attitude toward him; a −3, which means you have an extremely negative attitude toward him; or anywhere in between. If the speaker were President Ford, what would be your attitude toward him? Do you think he's extremely good, extremely bad, or somewhere in between? In the same way your attitude toward any topic might range from extremely favorable to extremely unfavorable. For instance a topic of a speech might be "Legalization of the Sale of Marijuana" (Figure 7.11). What's your attitude toward this topic? What number on the scale reflects your attitude?

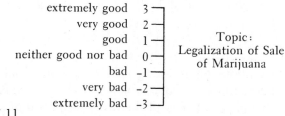

FIGURE 7.11

When a speaker gives a speech on a topic, he expresses his stand on the topic by mean of *associative* or *dissociative bonds*. An associative bond shows that the speaker has a positive attitude toward the topic: he favors the topic. A dissociative bond between a speaker and a topic indicates that the speaker has a negative attitude toward the topic: he opposes the topic. In Figure 7.12 we've illustrated an associative bond. In this case the listener has a +3 attitude toward the speaker and a +2 attitude toward the topic; the speaker is taking a favorable stand toward the topic. The connection be-

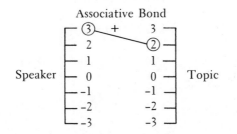

FIGURE 7.12

tween speaker and topic is shown by the line joining the numbers. Since it's an associative bond, there's a plus sign.

In Figure 7.13 we've illustrated a dissociative bond. The listener has a

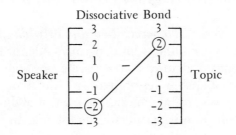

FIGURE 7.13

−2 attitude toward the speaker and a +2 attitude toward the topic; that the speaker opposes the topic is shown by a minus sign over the connection.

You, as listener, achieve congruity by, in the case of associative bonds, holding identical attitudes toward speaker and topic. Thus if you have a +3 attitude toward the speaker, a +3 attitude toward the topic, and the speaker favors the topic, you have a condition of congruity (Figure

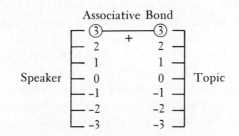

FIGURE 7.14

7.14). In the same way congruity would exist between a +2 and +2, a −2 and −2, a −3 and −3, and so on.

In the case of dissociative bonds you achieve congruity when your attitudes toward speaker and topic are of the same value but of opposite sign, that is, attitudes toward speaker and topic are in mirror-image

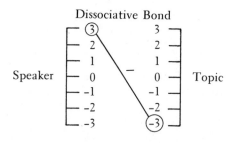

FIGURE 7.15

positions. For instance, if you have a +3 attitude toward the speaker and a −3 attitude toward the topic and if the speaker opposes the topic, you're theoretically in a psychologically balanced or congruous state (Figure 7.15). Other conditions of congruity for dissociative bonds would be a +2 and −2, and a +1 and a −1.

Incongruity exists for all other relationships between speaker and topic. Except for the precise conditions for congruity—identical scale positions for associative bonds and mirror-image scale positions for dissociative bonds—all other relationships result in incongruity. Thus in the case of an associative bond, a +3 attitude toward the speaker and a +1 attitude toward the topic results in incongruity for the listener. In the case of a dissociative bond, a +2 attitude toward the speaker and a +1 attitude toward the topic also results in incongruity. What happens when incongruity exists?

Since incongruity is psychologically painful and unpleasant, a drive or desire to reduce or eliminate this tension will manifest itself. Since incongruity can result from both associative and dissociative bonds, let's first examine how incongruity is reduced under conditions of associative bonds.

Associative Bonds   Let's say that Bob Dylan is the speaker and the topic is country-western music. Let's also say that you have an attitude of +3 toward Dylan and a +1 for country-western music. Then you, as a college reporter, attend a press interview at which Dylan speaks favorably of country-western music. This situation of incongruity can be seen in Figure 7.16. With an associative bond, you will have a desire or drive to bring attitudes toward speaker and topic to a state of congruity, defined by identical scale positions. The first task is to determine the total scale distance keeping you from reaching a state of congruity. If you hold your attitude toward Dylan at +3, you can achieve congruity by changing your attitude toward country-western music to a +3. Then your attitude toward speaker and topic would be identical—a state of congruity. Note that the change

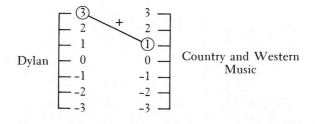

FIGURE 7.16

that you'd have to make toward the topic in order to reach congruity would be two scale units, from +1 to +3. You also can determine the total scale distance to be traveled to reach congruity by holding your attitude toward country-western music constant (that is, by keeping it at +1) and by lowering your evaluation of Dylan to a +1. You'd be in a state of congruity now, too, for your attitudes toward speaker and topic would be identical at +1. But how much attitude change will you make toward Dylan, and how much toward country-western music?

This theory, radically different from Heider's, states that attitudes toward *both* speaker and topic will change to achieve congruity. In Heider's theory, you either changed your attitude toward the topic or toward the speaker. Osgood states that you modify your attitudes toward both speaker and topic. The question then is how much change will you make toward the speaker and how much toward the topic? His basic rule is *total scale distance to reach congruity will be divided in inverse proportion to the respective polarization of scores toward speaker and topic.* "Polarization" refers to the extremity of the score: a +3 is more polarized than a +2; a +2 is more polarized than a +1; a −3 is more polarized than a −1, and so on. What this rule says, in essence, is that more extreme attitudes (scores) will change less than more moderate attitudes. It seems reasonable to assume that an extreme attitude, such as a +3, is more resistant to change than a moderate attitude, such as a +1.

The task now is to figure out what's meant by "inverse proportion." In Figure 7.17, you register an attitude of +3 toward Dylan, the most polarized positive score. Your attitude toward the topic is moderately favorable (+1). Thus Osgood's rule says that you're going to change your attitude toward Dylan less than toward country-western music. The amount each is to change must reflect a proportional relationship between the two scores of +3 and +1. All you do is add the two scores of +3 and +1. Thus the total scale distance to be traveled to reach equilibrium has to

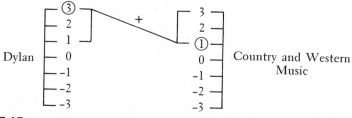

FIGURE 7.17

be (divided into) four equal subunits (Figure 7.18). To reflect the 3 to 1 proportion, attitude change toward one of the elements will be 3 of the 4 subunits, while attitude change toward the other element will be 1 of the 4 subunits. Osgood's rule states that the total scale distance to be traveled to reach congruity will be divided in *inverse proportion* to respective polarizations. We have scores of +3 and +1. An inverse proportion would thus

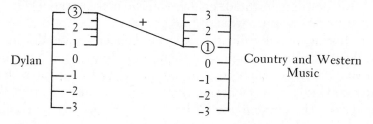

FIGURE 7.18

have the +3 move 1 of the 4 subunits, and the +1 would move 3 of the 4 subunits. You'd thus lower your attitude toward Dylan 1 of the 4 subunits and raise your attitude toward country-western music 3 of the 4 subunits (Figure 7.19). Congruity would thus be reached at +2½ on the original scale; attitudes toward both Dylan and country-western music would be congruous at +2½. What about incongruity resulting from dissociative bonds?

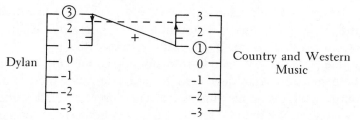

FIGURE 7.19

Dissociative Bonds   Let's have Dylan the speaker again, and you still have an attitude of +3 toward him. His hypothetical topic this time is "Legalization of the Sale of Marijuana" toward which you have an attitude of +2. Let's say that Dylan makes a statement opposing legalization of the sale of marijuana (Figure 7.20). His statement creates incongruity for you;

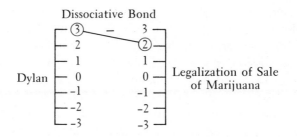

FIGURE 7.20

you'll attempt to restore psychological consistency by moving toward a position of balance. Since there's a dissociative bond in this case, you'll attempt to achieve congruity by adjusting your attitudes toward Dylan and toward marijuana so that your scores are in mirror-image positions (that is, identical scores but of opposite signs).

You first have to determine total scale distance to be traveled to reach congruity (Figure 7.21). This turns out to be 5 scale units. Second, you

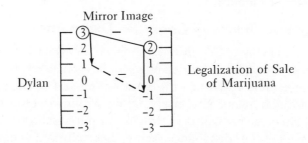

FIGURE 7.21

have to divide this total scale distance into subunits reflecting the proportions of the respective attitude scores toward Dylan and marijuana. Since the scores are +3 and +2, respectively, the total scale distance to be traveled has to be divided into 5 equal subunits. Finally, applying the inverse proportion rule, you'll change your attitude toward Dylan 2 of the 5 subunits and your attitude toward his topic 3 of the 5 subunits. We thus reach congruity at attitudes of +1 for Dylan and −1 for marijuana. Since, with dissociative bonds, we reach congruity when attitudes toward speaker and topic are in mirror-image positions, we now have congruity. Although we've omitted certain "corrections" to be applied, we've presented the essence of the theory. Congruity theory has many good features. First, Osgood specifies direction of attitude change. Second, he is willing to take the risk of predicting amount of attitude change. And finally, he makes the sensible assumption that the listener changes his attitudes toward both speakers and topics.

But congruity also has some flaws. The only way consistency can be obtained is by changing the listener's attitudes toward the speaker and the topic. There's no provision for trying to change the speaker's mind; this alternate is possible in Heider's Balance Theory, when P tries to convince O to change his mind. And probably the most significant deficiency is that congruity theory completely overlooks the degree of the bond existing between speaker and topic: nothing in the theory accounts for the degree of association or dissociation. For instance a speaker might oppose a topic with various degrees of rigor, for example Dylan saying he thinks marijuana has value of sorts or saying he thinks it's the greatest experience of all. What this all leads up to is that congruity completely overlooks the nature and strength of the bond between speaker and topic. This undoubtedly has an impact upon the amount of attitude change exhibited by the listener toward both speaker and topic.

We come now to the third intrapersonal theory, Festinger's Theory of Cognitive Dissonance.

Festinger's Theory of Cognitive Dissonance

Festinger's Theory of Cognitive Dissonance (1954) is the most controversial balance or consistency theories. While it has generated the most criticism, it has nevertheless spawned the most testing and research. Although its basic formulations are deceptively simple, it's the most complex of the consistency theories; we will only provide an introduction and cover fundamentals. Cognitive dissonance theory, especially as it's come to be revised and modified, may be applied to a range of situations and behaviors. We'll concentrate on basic definitions, variables, and propositions from the theory—and its direct applicability to intrapersonal communication.

Cognition refers to any knowledge, attitude, or belief about the environment, about oneself, or about one's behavior. The term *dissonance* refers to an inconsistent relationship between two or more cognitive elements. A cognitive element is one of these items of knowledge, or an attitude, or a belief about the environment, about oneself, and so forth. If you know you can only afford $150 for a TV set and if you find that you've just bought a color set for $450, dissonance will arise between these two cognitive elements. Two cognitive elements may also be *consonant* with one another. If you know that you've been overeating and if you find that your clothes are getting too tight, these two cognitive elements are considered consonant with one another.

Dissonance only occurs after a decision has been made. For example you only have dissonance after you realize you've engaged in behavior that's counter to other cognitions that you have. It occurs only *after* you've bought the $450 set that you couldn't afford and only *after* you've decided to go to a movie instead of working on a pressing term paper. The discomfort that you feel in these situations is what Festinger calls dissonance.

Dissonance is an uncomfortable psychological state; therefore a desire to reduce it builds up. In addition a person will actively avoid further situations or information that might increase the dissonance. The strength or drive to reduce dissonance is a direct result of the amount of the dissonance. *The greater the dissonance, the greater will be the drive to reduce it.*

We will summarize the basic points of the theory. (1) Dissonance occurs when inharmonious relationships exist between cognitive elements. (2) Dissonance only occurs after a decision has been made. (3) Dissonance results in a drive to reduce itself. (4) The greater the dissonance, the greater will be the drive to reduce the dissonance.

$$\text{Dissonance} = \frac{\text{Cognitive elements dissonant with decision}}{\text{Cognitive elements consonant with decision}}$$

The basic model of dissonance is this: Dissonance occurs after a person has made a decision or engaged in a behavior that is counter to other cognitions. Primarily two factors affect the size of dissonance. First, the *number* of elements involved in the relationship affects magnitude: the greater the number of elements in each cognition, the greater will be the dissonance. For example after you make a decision to buy a Porsche, you will experience less dissonance if there are only two conflicting cognitions (initial cost versus prestige) than if there are several conflicting cognitions (initial cost, high insurance rates, and expensive service versus prestige and luxury). Compare these two equations.

$$\text{Lower dissonance} = \frac{\text{Initial cost}}{\text{Prestige}}$$

$$\text{Higher dissonance} = \frac{\text{Initial cost, high insurance rate, expensive service}}{\text{Prestige, luxury}}$$

Second, the *importance* of the elements bears directly upon the magnitude of dissonance experienced. Less dissonance is experienced in choosing between two brands of shaving cream than in choosing between two very desirable women.

$$\text{Lower dissonance} = \frac{\text{Costs \$1.49, mint scent, stays moist, larger can}}{\text{Costs \$2.05, lemon scent, stays moist}}$$

$$\text{Higher dissonance} = \frac{\text{Beauty, intelligence, artistic interests, good cook}}{\text{Beauty, intelligence, athletic interests}}$$

If dissonance is related to the number and importance of the cognitive elements, what are the ways in which dissonance can be reduced?

Four methods of reducing dissonance are possible in this scheme. (1) You may change your attitude toward the decision or behavior. If you have previously had a negative attitude toward oysters but find yourself now eating them, you can tell yourself that they're not as disgusting as you had imagined. (2) You may change your behavior. If you smoke, knowing that smoking is bad for your health, you can attempt to stop smoking. (3) You may change your environment. If you're an athlete of only average ability—but you wish to make the varsity—you can go to a small school that lacks athletes and be the first-string quarterback. (4) You may add new cognitive elements. If you've bought a stereo system you can't afford, you might tell yourself that you will probably get a raise momentarily or that you will survive, after all, the expenses associated with an extravagant purchase.

We will turn our attention now to dissonance as it affects intrapersonal communication, restricting our discussion to the first method of reducing dissonance—by the individual changing his attitude toward the decision or behavior. An individual's attitude change, which comes about after he has made a difficult decision, is explained very well by means of dissonance theory. After a decision is made that results in dissonance, a common means of reducing this dissonance is for the individual to change attitudes to be consistent with his recent behavior. If he's put in many Saturday nights studying instead of going out—and he'd rather be going out—he's probably developed more positive attitudes toward studying. Although it's impossible to change his behavior once he's acted, he can still change his attitude toward the behavior: "After all, the time spent studying in the long run should be good for me. All I've lost is a little pleasure."

In explaining the relationship of incentive or reward (or punishment) to attitude change, dissonance theory leads to predictions that run counter

to expectation or common sense. Dissonance theory suggests that, if someone is induced to engage in behavior that he finds distasteful but is given a
large incentive or reward for doing so, he will *not* change his attitude in a
favorable direction toward the behavior. If he was persuaded to tell other
students that a tedious and dull communication experiment was interesting and was promised $100 for doing so, he'd experience little dis-
sonance—probably reasoning that he only did it for the money. On the
other hand, if he were persuaded to do so for only, say, $2, he'd be troubled
with a fair amount of dissonance. And the greater the dissonance, the
stronger the drive to reduce it. Since he can't take back his behavior, or his
act already committed, a common way of reducing dissonance would be
for him to change his attitude toward the behavior. He'd probably
rationalize to himself that the experiment wasn't all that dull; in fact it
could be very interesting if the student went into it with an open mind.

Dissonance theory also has useful applications in explaining the relationship of threat to attitude change. If you find yourself engaging in behavior that disturbs you, because of high threat from an outside source,
little dissonance arises since you were *forced* to comply; you would experience little or no attitude change favoring the behavior. But if the threat was
of a lesser degree, then you'd experience greater dissonance. One way out
would be to change your attitude—toward a more favorable attitude toward
the behavior. For example, if we assume that Penny doesn't like to take
exams, she'll experience less dissonance if she takes exams under high
threat of failing a course than under the low threat of an extra work assignment or report. In the case of high threat, we would expect Penny to experience little or no attitude change toward taking exams, but in the case of
low threat, we might expect greater dissonance and more attitude change
on her part toward taking exams—even a change toward a more favorable
attitude about them.

We have seen that the dissonance theory explains the relationship between the size of the incentive—or the seriousness of the threat—and the
amount of attitude change. It also has direct implications for the way people respond to certain persuasive messages. In listening to a message using
high reward or high threat to persuade you to do some objectionable act or
behavior, you're not likely to change your attitude into one favoring the
behavior. You're likely to experience little or no dissonance since you
could justify the behavior in terms of the sizable reward or intolerable
punishment.

Finally, dissonance theory offers a reasonable account for the common finding that extremely discrepant messages often result in attitude

change in the direction advocated by the message. A message favoring a stand extremely opposed to your own—a discrepant message—will create much higher dissonance than a message advocating a stand only slightly different from your own. The greater the dissonance, the greater will be the drive to reduce it. Provided that you don't choose some other means of resolving dissonance, one available means of reducing dissonance would be to change your attitude toward the direction advocated by the message.

Thus dissonance offers plausible explanations for the relationships between an individual's attitude change and the type of message: (1) the effect of messages offering high rewards or making strong threats upon attitude change, and (2) attitude response to highly discrepant messages.

But as is true of all theories, deficiencies exist. The one weakness we'd like to stress in dissonance theory is that *the method an individual uses to reduce dissonance is very difficult to determine* or predict; all options are possible to him. Festinger provides no rank ordering of the possible means of reducing dissonance.

We've presented theories that have been used to explain attitude responses in intrapersonal communicating contexts. Let's move on to a consideration of internal and external cues relevant to attitude change. We'll begin with a discussion of internal stimuli.

Intrapersonal Communication: Internal System

Internal cues or stimuli are those characteristics we bring with us to a communication situation. They are the sum total of our past perceptions, experiences, and feelings. We don't use all of them in every communicating transaction; we use only those that seem to be relevant to us at that time.

So far in this chapter we've focused on the communication factor of attitude and how attitudes may be changed or balanced. What we'd like to do in this section is mention internal stimuli that seem closely related to attitude response. We'll concentrate on three internal elements: personality, intelligence, and ego-involvement. Since two of these elements have been described in Chapter 4, we will not go into them at great length.

Personality traits, the elements we bring with us to any communicating environment, are relatively constant and have a direct bearing upon our intrapersonal communication. Two personality traits appear to be especially important in affecting our attitude changes—self-esteem and dogmatism.

Self-esteem

As we've seen in Chapter 4, self-esteem refers to perceptions a person has about himself—his feelings of self-respect and self-confidence. As might be expected, a person's level of self-esteem affects the amount of attitude change he experiences in response to persuasive messages. In general people with low self-esteem are more easily persuaded; they change their attitudes more readily than those with strong self-esteem when receiving persuasive messages. Furthermore people with low self-esteem conform more to group norms than those with strong self-esteem and are more susceptible to messages emphasizing social standards. Persons with strong self-esteem are more difficult to persuade; their attitudes on an issue are generally harder to change. Since they have more confidence in themselves and their opinions, they are less easily influenced by messages attempting to persuade them to change their stands or standards.

Dogmatism

Another personality trait that's related to attitude change is dogmatism. In our use of the term, dogmatism refers to a person's open- or close-mindedness. Someone who's open-minded is less rigid and more flexible in his approach to people and ideas. A close-minded person tends to be more rigid and set in his thinking: he knows what's right and what's wrong. And that's it!

It is known that strongly dogmatic people are highly suspectible to certain kinds of appeals by sources perceived by them to have high credibility. Unfortunately research findings have not as yet produced any clear-cut relationship between levels of dogmatism and persuasibility. Some findings show that attitudes of highly dogmatic people are more easily influenced; other studies demonstrate that attitudes of less dogmatic people are more easily affected. The influence of dogmatism upon attitude change seems to depend upon how dogmatism combines with other variables, for example, the authority of the message source. In the last section of this chapter, using the Trans-Per model, we'll see how dogmatism, an internal cue, and authority, an external cue, blend to influence attitude change.

Intelligence

It seems reasonable to assume that intelligence may be consistently related to attitude change—that highly intelligent people are either more easily or less easily persuaded to change their attitudes than people with low intelligence. In general it appears that people with low intelligence are more readily influenced. Unfortunately we cannot make unqualified statements since there are conflicting findings in this area. Some studies show that highly intelligent people are more difficult to persuade; other studies show that people with high intelligence are more easily persuaded. Apparently intelligence, like other internal elements, doesn't operate independently to affect attitude change; it combines with other cues or variables.

Ego-involvement

Ego-involvement, as you may recall, is the individual's commitment to the issue or topic being discussed—how relevant or how significant the topic is to him. Strongly ego-involved individuals are far more deeply concerned with specific issues than weakly ego-involved persons. Highly ego-involved persons have large latitudes of rejection: other than the view they consider most acceptable, they find almost all other points of view on the topic unacceptable. Weakly involved persons, on the other hand, have small latitudes of rejection—and large latitudes of acceptance and noncommitment. They find many positions on a topic acceptable other than their most acceptable position. As might be expected, weakly involved persons are much more inclined to change their attitudes than are highly involved individuals.

   Although we have described four particular internal elements that affect attitude response, we'd like to emphasize that *all* internal stimuli have the potential to affect attitude response. The elements we've chosen to discuss are those that seem to be more extensively researched—and not necessarily more significant than others we have not touched upon.

Intrapersonal Communication: External System

We'd like to discuss four external cues whose relationship to attitude change has been extensively researched, credibility, message appeals, evidence, and message organization.

Credibility

Although credibility may also be considered a meaning created through perceptual activity, we'd like you to think about credibility in this section as an external cue: we want you to focus on external qualities that communicators exhibit. Two kinds of external cues affect an individual's perceptions of another person's credibility: qualities the person brings with him to the communicating situation and what the person says and does when actually communicating.

   The classification of what a communicator brings to a situation is end-

less: he brings his appearance, clothing, grooming, education, religion, age, race, marital status, occupation, and so forth. Someone who is white, carefully dressed, and obviously wealthy may have a troublesome problem establishing a high level of credibility when communicating with someone who is part of a racial minority living in an inner-city ghetto.

In addition to qualities a communicator brings with him, characteristics exhibited by the communicator while he is in the process of actually communicating affect the listener's perceptions of his credibility. Does he look at you when speaking, or does he avoid eye contact? Does he seem calm and assured as he communicates, or does he exhibit nervous mannerisms? The type of language used is also germane. Is it understandable? Is it profane? Is the speaker fluent? Does he organize his ideas into a coherent pattern, or do his thoughts seem jumbled and rambling? You may include here all of the verbal and nonverbal elements discussed in Chapter 5 on the External System.

It's difficult to specify what external characteristics lead to one person's perceptions of another's high or low credibility. The best we can say is that "it depends." It depends upon how the external characteristics blend with the internal cues of the receiver. The president of Standard Oil of California may have high credibility to his stockholders but may have extremely low credibility to a U.S. Senator, who believes that the oil companies are attempting to profit excessively from an oil shortage. Knowing that both a variety of external cues and a variety of internal cues contribute to our perceptions of another's credibility, can we then specify what are the dominant factors that influence our perceptions of credibility?

Research has consistently identified at least two general dimensions of credibility, character and authoritativeness. We use the term *character* to refer to our perceptions of an individual's honesty or trustworthiness. If we pick up cues that lead us to believe that a communicator is telling the truth and that he has our best interests at heart, we tend to regard him as a person of high character. The other dimension of credibility that has been identified is authoritativeness. The term *authoritativeness* refers to those attributes of the communicator that lead us to believe he's competent, intelligent, well trained—and knows what he's talking about. Futhermore the two dimemsions of credibility appear to have different effects upon bringing about attitude change in the listener—depending upon the message. The character of the speaker seems to have more effect upon the listener if his message is concerned with values; his authoritativeness seems to have more effect if the message is concerned with facts or beliefs.

Other dimensions of credibility have been identified, but they haven't appeared with enough consistency for us to speak with any certainty. One of these is *dynamism*, a personal quality that leads us to perceive that the speaker is vigorous, energetic, and forceful. Keep in mind that these are our personal perceptions—and only that—of the speaker at the time of the communication. The speaker may not be, in fact, honest or trustworthy; he may not be, in fact, qualified or competent.

You might ask at this point what credibility has to do with attitude change—what we're most concerned with here. The credibility of the speaker strongly influences any attitude change that takes place in his audience. Although research findings are once again inconclusive and incomplete, we can say, in general, that a speaker who is perceived as a person of high credibility is more persuasive than a speaker who is perceived as a person of low credibility. We would like to consider now additional external cues that effect attitude change in the listener.

Message Appeals

A wide variety of *message appeals*—humor, pity, love, hate, and prejudice—often appear in daily communication. However only a limited number of message appeals have been studied as they affect or change the attitude of listeners; among these are logical versus emotional appeals and threat appeals.

Logical versus Emotional Appeals   Although it seems eminently sensible to distinguish between logical and emotional appeals, immediate problems arise in attempting to differentiate between them. What's logical to Jack may seem emotional to Robert. Research indicates that most people are not able to distinguish clearly between a logical and emotional message. People trained in argumentation and debate seem to do a little better, but even they still have trouble in distinguishing between the two. If a speech about wartime atrocities presents statistics dealing with thousands of women and children deliberately killed, is the appeal logical or emotional? If we're shown pictures of civilians who have been shot in the face, is that logical or emotional? Any distinction in these cases is purely arbitrary. Although the distinguishing between logical and emotional appeals seems to make good sense intuitively, it often doesn't help very much.

Perhaps the only distinction worth making—between a logical and emotional appeal—is the way a message *appears* to the listener. A seemingly "logical" message is sometimes effective with certain kinds of listeners; for example, messages using statistics and authoritative sources are relatively effective upon a highly educated audience.

Threat Appeals   Threat appeals emphasize that harmful results will befall the receiver if he doesn't accept the recommendation of the message. Such messages are intended to create anxiety and fear. Much research has delved into the effect of threat appeals upon attitude change. Studies have been devised to compare the effects of high-threat messages to those of low threat. For instance a verbal message that talked about the harmful consequences that might result if passengers neglect to use seat belts might be considered a low-threat message. The same message presented with pictures in full color—of an accident scene with several draped bodies—might be considered a high-threat message.

A major difficulty for researchers seems to be that people don't perceive threat in the same way. What's a highly threatening message to one person may not be so awesome to another. Universally perceived fear appeals have not been uncovered thus far. Obviously perception of threat depends upon the Internal System that the receiver brings with him to the communication.

One finding that seems relatively certain is that threat appeals are most effective if they contain means for alleviating the anxiety produced by the threat. In other words the message is more effective if it provides a way for the receiver to take action so that he can avoid the harm or punishment that may result. If the message doesn't offer a means of avoiding the harm, the receiver may simply screen it out as psychologically too painful to confront. Since he can't do anything about it, what good does it do for him to worry about it?

As to the effect of threat appeals on bringing about attitude change in the listener, present findings conflict. Early research seemed to demonstrate that low-threat messages were more effective than high-threat messages in influencing attitude change; more recent research seems to demonstrate the opposite. At this point all that can be said is that the findings are inconclusive, and the issue remains unsettled.

Evidence

By evidence we refer here to facts—generally statistics and opinions of experts—that are presented in a message. Messages can vary greatly in the kinds and amounts of evidence used. Much research has been devoted to the role of evidence in affecting attitudes; but, as with other external cues, results again are mixed. Again the effect of evidence depends upon what other internal and external stimuli are combined with it. When a person blends his own internal cues of intelligence and knowledge with the external cues of a speaker's credibility as well as a speaker's use of supporting evidence, his attitudes may shift markedly. We'll examine the blending of these variables, and the effect of blending on attitude change, in the Trans-Per section.

Message Organization

We will discuss one other external element that affects attitude change —message organization or message arrangement. Two widely studied aspects of message organization are message sidedness and order of presentation.

Message Sidedness   What kind of message is most persuasive in effecting attitude changes? If a person is writing a speech advocating the legalization of marijuana, will it be more effective if it only contains reasons in behalf of legalization, or will it be more effective if it also mentions reasons against legalization? Here too findings are mixed: a one-sided message has no clear advantage over a two-sided message. Again it seems to depend upon the Internal Systems of the receivers of the message. For instance highly intelligent listeners are often suspicious of messages presenting only one side. People with low intelligence seem less suspicious of and less disturbed by one-sided arguments. In general the two-sided message seems a safer approach: the listener probably perceives it as a fairer presentation than the one-sided message and responds with higher perceptions of trustworthiness. These perceptions of trustworthiness in turn have an effect upon the listener's possible openness to attitude change. In taking a two-sided approach, one can not only mention the opposing position but also take the opportunity to refute claims made in its behalf.

Order of Presentation   When a message is to contain a number of arguments of different strengths, is it more effective to present the strongest argument first, last, or in the middle? When the strongest argument comes first (primacy effect), it can capture attention immediately and thus have great initial impact. But does the effect of the strong argument wear off? And what happens when the receiver finds the speaker's remaining arguments weak and loses interest? If, on the other hand, the strong argument comes last (recency effect), the message can end with a bang. The danger is that the listener may have become disinterested or worn out from the preceding weaker arguments and may have already turned the message off—before the strongest argument is finally presented.

As you can probably guess, research doesn't clearly support the advantage of either the primacy or recency effect in bringing about attitude change. Some studies have supported the practice of putting the strongest argument first; other studies have supported the practice of putting it last. Everyone seems to agree that putting the strongest argument in the middle is not the way to be effective.

Another order of presentation that has proven effective in practice is for the speaker to create a need and then to attempt to satisfy that need. Generations of students in public speaking classes have learned these steps in organizing persuasive messages: (1) gain attention (2) show a need (3) satisfy the need through a solution (4) describe possible results of the proposed solution and (5) stimulate action toward effecting the solution.

At this point we've touched upon a variety of internal and external stimuli that may potentially bring about a change of attitude in the listener. In our final section we will illustrate the blending of internal and external cues and the effect of blending on attitude change—through the use of the Trans-Per model.

Intrapersonal Communication: Trans-Per

The *meaning or communication factor* we've focused on so far in this chapter is *attitude change* or response. We will consider attitude change to be within that portion of Trans-Per represented by the overlapping of the Internal and External Systems.

What we'd like to do now is illustrate how particular internal and external stimuli combine to affect a communicator's attitudes and reactions. We will set up a communicating context in which those internal and external stimuli particularly relevant to affecting attitude change are operating. Although any and all internal and external cues may have a potential relationship to attitude change, we'll select only those cues that can be conveniently illustrated. We'll show how different combinations of internal and external stimuli tend to affect attitude change or attitude response.

Dean Deveauraux of the college of arts and sciences, a well-respected educator, called a meeting of all undergraduates and gave a talk on a new academic policy she hoped to adopt. Her talk advocated doing away with the current practice of majoring in any one specific discipline, such as the traditional psychology, anthropology, or political science major. Instead she proposed to have majors in broad interdisciplinary areas, that is, in the social sciences, humanities, or physical sciences. In essence she spoke against specialized training in any single discipline in favor of a more general education across several disciplines. After carefully researching her ideas, she developed a talk supported by much strong evidence: she used arguments from the writings of other educators and university professors who also favored general education. Speaking vigorously in behalf of her proposal, she attacked the present practice, which she felt resulted in a too one-sided education.

In the auditorium listening to her speak are Jean and Rosemary. Both major in psychology and generally favor the current policy; both perceive Dean Deveauraux to be highly credible. However Jean and Rosemary differ in some significant ways: Jean has a highly dogmatic personality, an average IQ, and isn't particularly involved in the issue. Although she wants to keep the discipline major, the issue isn't all that important to her; what she wants to do is try to be a professional photographer. Finally most of the information presented at the meeting is completely new to her. She has never thought much about any type of major other than the traditional kind.

Rosemary, on the other hand, is a weakly dogmatic person. Very intelligent, she is highly ego-involved in the topic. Philosophically opposed to generalized training, she believes in majoring in a single discipline because she personally wants depth in her education. Her high involvement in the topic had stimulated her to do some reading and thinking in the area as soon as the meeting was announced; the ideas of Dean Deveauraux weren't completely new to her.

After listening to the talk, Jean was strongly persuaded by the arguments and changed her attitude completely. Rosemary, on the other hand, became even more entrenched in her own position. Let's examine their attitudes and reactions to Dean Deveauraux and her speech. Jean has a highly dogmatic personality; highly dogmatic people tend to accept recommendations from individuals with high credibility who are in positions of authority. In addition a highly dogmatic person feels that she understands less about what's good for her than those in positions of authority. Furthermore a highly dogmatic person has great difficulty in distinguishing between the authority and what the authority says; both get mixed up in her mind. When an authority says something counter to her own attitude, a highly dogmatic individual tends to change her attitude.

Contributing to Dean Deveauraux's effectiveness in influencing

Jean was Jean's average intelligence. Using a one-sided approach, Dean Deveauraux spoke only in favor of the position she was advocating—and said nothing in favor of continuing the present system. People of lower intelligence tend to be more influenced by one-sided messages than those with higher intelligence. Jean also was unfamiliar with the evidence presented: evidence tends to have a much greater impact when it's unfamiliar to a receiver. Finally, Jean wasn't involved in the issue and had a very wide latitude of acceptance. Thus the speech produced a very large shift in Jean's attitude: the particular combination of internal and external cues led to Jean's dramatic change of attitude—toward one in favor of general rather than specialized majors.

Rosemary, on the other hand, didn't change even slightly her attitude on the issue after hearing the talk. What put the most pressure on her—and caused her to reconsider her attitude somewhat—was her perception of Dean Deveauraux as a person of highest credibility. However other combinations of stimuli led her to a firm and final rejection of the proposal. As a weakly dogmatic personality, Rosemary has the ability to differentiate between who is presenting a message and what the message contains. And if a speaker, even a highly credible one, takes a position opposing her own, the weakly dogmatic person tends to lower her evaluations of the speaker, as a means of maintaining psychological balance, rather than to change her attitude toward the issue. Rosemary, like other people with high intelligence, is suspicious of individuals who present only one side of an issue. In addition she had some knowledge of the educational issues involved and had previously read some of the arguments that Dean Deveauraux used. Evidence tends to be less effective with people who have been previously exposed to it. Having been exposed to some of the arguments used, Rosemary may have already thought about counterarguments; she may have already insulated herself against the arguments in the speech. Finally Rosemary was highly involved in the issue and had a very wide latitude of rejection. Messages falling into one's latitude of rejection have no chance of producing substantial change in one's most acceptable position. Thus this combination of internal and external stimuli negated the possibility of attitude change in Rosemary.

We might have set up communication situations in which different cues were operating. What we hoped to get across from our example, however, is that attitude change or response is a result of a mix of internal and external cues: these cues are interdependent and interrelated. Since particular combinations produce unique reactions, we must be very careful about forming imprecise generalizations—such as that a certain internal or external cue invariably leads to a certain attitude response. Accounting for what influences or changes attitudes is a complex affair. Depending upon the cues coming into the blend, responses of individuals can be quite different.

In the next chapter we'll consider communication in the interpersonal context. Everything we've learned about intrapersonal communication applies to interpersonal communication as well. Interpersonal communication is not distinct from intrapersonal communication; it incorporates intrapersonal communication.

Although interpersonal communication is more complex—and will challenge you more—it's a fascinating communicating environment. So many of our strongest feelings and emotions come about from our interpersonal communication.

Additional Readings

Bettinghaus, E. P. *Persuasive Communication.* 2d ed. New York: Holt, Rinehart and Winston, 1973.

Chapter 5, "The Influence of the Communicator," is a brief summary of the nature of source credibility and includes major findings on the persuasive effect of source credibility. Chapter 7, "Structuring Messages and Appeals," is a good synthesis of research on the external cues of message organization and message appeals.

Brown R. "Models of Attitude Change." In *New Directions in Social Psychology*, edited by R. Brown, E. Galanter, E. Hess, and G. Mandler. New York: Holt, Rinehart and Winston, 1962.

A well-written, interesting, advanced treatment of the theories of congruity, dissonance, and balance.

Kerlinger, F. *Foundations of Behavioral Research.* New York: Holt, Rinehart and Winston, 1973.

Chapters 1, 2, and 3 are excellent fundamental studies of the aims and methods of science and include a fundamental treatment of the nature and role of scientific theory.

McCroskey, J. C. "Studies of the Effects of Evidence in Persuasive Communication." *Quarterly Journal of Speech* 55 (1969):169–176.

A descriptive evaluation and review of research on the effects of evidence.

Zajonc, R. "The Concepts of Balance, Congruity, and Dissonance." *Public Opinion Quarterly* 24 (1969):280–296.

A simplified review and evaluation of the intrapersonal balance theories of Heider, Osgood, and Festinger. Also found in *Foundations of Communication Theory*, edited by K. Sereno and C. D. Mortensen. New York: Harper & Row, 1970.

Applications

Exercise 1

Sometimes the communicating behavior of other people baffles us. Do you ever create your own "theories" to explain the behavior of, for example, your mother, your friends, your boss, your teacher? In a sense, do these theories have constructs, propositions, predictive power, explanatory power? Do you ever create theories to explain your own communication behavior?

Exercise 2

Think about the following situations and draw a model for each, using Heider's Balance Theory (P, O, and X). Then determine how you would probably balance each of the following situations, according to Heider's theory:

a. You like Charles. You dislike Ford. Charles likes Ford.
b. You hate and avoid cocktail parties. Katy hates and avoids cocktail parties. You like Katy.
c. You think Mr. Rush is the worst teacher you've ever had. He thinks Beethoven is the best composer of them all. So do you.

Do you think that this theory explains all the possible outcomes?

Exercise 3

Divide into small groups and think of several topics that are probably controversial among members of the class. Then combine all the topics from all the groups onto one list; next to each item on the list indicate a scale from +3 to −3 (indicating very positive to very negative attitudes). Have everyone in the class fill out the questionnaire by numerically indicating his attitude toward each topic.

Next have each member prepare and give a speech on a topic he chooses from the list. Before he begins, he must state at what point on the scale he has registered his own attitude. After each speech, decide how you feel toward the topic. Compare your attitude on the scale after the speech with your attitude before the speech.

Do you have an associative bond or a dissociative bond with each speaker? Is there congruity?

Exercise 4

Discuss some situations that have produced dissonance for you lately. How strong was the discomfort? Did you do anything about it?

Exercise 5

How could dissonance be reduced in the following situations? (Or would there be dissonance in the first place?)

a. You have a test in chemistry tomorrow, but you yield to pressure from the group and go to a double feature movie.

b. Asking for a job that he badly wants as a swimming instructor, Sam has just told the interviewer that he's had similar jobs before. Sam has never been a swimming instructor although he does know how to swim.

c. Jan tells her statistics instructor that she finds statistics "quite interesting," and that she's "certainly learned a lot of new material in the class." She hates statistics; she likes good grades; and it's near the end of the semester.

CHAPTER • 8

Theoretical Approaches to Interpersonal Communication
Attribution Theory
Game Theory
Social Comparison Theory
Newcomb's Balance Theory
Four Factors of Interpersonal Transaction: Attraction, Understanding, Trust, Anxiety
Attraction
    Attraction: Internal System
    Attraction: External System
    Attraction: Trans-Per
Understanding
    Understanding: Internal System
    Understanding: External System
    Understanding: Trans-Per
Trust
    Trust: Internal System
    Trust: External System
    Trust: Trans-Per
Anxiety
    Anxiety: Internal System
    Anxiety: External System
    Anxiety: Trans-Per
Summary
Additional Readings
Applications

Communication in the Interpersonal Context

Few of us would argue with the claim that our most exhilarating moments come through our interpersonal relationships. Our feelings of greatest happiness, joy, contentment, and satisfaction are typically experienced in our relationships with others. On not such a happy note, few of us would argue with the lament that our most serious depressions come about as a result of our interpersonal relationships. The feelings of anger, despair, loss, and distrust are also possible consequences of interpersonal relationships. In our relationships with others are found all the most beautiful and the most ugly experiences we have as human beings. Of particular interest to us is the fact that communication is the process by which we establish, maintain, and terminate our relationships with others. What is interpersonal communication? What does it involve?

Communication in the interpersonal context is relatively unstructured and informal communication in which we engage another individual face to face. When speaking face to face (as opposed to listening to a speaker on TV or radio), each person in the transaction supplies the other with a rich source of cues or stimuli—not only what each says through words (verbal content) but also what each expresses through the vast range of gestures, body movements, and other behavioral cues (nonverbal content).

When two people are communicating on an interpersonal level, they take turns speaking and listening. A give-and-take is evident in interpersonal communication that's not matched in any other communication context. But to say people take turns speaking and listening is not quite precise: it implies that someone is first a sender of a message and then a receiver of a message. In actuality people engaged in interpersonal transaction are simultaneously sending and receiving messages continuously. Simply because one person happens to be speaking doesn't mean that the other person isn't sending a whole slew of nonverbal messages. In other words people are always simultaneously sending and receiving messages.

In addition interpersonal communication is characterized by fairly *frequent changes of topics*. For a wide variety of reasons the topic may change back and forth. Let's observe a couple talking over an excellent steak dinner in a quiet, uncrowded restaurant. They're presently talking about how much they're enjoying the meal and each other's company; they remember earlier meals in other pleasant settings that they have shared in the past. Suddenly the entrance of another couple interrupts the flow of their conversation. The man coming in is about fifty-five, overweight, smiling, energetic, and appears to enjoy the good life. His companion is about twenty-four, underweight, prim, and looks as if she prefers libraries to parties. The conversation immediately shifts to the entering couple —who they could be, what they see in each other, various other speculations. After reaching the conclusion that "opposites attract," they return to their previous conversation. And so it goes—the conversation shifting from topic to topic.

Frequent changes of topic are generally caused by changes in the External System in the form of new verbal and nonverbal cues. The two newcomers who entered the restaurant are considered part of the External System. (A new person would be considered as an additional Internal System only if he entered into face-to-face communication with the original communicators.) Since no formal agenda is followed in the interpersonal context people are more responsive to changes that occur in the environment. Indeed in this example the original couple was communicating mainly about certain external stimuli in the External System—the uncrowded restaurant and the quality of the dinner. Changes in their External System will naturally be reflected in their communication transaction.

When writers use the phrase "interpersonal communication," they're typically talking about communication taking place between two people although more are sometimes included; however in this chapter we're taking the two-person stance. In addition other researchers may use the term interpersonal communication to refer to conversations between strangers, acquaintances, friends, or lovers. We're focusing just upon conversations between people who are deeply attached to one another: friends, lovers, married couples, and close relatives. The reason we prefer to focus on conversations with close friends, or people with whom we have or wish to have intimate relationships, is that these transactions are the usual sources of the soaring pleasures and the deep unhappiness we experience as human beings.

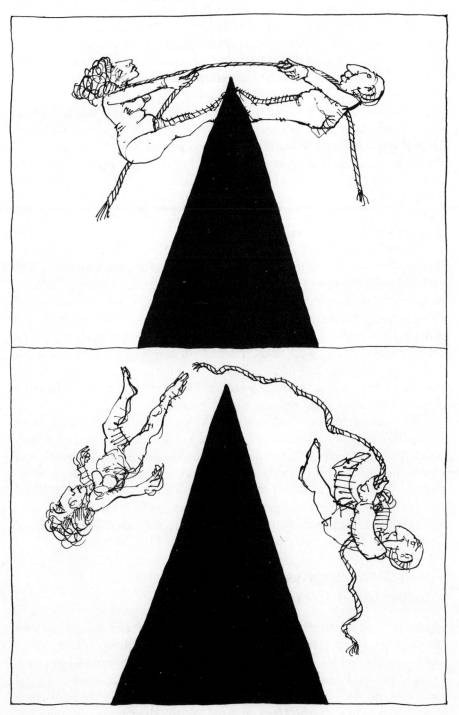

Before probing further into the nature of interpersonal communication, let's take stock of where we are in our study of the process of human communication. Recall that intrapersonal communication refers basically to how we "talk" to ourselves and concerns itself with what we broadly call self-maintenance—how we maintain our own psychological balance or stability. In our study of the intrapersonal context we described the various theories presently available that attempt to explain how we maintain psychological balance or stability among our attitudes.

In the present chapter we are going to build on our previous findings and observations. Interpersonal communication is a natural extension of intrapersonal communication. We have previously observed that communication in the intrapersonal context is essentially concerned with the evolution of meaning taking place within the individual. Obviously this process still occurs in interpersonal communication: it doesn't stop or disappear when we enter into communication with another individual. What we have now, however, are *two* intrapersonal systems operating within a larger, more complex communication system. Everything we've learned about intrapersonal communication applies as well to the interpersonal context. Although we may not keep referring to the ongoing intrapersonal communication process, it's assumed that you are aware that it's operating at the same time as, and in addition to, the interpersonal system. For in essence the interpersonal system is formed by the joining up of two Internal Systems that share a common External System.

We want to deal next with some of the major theories that have been used to help explain interpersonal communication. Theories, as you may recall, are general explanations that are able to account for a wide variety of specific behaviors—in this case communicating behavior in an interpersonal context. We'll look at four theories which provide seemingly different, yet fundamentally related, views of the significant determinants of interpersonal communication: Attribution Theory, Game Theory, Social Comparison Theory, and Newcomb's Balance Theory.

Theoretical Approaches to Interpersonal Communication

Once again we're using the phrase "theoretical approaches to" rather than "theories of" interpersonal communication. It would be technically incorrect for us to label all four theories we will take up as theories of interpersonal communication. The theories are all actually psychological theories—but they all can be used to shed light on interpersonal communication. They are, however, not specifically theories of interpersonal communication: a theory of interpersonal communication would be one whose primary aim is an explanation of the process of interpersonal communication. All of the theories we'll consider have as their primary aim an understanding of psychological or of mental processes. What's of interest to us is that they may be applied to communication processes.

For instance, recall the psychological theory that deals with the relationship of frustration and aggression previously discussed in Chapter 7. A basic proposition from this theory is that frustration leads to aggression. Now a theoretical statement such as this can be used to help us understand, explain, and predict certain communicating behavior. For example if we identify certain communicating behavior that leads to frustration for the listener—like interrupting him continually—this theory would lead us to predict that an aggressive type of response might occur. (What the specific response might be in the specific communicating situation varies.) Although the theory is basically directed toward explaining the psychological processes of frustration and aggression, it allows us to understand certain forms of communicating behavior. In a similar way all the theories we will present are means of helping us understand what's happening in the process of interpersonal communication.

If we had to sum up the essence of theory, a theory is used to help explain behavior—in this case psychological processes. We caution you that none of the following theories accounts for *all* interpersonal communicating behavior. Since it's very difficult to create a scientific theory that includes every possible variable, they're all somewhat limited in scope or in range of variables considered. Another limitation we must bear in mind is that most theories work only when specific variables are allowed to come into play while all the others remain unchanged. Called by scientists the *ceteris paribus* requirement, it means that all variables other than the one being studied have to be held constant or have to be equal. The problem is that a whole complex of variables operates in different communicating situations; variables are never constant or equal unless the scientist exerts tight control over them in a laboratory context. They cannot control or block variables in the real-life setting of a typical interpersonal communication. Despite the fact that these theories do not explain everything connected with interpersonal communication, they do explain a good deal.

Attribution Theory

To communicate on an interpersonal level, we have to interpret the words and actions of the other individual involved. We try to make sense out of what the other person says and does. Making judgments or inferences from the actions of another person about his or her motives is the process of attribution. For example one person must decide the extent to which what the other person says and does is to be believed. He has to figure out how much of what the other person says and does reflects his true feelings and how much his behavior is caused by the role or situation in which he finds himself.

In making judgments of the motives or intentions of the other person, the total situation must be considered. What may be interpreted positively in one situation may be looked at with a jaundiced eye in another. When our boss gives us compliments, we react quite differently if we believe the praise is sincere on her part rather than motivated by her wanting us to work harder and faster. Our increased production would make her look successful at her work and ripe for a raise. If we interpret her praise as being motivated by self-interest rather than concern and care, we may react in an opposite manner from that which our boss had intended. We may work less and try to get away with more. A message, such as praise, is interpreted in relation to the specific situation in which it occurs. We are disconcerted by what we interpret as insincere compliments. On the other hand we may not be too disturbed by criticism if we believe the criticism was sincere and was given with our best interests at heart. The fundamental idea of Attribution Theory is simply that interpretation of motives arises out of the total situation: a person evaluates and interprets the psychological state—motives and intentions—of the person he is talking to by putting what the person says and does into a total context.

Two propositions from Attribution Theory may be applied to the study of interpersonal communication. First, we tend to believe what a communicator says when his message seems to be internally motivated and when we perceive he is saying what he truly feels. Second, we tend to distrust what a communicator says when we feel that the message was externally motivated or that his actions were caused by a role he had to play or by external pressures. In essence we believe messages when we feel that the message reflects how the communicator truly feels. Conversely we distrust messages if we perceive them to be insincere, that is, caused by circumstances and not by honest inner feelings. In making these judgments the cues we use are selected from the total situation.

An important derivation from Attribution Theory is the hypothesis that, when people exhibit behavior contrary to role-expected behavior, the unexpected behavior is much more likely to be believed. The first time we attend the taping of a Hollywood game show and observe that our friendly TV host—after saying "we'll be right back, folks, after this word from our sponsors"—drops his face-wide smile and totally ignores contestants and audience, we tend to believe these out-of-role behaviors. We tend to think of him as unfriendly, hypocritical, and worse.

In interpersonal communication the process of attributing motives does not usually come into play in the discussion of mundane, routine matters. We mean those passing conversations of saying hello to a friend in the corridor, or making small talk in the elevator about the weather, or when waiting in the cafeteria line talking about how the food in the cafeteria is not worth eating. But attributing motives is a crucial behavior in more permanent and significant interpersonal relationships. Although it doesn't matter how the cab driver responds, it does matter when talking with close friends to keep our eyes and ears tuned to out-of-role behavior from which the other person's inner feelings may be determined. When Sara says "I don't mind that you're going to the party alone. I can use the time to finish this paper that's due on Monday. I heard Joan will be there, and you haven't seen Joan for a while. You two will have a good chance to talk," it's the insensitive friend who believes what he hears although he may want to believe it. Sara, hoping to please her boyfriend, is playing a "good woman" role: she's saying what she feels is expected of an open-minded person. Nevertheless she is playing a role rather than expressing her true inner feelings. If her boyfriend continually fails to recognize the true feelings of Sara, his insensitivity will lead eventually to a deterioration in their relationship.

When communicating with a person of significance to you, it's useful to go behind the surface of his words—to what he is feeling inside. In attempting to understand what someone honestly feels, you have to take into account all that is feeding into his or her messages and behavior; you must assess the relationship of the person you care about to the specific situation. If you perceive, for example, that the other person's behavior may be accounted for by self-interest or by external pressures, your perception of insincerity typically creates an interpersonal barrier. If you attempt to understand the total situation and the motives of the participants, including your own, you have a better chance of removing communication barriers in the interpersonal context.

Game Theory

Games, as we refer to them here, involve struggles in which people oppose one another and in which participants seek incompatible results. Typically each person seeks to maximize his gains, which may be physical or psychological, while minimizing his costs, which may also be physical or psychological. Put more simply, each person seeks as much reward as possible while trying to avoid punishment. These struggles, however, are kept within the boundaries of accepted rules.

In Game Theory a basic distinction is made between the zero-sum game and the non-zero-sum game. The *zero-sum game* is one in which one person wins and the other loses; an example of a zero-sum game is chess. Each player in chess is out to defeat the other; mutual cooperative agreement is not the point. Nothing is to be gained in trying to reach a cooperative agreement with the other player, for in the end, there can only be one winner. The likelihood for fruitful interpersonal communication, which depends on mutual agreement, in such a situation obviously is almost nonexistent.

The *non-zero-sum game* is neither purely competitive nor wholly cooperative. It's a game that scientists call a "mixed motives" game. Each of the players tries to win as much as he can, but what each wins depends upon the combined decisions of the two players. If Benjamin makes a one-sided or selfish move that is best for him without considering Jay's needs or desires, Jay may disrupt his plans by selecting a move that deals Benjamin an unexpected blow. If Benjamin generously selects a move that will benefit Jay the most, Jay, after deciding Benjamin is a fool, may take advantage of his weakness and generosity. Thus how Benjamin or Jay decides to move depends upon each one's estimate of what the other will do. So the game goes.

Whereas the zero-sum game—unconditional surrender of the loser—doesn't appear too often in "real life" interpersonal situations, the non-zero-sum game may be applied to many daily interpersonal transactions. For example the decisions reached by husbands and wives are typically explained as non-zero-sum games. Shirley wants to wear her new blue dress and try a new Chinese restaurant for dinner; Walt wants to stay home with his beer, without his shoes, and pick up the Monday night game. As a compromise, Shirley and Walt may agree to watch the TV game together on Monday night and to go out to dinner on Saturday night—during which Walt will forgo another critical game on TV. Or they might reach some other compromise. The point is each wins a little and loses a little; it is even possible that they might reach an agreement where both gained. Couples differ in their compromises and decisions depending on whether there is no communication, one-sided communication, or full communication between them.

In determining a strategy to use, we must make some judgments about the other person—first and most basic, whether we can trust the other person or not. Second, we must determine if someone is selfishly looking out for his own personal well-being or unselfishly looking out for the mutual welfare of both, that is, if the individual is individualistically or cooperatively oriented. Research in this area tends to demonstrate that when two people repeatedly exhibit a cooperative approach toward one another, mutual trust develops, and consequently decisions are made of greater mutual benefit to both. Third, we should also be attuned to methods by which another person may attempt to control, demand, threaten, manipulate, or promise in order to realize his own ends.

Underlying all game behavior is the notion of rewards and costs: we balance what we may gain if we play a certain move against what we may possibly lose. Any interpersonal communication we have with another can be evaluated in terms of the rewards and cost—both psychological and material—derived from that encounter. Judgments we make about possible benefits or costs of an encounter will determine whether we seek out a certain person for future communication. If Johnnie has had an unpleasant, costly conversation with Morris, Johnnie may—although he may just as likely not—decide to give Morris one more chance. But if the second experience is also unpleasant, we may assume that this is the end of any relationship between them.

In addition experiences of painful costs incurred during previous encounters with a certain individual will have a profound effect upon our future behavior toward him. For instance, if we've been taken advantage of in past communicating encounters, we're likely to be cautious and distrustful—likely to play our cards close to the vest. This caution obviously does not help open and honest communication but is a reasonable approach given past experience.

Thus Game Theory can be applied to the study of interpersonal communication since transactions between two people often can be thought of as a balancing of possible gains and losses, typical of the non-zero-sum game. Game Theory can be used to describe the moves, the strategies, and the basic approach we take with another person. It gives us insights into dealing with the other person and allows us to make cooperative decisions and fruitful compromises.

Social Comparison Theory

A fundamental assumption underlying Social Comparison Theory is that all of us are uncertain of our own opinions and abilities. We care deeply about whether our opinions are considered valid by others and whether we actually have the capacities or abilities we like to think we have.

When we're wondering about the length of a sofa we've bought or the time it takes to drive to school in the morning, we don't have to ask someone's opinion about it or to argue with someone over it. We can take out a yardstick to measure the sofa and keep an eye on our watch to time the trip to school. No problem arises when we have to make judgments about physical things or when we can check out facts for accuracy. For example we can easily determine what was the hottest day in any given year or whether Notre Dame ever beat Alabama in football before 1974. But what about our political opinions? What about our abilities as writers, artists, or musicians? What about questions of values, faith, and religious belief? In these instances no firm standards exist by which we can judge for ourselves. These intangible values—the ones that are not open to verification—are dealt with in Social Comparison Theory.

In these areas we learn about the correctness of our opinions and about our abilities by finding out from other people what they think about our opinions and our abilities. In the absence of clear, objective criteria, we come to evaluate the "correctness" of our opinions and the approximate level of our talents by talking to others. Since there's no definitive means of testing our views of the Mona Lisa or Jim Croce—or whether there's life after death—the best we can do is compare our views with those of others and obtain from them some "social" validation of our views. Most of us are unsettled by uncertainty; we seek out psychological closure.

We are especially concerned with confirming our views about ourselves. We not only have the need to make sense of the world we inhabit but also have the desire to make sense of ourselves. Who are we? How do we fit into the world? Where are we going? Unfortunately we can't find out about ourselves as easily as we can find out whether or not a door is locked. The key that unlocks the door to our inner selves is to be found in our transactions with others. We come to know who we are through others.

Two implications derived from Social Comparison Theory can be applied to interpersonal communication. First, Social Comparison Theory attempts to account for why we communicate with one another: we communicate in order to verify our perceptions of the world and our assumptions about ourselves. Thus we seek out others to reduce uncertainty, to confirm our opinions, and to establish our identities. Second, it then follows that much of the content of interpersonal communication concerns just such matters as our identities, opinions, and assumptions. Think about your recent interpersonal communication encounters. Weren't they concerned with your and your friend's opinions of such things as movies, politicians, and members of the opposite sex? You both wished to determine whether or not your opinions were shared by the other person.

Newcomb's Balance Theory

Newcomb's Balance Theory is probably the most widely known of the four theories discussed in this chapter and is frequently used to explain and interpret interpersonal communication. Newcomb's theory is an extension of Heider's original theory, which we examined in the previous chapter. Whereas the balance theories you're familiar with, those of Heider, Osgood, and Festinger, were applied to intrapersonal contexts, Newcomb's theory will be applied to an interpersonal context. Newcomb doesn't look at what's happening merely from the point of view of one individual; he explains what's going on in the minds of two people involved in a transaction. In other words this theory explains the thinking processes of two people who are reacting to one another simultaneously.

The elements are similar to those of Heider: whereas Heider had a P-O-X system, Newcomb changes it to a highly creative A-B-X system. A and B, as you might imagine, are the two people involved in the communicating act, and X, as in Heider's notion, is the thing or topic talked about. As is typical of all the other balance theories, the assumption that people need psychological balance or consistency holds true. Researchers agree that imbalance and psychological inconsistency are painful, unpleasant states—much to be avoided.

To illustrate the system, we will say that Herb (A) responds to X, a proposed political campaign, in the light of his reactions to Dave (B); that is, his attitude toward the political campaign is tied in with his attitude toward Dave. In the same way Dave's attitude toward the campaign is affected by his attitude toward Herb. The attitude changes and reactions of both are going on simultaneously.

The most useful concept to come out of Newcomb's theory is the idea of *co-orientation*. Co-orientation is the simultaneous orientation or focusing of Herb and Dave upon the campaign and each other. Herb doesn't think about the campaign apart from how he feels about Dave and how Dave thinks about the campaign. The same is true of Dave. Restated in general terms, each person simultaneously takes into account his attitude toward the topic being discussed, his attitude toward the other person, and the other person's attitude toward himself. This meshing process is co-orientation.

A basic proposition of the theory is the notion of *strain toward symmetry*. Within the A-B-X system, certain forces cause "strains" toward preferred states of balance or of symmetry. These forces tend to move two people toward a similarity of co-orientation. What's meant here is that the two people who are deeply attached to one another will move toward similar views about X. Elizabeth and Edward, a well-known theatrical couple, will move toward similar views of money, paintings, vacations, friends, and so forth. Two advantages come about as a result of this strain toward symmetry. First, if Elizabeth's attitude toward the manner in which money should be spent is similar to Edward's, she can more easily predict his behavior in this area. The closer the attitudes of two people, the less the need for either of them to struggle with interpreting X in terms of the other person's orientation. This means there's less chance for error in translating what the other person means and less chance for faulty co-orientation.

A second advantage of this movement or strain toward symmetry of co-orientation is that each one has the chance to have the other validate his attitudes toward X. In the case above, Elizabeth, who likes to surround herself with antiques and tapestries, has the opportunity to confirm her views on acceptable ways of spending money. (Notice the close similarity here to Social Comparison Theory.) If Elizabeth and Edward agree, the more confident each can be of his or her own attitude—now confirmed by the other. They're able to say to one another: "We are indifferent to what other people may think. We know what we want to do." As a result of this strain toward symmetry of co-orientation, they find their agreement rewarding in and of itself. The increased mutual agreement in turn leads to even greater symmetry of co-orientation.

Of interest to us is the notion that symmetry of co-orientation is achieved primarily through the process of communication. Since symmetry is a rewarding state, people hope to work toward achieving it in their communication. If two people with similar interests and viewpoints talk with one another at great length, the possibility that symmetry will develop increases. In conceptual terms, if two people talk for long periods about a topic of mutual interest, the possibility arises that one or the other will change his attitude toward X and that both will move toward increased symmetry.

We shouldn't assume at this point, however, that interpersonal communication always leads to symmetry of co-orientation. We all know that sometimes it doesn't. Strain toward symmetry will be helped tremendously if the two people develop respect or liking for one another; conversely the force to achieve symmetry will be weakened in the case of two individuals who are unsympathetic toward one another. Since the drive toward symmetry of points of view is such a strong impetus, the possibility always exists that two people who don't particularly care for one another at first may begin to like each other more after getting to know one another better. The strain toward symmetry leads to further increases in their liking for one another. Many forces operate when two people engage in interpersonal communication—the development of liking for one another is merely one.

Some of the other forces affecting the strain toward symmetry are constraint, role relationship, and threat. If two people are forced to communicate, the *constraint* of the relationship may adversely affect the strain toward symmetry. If two people are forced to associate with one another as co-workers, particularly as bosses and workers, they may not always feel a strong drive to reach symmetry. Although they're required to talk to one another to get the job done, they don't have to like one another. Nor do they have to reach agreement on topics other than those directly relating to the job.

Couples who've been married for a long time know from experience that they can't reach symmetry of co-orientation on certain topics. Both Harold and Mary know that they will never reach agreement about the motives or the opinions of Mary's mother. Since Harold and Mary are "constrained" to associate with one another, they've reached an understanding that they will discuss Mary's mother as little as possible. The same policy may work for them on such other sensitive topics as politics and religion. Since people have to live with one another, they may simply agree to disagree; they recognize that they will not reach symmetry of co-orientation in certain areas.

A second force affecting strain toward symmetry is the *role relationship* that the two people have to one another. The role relationship may require that the two not reach an identical view toward X but rather that each develop a stance appropriate to his role. For example a mother and her thirteen-year-old daughter may reach an agreement on smoking and makeup: both agree that they should conform to norms that prescribe different behaviors for older and younger women in these areas.

A final force affecting strain toward symmetry is the element of *threat*. It's possible that if symmetry were achieved on a certain topic, it would be threatening to one of the parties. Chris doesn't always tell the truth when he breaks something because his dad may punish him. So although he and his dad theoretically agree that telling the truth is a good thing, the dish "somehow seemed to fall all by itself." So implied threat may be another impediment to the achievement of symmetry of co-orientation. Despite the fact that (1) constraints of an association, (2) role relationships, and (3) threat may limit the strain toward symmetry, we still find a strong drive within individuals to achieve harmonious and symmetrical points of view.

In an interpersonal context a variety of attempts will be made to achieve symmetry toward X. One attempt may take the form of your trying to convince the other person to accept your point of view. Another attempt may take the form of the other person convincing you to accept his viewpoint. Or it's even possible that you might unconsciously distort the other person's view of the topic—so that it fits more closely with yours. Another likely behavior to occur in an interpersonal communicating context is that you may change your mind about how attractive you find the other person. If you find that you and your boyfriend can't seem to get together on the matter of outside dating, one possible result is that you may find him less attractive. If you find him less attractive and of less interest to you, you no longer feel a need to agree with him. The tendency to persuade the other person, to change your own attitude, to distort the other person's viewpoint, and to change your judgment of the other person's attractiveness —all these are very possible efforts you will make to achieve symmetry toward X.

In the course of this section we've looked at four theories: Attribution Theory, Social Comparison Theory, Game Theory and Newcomb's Balance Theory. In Attribution Theory we saw how we need to know the whole social context or situation to help us interpret the messages of the other person. We observed that if what an individual said could be accounted for by self-interest, by external pressures, or by demands of his role, we're likely to be wary and distrustful of his communications. Game Theory gives us insights into how our evaluations of rewards and costs are a part of any interpersonal communicating encounter. Compromise often goes on in interpersonal communication—with participants typically both winning a little and losing a little in a non-zero-sum game. An assessment of our rewards and costs affects whether or not we wish to talk with another person again and also affect the strategies we will take with him if we do communicate again. Social Comparison Theory helps us understand why we seek out others and why we need and wish to communicate with others: we need others to help us confirm and validate our opinions, beliefs, and values—those intangibles we cannot test for ourselves against objective criteria. We observed that the content of much interpersonal communication consists of our personal attitudes and subjective opinions—and particularly concerns those areas in which we wish to hear another person's viewpoint or evaluation. Finally we've noted in Newcomb's Balance Theory that each person simultaneously takes into account his attitude toward the topic, his attitude toward the other person, and the other person's attitude toward himself. In our associations with others, we strive to achieve psychological balance, explained in Newcomb's theory as a strain toward symmetry of co-orientation. This strain toward symmetry affects interpersonal communication by affecting the individual's attempts to change his own attitude or the attitude of the listener in order to reach a harmonious viewpoint toward any given topic.

Four Factors of Interpersonal Transaction: Attraction, Understanding, Trust, Anxiety

For our discussion of the interpersonal context, we have arbitrarily chosen four communication factors or meanings that are typical outcomes of interpersonal transactions: attraction, understanding, trust, and anxiety. What all four have in common is that each may be considered an actual meaning that is generated or assigned by the communicators during a communication transaction. In our Trans-Per model the communicator assigns meaning as he blends internal and external cues. The meanings we'll examine will all fall into the overlap of the diagram—that area in which the two Internal Systems and the External System coincide. The kinds of meanings that we will consider are those that are a consequence of two Internal Systems transacting.

Out of all the multitude of meanings that may develop during interpersonal communication, we have arbitrarily chosen for our analysis four meanings that researchers generally agree are significant and useful. Since we are not attempting to be comprehensive or to consider all the major meanings that might arise during interpersonal communication, we may have omitted several meanings that other authors might consider more significant than the ones chosen. Although we believe our selective choices are sound, the meanings we have chosen—we admit it—reflect our joint biases. Our goal here is to present a simple, representative, and accurate modeling of interpersonal communication.

Each of the meanings we discuss—attraction, understanding, trust, and anxiety—not only may be looked upon as a meaning that arises during interpersonal transactions but also may be analyzed as either a cause or an effect. For instance attraction may be an *effect* of the communication, the result of two communicators finding out that they fulfill needs together that each is not able to fill alone. Attraction, on occasion, may also be a *cause*—influencing further developments of interpersonal communication. Individuals who are attracted to one another, for example, might engage in more trusting and self-revealing communication than they would have otherwise. We want to suggest the possibility that each of the four communication factors or meanings may be either cause or effect—or both—depending on the specific transaction. How do we resolve this problem of determining cause, effect, or meaning? In systems—and we have defined Trans-Per as a system—every element affects every other element. Therefore each specific communication requires an analysis of all contributing elements and their interrelationships. In this present chapter we will consider the four terms, attraction, understanding, trust, and anxiety, only as *meanings*, meanings that are the outcome of each individual's perceptual blending of the available stimuli.

We'll begin with a general description of each of these four meanings—a definition, if you will. After defining each meaning, we'll show how each one arises or comes about during transactions. Using Trans-Per again, we'll take each meaning and examine the internal and external elements contributing to it. For instance we'll see what blends of internal and external elements lead to meanings of mutual attraction for two people engaged in interpersonal communication.

As we've said before, this process of identifying internal and external elements related to each meaning is admittedly artificial and static. Keep in mind that we will make some arbitrary decisions about whether to consider various elements as internal or external in our Trans-Per model. For example, where do we place *attitude?* As you may remember, we explained previously that attitude may be considered as an internal element, as an external element, or as a meaning. As an internal element, preconceived attitudes are cues we bring with us to a communicating situation. But these attitudes weren't always "between our ears." They were learned at some time or other in our past. At the point when they were becoming learned, attitudes were the meanings that arose as the result of the blending of other internal and external elements. Thus they would have then gone into the "meaning" or overlap portion of our model instead of into the internal element area of the Internal System.

However, attitudes may also be viewed as external elements in the analysis of those transactions in which individuals express outwardly (by various verbal and nonverbal cues) certain explicit attitudes—whether toward Women's Liberation or environmental protection or any other topic to which they are committed. So attitude may be analyzed as an internal element, an external element, or a meaning. And attitude may be placed in the circle of the Internal System or the circle of the External System—or it may be placed in the overlap of Trans-Per, depending always upon the particular communication. It's possible—in fact it's likely—that each element we classify as external may, under different conditions, be classified as internal. The elements we discuss will include those already presented in the chapters specifically dealing with internal and external stimuli. Internal elements, as you'll recall, are classified as attitudes, personality traits, sexual role, IQ, knowledge, and so forth.

External elements include all the verbal and nonverbal stimuli potentially available within the communication environment. In an interpersonal context *feedback,* a major external cue, can be viewed as the reactions a receiver sends back to the source of a message. These responses allow the source of the message to make a judgment about whether he's being understood or not. In our transactional approach the source and receiver are regarded as sending and receiving simultaneously; we speak of these as separate events only for the purposes of analysis. A communicator can do a variety of things once he begins to get some feedback. He can continue as he's been doing; the feedback in this case presumably has been of the "I follow you. Keep going" variety. If the feedback has been of the "I'm not sure I follow you" or "wait a minute" variety, the source might repeat, expand further, or provide more information on what he's saying.

Feedback in interpersonal transactions usually takes the form of a combination of verbal and nonverbal cues. When trying to follow another's point, you might say, "uh . . . huh," "go on," or some such expression. Usually such expressions are accompanied by appropriate facial responses and body movements that indicate you're receiving the message. For instance the vocal expression "um . . . hmmm" might be accompanied by direct eye contact and positive head nods. Combinations of verbal and nonverbal cues are also used to show failure to understand.

That feedback has a direct relationship to comprehension has been shown in a variety of studies in which kinds and amounts of feedback were manipulated by researchers. For instance they might allow zero feedback, in which case the receiver can't be seen by the source and says nothing to him—for example, when the source speaks on radio or TV. Researchers might also allow a limited type of feedback in which the speaker can see the listeners, but the listeners say nothing to the speaker. This is the case in typical public-speaking situations. Third, feedback might be limited to "yes" or "no" responses in reply to questions from the source. Finally feedback may occur under what's called *free conditions.* Here the receiver may interrupt, ask questions, nod agreement, shake his head in disagreement, and so forth. Results seem to show increases in understanding as feedback changes from zero to free conditions; however results of this type must be used cautiously. The tasks in this kind of research typically involve such problems as the source communicating the shapes of geometric patterns, such as six equal rectangular elements, and describing the spatial relationships of the elements in different configurations. It does seem reasonable to assume, nevertheless, that when a source is better informed of his progress, he should be able to do a better job of making himself understood.

In our discussion of the four communication factors, we may bring in cues that we haven't mentioned before—cues that are particularly relevant to the meaning under consideration. Since research and theory have not shown how all potentially relevant internal and external stimuli affect each specific meaning being analyzed, we won't be able to be as conclusive as we would wish. For us to speak more definitively of our modeling, we await the results of further research in many of the areas where we have mentioned inconclusive or conflicting results.

We want to emphasize, however, that you should clearly understand that *all internal and external stimuli have a potential bearing* upon each of the four interpersonal meanings that we will analyze.

One further general comment on the interpersonal factors of attraction, understanding, trust, and anxiety: notice that each of them falls on one side of a continuum. Attraction, for instance, is the opposite of repulsion or rejection. Understanding is the opposite of misunderstanding or confusion; trust and anxiety are the opposites of distrust and relaxation. We want to point out that, although each of our factors expresses only one side of a continuum, in a sense we can gain insights about the other end of the continuum from the same information. For instance when we learn that closer distances and longer eye contact generally are signs of attraction between two communicators, we can also infer that wider distances and less eye contact generally indicate a lack of attraction or even possibly rejection. The same inferences can generally be drawn from the research we present about any interpersonal factor. If we know that certain internal and external stimuli increase understanding or trust, we can make fairly sound estimates about how these same stimuli might be related to misunderstanding and distrust.

Before getting into each specific interpersonal meaning, one last observation: you should avoid looking at our point of view as the only way to approach interpersonal communication. We hope you keep in mind that other researchers take other legitimate approaches. We believe, however, that our Trans-Per approach will give you insights into what is taking place during an interpersonal transaction. We feel our model will help you deal with the complexity that characterizes interpersonal communication in a manageable and sound manner. Finally we hope that our approach is helpful to you in terms of practical use. Although we cannot tell you how to improve your interpersonal communication, we will try to bring to your attention the prominent variables that typically influence interpersonal transactions. How you use this information is up to you. What's right for you may not be right for someone else. By being more conscious of the communicating process, perhaps you will help yourself be a better communicator and in that way improve your relationships with others and your knowledge of yourself.

Attraction

A major *purpose* of interpersonal communication may be to increase the initial attraction felt between two people who are drawn toward one another. In the case of the coed and the varsity hockey player who have recently met, their attraction for one another causes increased need for communication. The desire to feel attractive to the opposite sex is one of the strongest needs, particularly among adolescents and young adults. In addition, a strong and continuous attraction felt by two people toward one another has a dramatic effect on how they communicate with one another and affects the future developments of their interpersonal communication. Attraction. What is it? How can we describe it?

We will make three subdivisions under the general communication factor of attraction and speak of *affection, respect,* and *love.* To illustrate, Rita's attraction for Carl may be warm affection; it may be honest respect; or it may be passionate love.

Affection refers to the warm, quiet liking you feel toward someone else, based upon how the other person relates to you directly and upon personal experiences you've shared. Thus Rita may feel warm affection for Carl because he is amusing, agreeable, interested in others, and seems to care about how she feels.

Respect is another kind of attraction one individual develops toward another individual. It is based upon admirable characteristics or actions that reveal themselves in spheres other than those relating to you personally. You may have respect for a politician because you're familiar with what he's accomplished for underprivileged minorities or what he's achieved in the area of disarmament. And yet you've never met him.

Love, a third classification within attraction, may be subdivided into two further components: attachment and caring. In our use of the term *attachment* refers to an individual's romantic feelings of ecstasy and joy and his strong desire to be with the object of his love. Since we include with attachment the selfish part of love, it is primarily concerned with an individual's desire to make himself completely happy. As a result attachment often carries with it feelings of possession, envy, and jealousy. Although we commonly describe attachment in terms of the positive, impassioned, romantic feelings associated with it, it may give rise to negative side effects. *Caring*, as opposed to passionate attachment, involves genuine feelings of concern for the other person and a selfless interest in the other person's well-being. Love, in this sense, is not based upon a *quid pro quo* relationship: "What will you do for me in return for what I do for you?" Sydney Carton, who loves Lucie in an unselfish caring sense in *Tale of Two Cities* by Dickens, wants to see her happy—more than he wants to see himself happy. Even if it means with another man. But that behavior is for heroes. Most of the time love involves a combination of passionate, selfish attachment and selfless caring.

In making these distinctions between affection, respect, and love our intention is to describe with as much precision as possible the kinds of attraction operating in interpersonal encounters. Obviously the kind of communication that occurs when the form of attraction is respect will differ from that which occurs when the attraction is passionate attachment or gentle, detached affection. Admittedly we've made some fine distinctions here that aren't that easily applied to our own personal experience. Furthermore the possibility exists that several or perhaps all of these three types of attraction may operate simultaneously: individuals like Sydney and Lucie may experience—all at once—feelings of affection, respect, and love for one another. We will now look at the kinds of internal stimuli —those things we bring with us to an interpersonal environment—that give rise to feelings, responses, and meanings of attraction.

Attraction: Internal System   In this section we'd like to illustrate some of the in-the-head internal stimuli that people bring with them to interpersonal encounters—and particularly those stimuli that influence attraction. As you will recall, the significant internal stimuli include attitudes, personality traits, sexual role, intelligence, knowledge—all previously mentioned in Chapter 4. Among these internal stimuli, the attitude element strongly influences our feelings of attraction—or repulsion.

That *preconceived attitudes* we bring to an interpersonal environment affect attraction is beyond question. An attitude, as you'll recall, is a tendency to evaluate an object, issue, or person in a favorable or unfavorable manner. If Joyce has heard that Allan is a "lady's man," who tends to take advantage of women, she's going to bring a negative predisposition or attitude to any transaction that she may have with him. She's prepared not to like him. With such a preconceived attitude, she'll probably notice those things he says and does that support her negative feelings. It's also likely that she won't be able to hide her feelings very well and that she will behave with a certain coolness that Allan will feel. Allan, in sensing her negative attitude toward him, will respond in kind. So it wouldn't be surprising to find that, after a first meeting, Joyce and Allan didn't respond to each other. Joyce went into the conversation not expecting to like Allan, and she didn't. This common phenomenon is called by scientists the "self-fulfilling prophecy."

If Hubert and Molly are having trouble with their marriage, Molly may suggest counseling; however if Hubert doesn't have much confidence in marriage counseling or marriage counselors, his preconceived attitude can prevent any good at all coming from the counseling. His negative attitude will probably prevent him from developing any respect or liking for the counselor and can cause him to reject much of what the counselor suggests.

Preconceived positive attitudes, on the other hand, may help to foster an initial attraction. Jan dislikes lecture classes in which the instructor, by and large, repeats what's already explained in the textbook. She prefers by far classes in which a great deal of give-and-take takes place between students and instructor, Thus when Jan registers for Professor Gill's interpersonal communication class and finds that Gill encourages students to share their ideas, her positive attitude toward his method of teaching contributes to her respect for him. She concludes that Gill knows how to teach effectively and that she wishes she could know him on a more personal basis.

Another set of internal cues that have a bearing upon attraction are the psychological and physical *needs* that people bring to a communicative situation. We may think of needs as desires people all feel, wants they wish to satisfy, or goals they pursue. In the case of physical needs we fulfill them through food, water, clothing, shelter, and rest. In the case of psychological needs we fulfill these for the most part with and through other people. Our psychological needs often determine what kinds of people we find attractive as communicators, as friends, as lovers, and as mates.

People have differing psychological needs. Whereas some individuals need to dominate—those with an inordinate need to dominate are called highly Machiavellian by personality theorists—other people have no desire to exert control over others. Still other individuals have a need to defer to or to depend upon another person. If Bob and Bette both have strong needs to dominate, it's reasonably safe to assume that they will not be attracted to one another.

We all have a need to pursue our innate talents and natural interests, whether they be athletics, reading, music, TV, travel, good living, or what have you. Shared or common interests, without a doubt, affect the amount of attraction two people may develop toward one another. And not to be overlooked is the need or wish to feel attractive and desirable to the opposite sex. We have talked enough about needs to make our point: the needs we bring to an interpersonal transaction have a major impact upon how much attraction we feel toward another individual. We gradually determine whether or not we can fulfill our personal needs with and through him. You may wish to add to this abbreviated list many more of the internal stimuli people bring with them when they communicate in an interpersonal context.

Attraction: External System   One category of external stimuli that gives rise to feelings of attraction are *external personal traits* that others display and we pick up, interpret, and blend. What are some external personal traits that contribute to the development or the nondevelopment of attraction?

Physical attractiveness is an obvious external stimulus that we respond to. There is no doubt that good looks are a useful asset for generating initial attraction. Physically attractive people have an advantage in getting to know others—since people tend to seek them out. Not being able to get to know others easily is a barrier that plainer people are all too familiar with. In our culture we have a tendency to think of attractive individuals as agreeable, pleasant, and trustworthy—and to regard plain or ugly people as disagreeable, dull, or sinister.

Other external traits that individuals exhibit—and that we're inclined to notice—are how outgoing or withdrawn they are, how much or how little confidence they display, and how aggressive or dependent, how introverted or extroverted, how mature or immature they appear. Again you could probably expand this list without too much trouble.

In addition we tend to be attracted to individuals who exhibit personal traits of intelligence or competence and trustworthiness. We tend to like people whom we perceive to be competent and honest.

Another external cue that individuals exhibit and that influences our feelings of attraction toward them is *reinforcement*—social approval of us and our actions. This approval may be indicated by such phrases as "nice going" and "you've been a big help." Approval can also be shown by nonverbal reinforcements such as "um. . . hmmm," and "uh . . . huh," by head nods and smiles—or by combinations of all of these. We tend to find people attractive if they approve of us; as you might expect, we tend to find people less attractive if they disapprove of us.

Generally research on attraction has shown that facial expressions, posture, bodily positions, and body movements are good indicators of degree of attraction. These external cues have been found to be fairly consistent indicators of positive or negative attitudes expressed by the source that are picked up fairly readily by receivers. The attitudes expressed by facial expressions and body postures have an influence upon how attractive the source exhibiting these nonverbal behaviors will be found by the receiver.

Distance, eye contact, arm position, body orientation, and degrees of relaxation have been consistently interpreted as revealing the communicator's conscious and unconscious attitudes. Generally it has been found that the more someone is attracted to another, the closer in distance he seeks to be. Individuals who are attracted to one another usually tend to maintain longer and more frequent eye contact and are inclined to smile at each other more frequently than those who are not. Arm arrangements, interestingly enough, also indicate attitudes of attraction or rejection: an open arrangement of the arms tends to show more positive feelings toward the other person than a closed position. Body orientation—the manner in which one person aligns himself in relation to another—seems to be another indicator of attraction or rejection. Body orientation tends to be least direct with people one dislikes and most direct with people one likes and finds attractive. Finally the amount of recline or lean of the body is related to attitudes: moderate amounts of recline or sideways lean tend to convey positive attitudes; excessive amounts of recline or lean—or completely erect positions—tend to reveal negative attitudes.

Now that we have reviewed some internal and external stimuli that affect attraction, we will use Trans-Per to illustrate the dynamic interplay of stimuli—how each communicator assigns meanings of attraction to his own blend of internal and external stimuli and how both communicators share meanings of attraction.

Attraction: Trans-Per   Since he was in her brother's group of close friends, Joy had heard about James from her brother—even before she met him. Every Tuesday evening, no matter what the group had planned, James would slip away. The others thought he must have a mysterious, serious girlfriend, but one of them found out that James regularly saved Tuesday nights to spend with a childhood friend, totally deaf, who could only use sign language and make strange, muffled sounds. So even before she met him, Joy had a favorable, preconceived attitude toward James —that it was decent of him to remember the loneliness of his childhood friend and take the time to be with him. Joy had, in addition, heard her father, a man who rationed his praise, comment: "Not too many boys in his age group would be that considerate."

The first time that our couple, Joy and James, communicate directly, James is waiting in the living room for Joy's brother. Joy, who answered the door, waits with James for her brother to arrive. They find one another slim, clean, and physically prepossessing. Having planned to play tennis with her brother, James is all in white and has his racquet with him.

JOY: I'm sorry he's late. The coach won't release him from prac-
        tice until he's finished his laps, no matter how tired he is.
        (*Pause. Each is thinking of a topic of conversation.*) Do you
        play much tennis?

JAMES: Quite a bit. Now that I've fixed up my serve. I had a lot of
        trouble learning to control it. I finally have, after seven or
        eight years of trying to develop it. You might say (*here James
        laughs and gestures helplessly*) I'm a slow learner.

JOY: I had the same problem with golf. I couldn't at first even
        come near the tee with my club. I'd just keep chewing up the
        divots all around. My brothers gave it to me unmercifully.
        They have no qualms about hurting people's feelings. I de-
        cided to take lessons from a pro and practice my swing, secret-
        ly, at a driving range. So my brothers would have to take it all
        back—that I was born a spastic. Now my golf is respectable,
        and no one laughs I'm happy to say. As a matter of fact I beat
        my father by one stroke last Sunday for the first time ever. He
        said "I'm quite impressed." It still makes me smile inside.
        (*Pause.*) My brother tells me you'd like to be a doctor.

JAMES: So far. If I can take the pressures, make the grades, be
        accepted to a med school—not easy these days—I'd like to be
        a doctor, maybe ear, nose, and throat. But I'm a slow learner
        in more than tennis. I'm slow in many subjects, particularly
        English, math, Spanish—to name a few. But I've noticed if I
        work away at a tough section of the book—plod away at it—I
        finally get it. I do occasionally wish I had attached myself to a
        mind with a better memory, but it's been good enough so far.

JOY: What made you choose medicine?

JAMES: It's hard to say exactly. John Kennedy's motto was tacked to our wall in grammar school—the one about ask what you can do for your country. I don't know why I'm pouring out all this. It sounds idealistic and childish both, but I honestly feel it . . . and I'll tell you. I would like to do something—as much as I can—for my country, and even all the people in it. Since I don't exactly know how to help the whole country, I've settled on trying to help along a few people, if I can. Ed, my deaf friend—he's shut off from everyone. It would be a great deal, as far as I'm concerned, if I could help out anyone like that. Everyone, of course, has to decide for himself what kind of a life is best for him. Kennedy's question isn't as simple as you think at first.

JOY: I've been mulling over the same questions. We're at that time of life. I agree with you. I'd like to do something useful, even if it is a small ripple. I haven't yet pinned myself down, perhaps a physical therapist or a doctor directly invloved in patient care—not in research. I hope I don't grow so callous that I forget the patient. Some people in those professions become so hardened. . . .

Joy's brother arrived home at this point in the transaction. James left to play tennis and wiped out his opponent with his hard, carefully developed serve.

Which internal elements can we analyze from this conversation that led each communicator to assign the meaning of attraction to the transaction? Joy had, as we have said, a preconceived attitude that was favorable to James. She admired his dedication to Ed—although she had heard some of her fun-loving friends fault James for being too wrapped up in Ed and for being too serious.

Each of our communicators is able to fill significant psychic needs of the other: both have strong motivations to pursue their major goals; both have similar goals of a basically humanitarian nature—of helping others. Very quickly each recognized in the other significant cues of the same major interests, the same motivations, and the basic similarity of attitudes. In terms of Trans-Per, a wide area of overlap—of shared meaning —develops in just a few minutes.

In addition each notices a similarity of approach to problems, as illustrated by that part of their conversation on learning to play golf and on learning to study. They had both discovered independently that if they work hard at a certain skill or task, even if they have no great natural abilities for it, they are able to achieve gratifying results. So another area of shared meaning emerges in this recognition of a similar viewpoint of how to learn a skill.

Most important both discover that they share the same basic attitude toward a useful life: both feel a need and predisposition to spend their time helping others—in preference to any other possible life-style. By nature both prefer service to others to pleasure and parties.

As for external elements we will assume that they find one another physically attractive. You may imagine Joy and James as a pleasant couple with regular features and ready smiles. James radiates cues of self-confidence, maturity, stability, and trustworthiness that Joy finds agreeable. She likes the idea that he says what he means—outright and directly. Even if he feels he might be disclosing what certain of his sophisticated friends would interpret as idealistic or naive, he is willing to risk telling Joy his honest inner feelings—mainly because she in turn gives off cues of an earnest seriousness and a caring for others that he picks up.

His nonverbal cues—moving closer toward her when he discloses his personal master plan, listening to her attentively, and lifting his eyebrows in a silent reaction to her words—are some of the myriad stimuli bearing on the meaning she will assign to the transaction. By observing his gestures, his posture, his body orientation, the timbre of his voice, she is consciously and unconsciously bombarded by nonverbal stimuli that elaborate upon his verbal message. She notices that he crosses his arms in back of his head when talking about tennis; he spreads his arms wide to explain his interest in medicine; he gathers his limbs into a tight formation when making significant disclosures. Each searches the other's face and physical presence for additional cues that will reinforce the ongoing verbal message being exchanged.

We mentioned that individuals have a need—an internal element —to express themselves, to receive praise, and to demonstrate skills. We see this need being satisfied by each explaining his level of ability at his chosen sport. Although they both keep silent about it, each wishes to demonstrate for the other his acquired skill and winning form. They probably will soon plan a golf or tennis match, or both.

On the way home from tennis, James teases Joy's brother good-naturedly: "How did a generally average person like you come up with that lovely sister? Do you think she's free this weekend?" So we can conclude in this case—we admit to prearranging the elements—that the blend of internal and external elements resulted in a large overlap; on a Trans-Per diagram, we would see probably more shared meaning than in any other of our examples. James and Joy each assign a clear and strong meaning of attraction to the communication.

Another meaning derived from interpersonal communication is *understanding*; we will attempt to describe the way in which people come to understand—or fail to understand—each other.

Understanding

We'd like to look at this business of understanding the other person. What do we mean by understanding? What processes heighten or decrease our understanding? Our concern here is to analyze the ways by which we can come to understand another individual.

We typically develop an opinion of an individual both from hearsay (by hearing what others say about him when his name comes up in a conversation) and from our own direct contacts with him (by listening to his own stated point of view). Either we can arrive at an understanding of his nature from our own limited perspective—or we can make a great effort to see the world from his point of view. Let's take a closer look at how we develop understanding of an individual—someone who is a close friend, someone whom we respect or love. (We can, needless to say, develop understanding of a young convict's behavior—that his complete lack of any advantages made it almost inevitable that he would grasp any means of helping himself.) We will limit our discussion, however, to the understanding of an individual with whom we have a close relationship.

When an individual who is unknown to us moves into our perceptual range, we perhaps at first learn about him from hearsay or indirect sources. We may hear others mention him in passing as the owner of an Alfa Romeo or as an excellent golfer. Or we may hear that his family owns a movie chain. Or friends, or others we talk to, may make more direct and personal comments about him to us—that he has a reputation for being first man in his class, or that he is only an average student although he lives at the library. What we're gaining here, however, is not necessarily an understanding of that person; instead we're getting someone else's viewpoint. It may tell us more about the person making the statement than about the person to whom he is referring.

We can also come to know and to understand someone from our own direct experiences with him. We look at him—what he says and what he does—from the limited perspective of our own background and point of view. We interpret what he says from our own experiences, biases, and prejudices. This approach doesn't necessarily provide a full understanding of that person because our attitudes and biases merely reflect our attitudes and biases.

Another way we can come to understand someone is to attempt to transcend our own limited viewpoint—and to try to understand things from *his* viewpoint. In this case we try to understand how he feels, how he thinks, and how he sees the world. The object isn't to agree or disagree with him: the goal is to try to view the world through his eyes. The word that's used to express this approach to understanding is *empathy*. It's the attempt to feel yourself into—to participate in—the inner world of the other person, especially his emotional state. You still remain aware of the fact that you're someone else.

We might illustrate the empathic approach this way: the pet dachshund of one of your authors ran away. So Ken tried to figure out where in the world Otto could be. He tried to get inside Otto's head. "Now Otto has plenty to eat. As a matter of fact, he's overweight. We don't beat or abuse him—too frequently. Then why did he run away? What possible reason could he have? Could it be another dog? That seems like a good possibility, worth checking out. So where are female dogs within scenting distance?" After having researched all the attractive female dogs in the neighborhood, Ken began his search. And sure enough Otto was soon found. Although we all recognize that Otto's not a person, the same process may be applied to human interpersonal relationships. Empathy requires viewing things from the other person's perspective—while being simultaneously aware that one is not that other person.

Now that we have some idea of what we mean by understanding, let's consider those major internal and external cues that may affect the development of understanding.

Understanding: Internal System　All internal cues or stimuli have a *potential* bearing upon our developing or not developing an understanding of the other person. From among all the potential internal elements, we'd like to choose two that seem particularly related to the assignment of the meaning or communication factor of understanding.

Empathy, which we've already discussed, is one of the key internal elements contributing to one individual's understanding of another. Empathy can be thought of as a tendency or predisposition to view what's happening from the other person's eyes. It's often quite difficult, if not impossible, to do—as in the case of a middle-class white attempting to view the world from the eyes of a Black or a Chicano. The typical middle-class white simply hasn't had the experiences of a typical Black person; thus it becomes almost impossible for him to see the world as a Black does. To view the world from another's perspective requires some common experiences, some shared feelings. Otherwise one couldn't possibly attempt to think, feel, or value as the other person does.

Another of the internal elements a person may bring to the interpersonal transaction, one which contributes greatly to the development of understanding, is an attitude of acceptance. To have an attitude of acceptance, means to view the other person as an equal and as entitled to his own point of view. Implicit in this attitude of acceptance is the feeling of sincere respect for the other person. To accept another doesn't mean to agree with him always. Nor does it mean to value precisely what he values. Rather it is to recognize that one person has as much a right to his particular ideas, feelings, and values as any other person. With an attitude of acceptance, you convey that you are open to possibility and willing to listen. Your replies would be something like: "I think I follow you," or "Is this the way you see it?"

One of the significant implications of having an attitude of acceptance is that *just having such an attitude* is of itself an enormous first step in gaining understanding. When your verbal and nonverbal cues reflect this attitude, your openness is picked up and reflected by the other person. And just knowing that an individual genuinely wants to understand you is of tremendous assistance in bringing about mutual understanding.

Understanding: External System Of the total range of external stimuli affecting the development of understanding in an interpersonal context, one external element, reinforcement, appears to be particularly significant.

By reinforcement, we're talking about another person's stated or implied approval of our actions or attitudes. Particularly appreciated is someone's support or approval when we feel that we have failed or when we're expressing something that is particularly painful or embarrassing to disclose. If Joy, when James attempts to explain to her why he did so poorly on his final exams, were to interrupt with a tactless "How could you mess it up like that?" her words would have a souring effect on James's ability to communicate openly. James would probably feel pushed, threatened, and prodded. He might sense that Joy has failed completely to understand how he feels—that he feels miserable enough without her disapproval. He already realizes himself that he has failed—without her explaining it to him. So he grows quiet. The chance to reach mutual understanding has been stymied.

A good deal of research on reinforcement demonstrates that negative responses cause breakdowns in communication. The person receiving the disapproval wants to get away, to escape. One way to do this is to say nothing. Disapproving or threatening responses also typically cause breakdowns in thought patterns (which obviously don't help understanding) and a wide variety of hesitations and verbal nonfluencies such as "ums," "ers," stutters, repetitions, tongue slips, and the like. In sum, disapproval—which is almost always perceived as threatening—consistently causes breakdowns in the development of understanding.

Understanding: Trans-Per   We will analyze another transaction of our same couple, which takes place several years later. Looking distraught, James arrives at Joy's home and flops in his favorite chair.

JAMES: I didn't pass my final exams.

JOY: Oh, James . . . (*silence*) . . . I'm sorry. You worked so hard for them.

JAMES: That's not all. I'll have to repeat my first year at medical school. I knew I didn't do well, but I expected to pass.

JOY: But James, remember you had distractions this year. Your father was in and out of the hospital. Your mother was continuously upset over your father—how he would never follow the doctor's orders. And Ed, when his mother remarried, needed your extra time and support. And on top of that, that job of yours as hospital orderly—to keep you going—it was too tiring for you to work night and study days. You're human, as they say. It's all those things together. James, don't be too hard on yourself. You'll do it next year. You know you can do it next year.

JAMES: I didn't spend enough time preparing the basic fundamentals. Particularly physiology. I didn't know the material as solidly as I thought. Well we know I'm a slow learner (*smiles briefly*) with a weak memory. I would have liked to keep it private. Now everyone knows.

JOY: Remember how you had to work on your tennis. And now you sweep everyone off the court. They wanted you to try out for a pro tour, but you told them you had other plans.

JAMES: Yeah, that's right. I beat everyone I play lately. Next year nothing will stop me. Next year I'll just redouble my effort. I'll show everyone I can do it. But for the time being, it's so ____ (*he pounds his fist onto his knee*) embarrassing to tell everyone. Really embarrassing to admit the whole class made it but you and one other person, who's too stupid to tie his own shoelaces.

JOY: James, I know it will hurt for weeks. You'll probably lose sleep and have some bad moments, some very bad moments. But remember your long-term goal, helping Ed or someone like him.

JAMES: You've calmed me down. Joy, you've helped me quite a bit. As you say, I'll have to wait out my feelings of self-disgust. And then plunge ahead with all my mottoes in full force. With vigor—as John F. Kennedy used to say.

James is profoundly troubled and shaken by his setback—one that can only be made up by great effort over a year's time. Joy brings to this transaction the internal element of empathy: she is able to feel herself into the inner world of James, particularly his emotional state. She also brings an attitude of acceptance and a desire to understand—key elements of all those operating in this transaction. She can understand how much this failure disturbs James; she senses the amount of anguish he feels. Blending these internal stimuli with the external cues provided by James—his unconsciously rubbing his forehead, his halting voice, his fleeting looks of deep misery—she creates a meaning of understanding that James shares. He responds to her understanding and sensitivity. On a Trans-Per diagram, their shared meaning would again be represented by a substantial overlap. Joy is able to provide both external verbal and nonverbal cues that were positive and supportive: the sincerity of her voice, the quiet reassurance of her eyes, the certainty she conveys in her statement that he will make it next year. Always providing positive feedback and reinforcement, she allows James to explain the situation and disclose his feelings of self-disgust and, for him atypical, low self-esteem. Notice she said nothing to reinforce his own strong ideas of inferiority and nothing to reproach him for what he hadn't done. Together they make productive, positive plans to overcome the problem; they offer one another helpful words to repair James's temporarily shattered future.

Trust

That trust is the most important relationship established between humans can be seen by looking at the works of poets, novelists, philosophers, theologians, psychiatrists, and others who attempt to describe the human condition. The development of trust or its opposite, suspicion, is one of the vital outcomes of intimate interpersonal communication; the presence or absence of trust can easily strengthen or destroy a relationship. What is trust? How can we describe this phenomenon?

One element that must be present for trust to exist is the idea of predictability: the person you trust can be counted on for certain predictable behaviors. You have absolutely no reason to suspect that he will harm or betray you in any way. Trust refers to feelings you have that the other person won't take advantage of you, has your concerns at heart, doesn't have any ulterior motives, can keep a secret, and so forth.

If what is expected or predicted doesn't occur, the person who trusts typically will suffer. For instance, if a wife trusts that her husband will deposit his paycheck and pay off their bills before anything else and if instead he fritters it away at the racetrack, the wife suffers. They may be evicted from their apartment or be hounded by creditors.

Trust is particularly necessary to interpersonal communication if the more significant and meaningful transactions that involve discussions of personal and intimate behaviors and feelings are to take place. To develop a truly close relationship with another individual requires the disclosure of what might be damaging information—if taken advantage of by the other person. Self-disclosure characterizes transactions between close friends; for self-disclosure to occur, trust must be present.

Trust: Internal System   As we have said previously, all the internal cues that we bring with us to a communicating situation have a potential bearing upon the meanings that we do or do not develop. Let's examine those elements that particularly contribute to the development of meanings of trust between two communicators.

Everything we've already said about a person's developing attitudes of acceptance and respect are prerequisites to the development of trust. The attraction one feels for the other person also contributes to the development of trust. (Notice what's happening here: we're using attraction as an internal element. In looking at attraction earlier in the chapter we viewed attraction as a meaning that evolved out of a transaction between two people. But, depending on the specific case, attraction can also be analyzed as an internal element, an inner cue that a person brings to a given interpersonal transaction.) In addition a feeling of affection or liking, and especially a feeling of care and concern, can do much to create an atmosphere of trust. Our internal feelings of affection and care are expressed through the external cues—words, gestures, positive reinforcement—that we provide the other person and that contribute to the development of trust.

We can summarize all the internal elements that contribute to trust simply as an individual's attitude of *positive expectation*. If he expects others to accept and respect him, if he expects others to like him, then he's likely to reciprocate this liking and respect and acceptance. When present in both communicators, such positive expectations contribute greatly to the establishment of mutual trust.

Trust: External System   Let's turn our attention to four external cues that are particularly related to trust: orientation, status and power, self-disclosure, and feedback. When we discussed Game Theory earlier in the chapter we mentioned three kinds of *orientation* described in communication research: cooperative, competitive, and individualistic. A cooperative orientation is fostered by a situation in which both persons recognize that each has something to gain or win if they work with, rather than against, one another. For example certain schools now allow team master's theses; the individuals working on this type of thesis realize that they stand to benefit most by cooperating with one another. Just as in the zero-sum-type game, a competitive orientation is one in which each individual experiences either complete victory or total loss. Unless he prefers to lose less than everything, he has no reason or desire to cooperate. Instead of being purely cooperative or competitive, however, most communicating transactions in daily life are usually a mixed-motive or non-zero-sum game. A third type of orientation is an individualistic one in which the individual primarily puts his own interests above anyone else's. Research suggests that mutual trust is most likely to occur under cooperative orientations, less likely to occur under individualistic orientation, and least likely to occur given competitive orientations. These findings are consistent with what we would normally expect to occur.

Another external cue, the relative *status and power* of the individuals involved, can markedly affect the development of trust. The more nearly two individuals are equal in power or status, the more likely they are to engage in trusting behavior. If obvious differences in power or status exist, as in the case of a boss and a worker, such differences make it more difficult to achieve trust, since the less powerful of the two tends to bring suspicious and distrustful attitudes to the transaction. Understandably his messages are more inclined to be evasive, compliant, and guarded. He uses these devices to conceal what he really feels—because he may not completely trust the more powerful person. For one in a subordinate position to disclose himself honestly to someone in a more powerful position increases his potential vulnerability.

If mutual trust is to develop, both parties must engage in a certain amount of *self-disclosure.* If Mercedes discloses intimate aspects of her thoughts and feelings to Lars but if Lars doesn't reciprocate in kind, Mercedes will tend to grow more cautious in what she continues to reveal about herself. The fact that Lars is unwilling to disclose himself could lead to a distrustful and suspicious state of affairs.

An external cue that comes into operation first at the interpersonal level and that contributes significantly to the individual's development of trust is *feedback.* When someone's speaking to you, if you sit impassively and give little verbal or nonverbal feedback, you're apt to make the other person feel disconcerted and uncomfortable. For when you do this, you're not revealing your reactions; you're not disclosing anything of yourself. The employee who's asking his boss for a raise will tend to engage in nervous and suspicious behavior after a time if his boss looks at him without any reaction—not approving, not disapproving. Even disapproval, although painful, might be preferable, for the employee at least has some idea of how his boss is reacting.

Let's now take a look at some of these internal and external cues as they might blend in an interpersonal transaction, the outcome of which is the development of trust.

Trust: Trans-Per   James has now successfully completed three years of medical school. Having moved near the top of his class, he feels fairly secure that his plans—now to be a surgeon—will work out satisfactorily. His self-esteem—at a low ebb after his poor freshman year—has been restored to its moderate level by his improved grades and his high class standing.

Joy has been appointed assistant head of physical therapy of a major urban medical center and finds her work infinitely satisfying. She gets to know many of her young patients well, as she guides them through their exercise programs. James and Joy see each other frequently.

Both bring to their transactions some very similar internal cues: they feel strong attraction, both the selfish attachment and the selfless caring that we discussed previously in our classification of *love.* They also both have true respect for one another's feelings. Their conversations reflect a warm mutual affection. Notice the good-natured bantering that takes place between them and their utmost efforts at honesty. Both try to understand things from the other's point of view; that is, each has empathy for the other. Most important, they both hold the attitude that, if they can express their inner feelings and talk problems out, everything can be worked out and clarified between them.

One night during dinner—James has cooked a favorite dish of theirs, shrimp pilaf—this transaction takes place:

        JOY: The shrimp is as good as usual. I'm glad to see you haven't

lowered your standards. But I need to talk to you about tomorrow night. Remember I told you about Robert Ray—the
person I was engaged to briefly—until he changed his mind.
Remember I told you how miserable I was for months over
him. I didn't want to eat, work, or sleep.

JAMES: Sure, I remember.

JOY: Well he called late last night—I had just fallen asleep—
from Cleveland and said he was coming here—on a tour of
his company's branch offices. He's a stockbroker, I think, or a
banker; even back then he was interested in investments and
economics. After five years of silence, he announces he
would like to see me . . . to catch up . . . I don't know what
else. I was so surprised . . . shocked . . . to hear from him.
Anyway I'd like to see him, and we're meeting at the Hotel
Plaza for a drink.

JAMES: Do you *have* to see him?

JOY: I want to. I think I want to see that I made a mistake in
loving him in the first place . . . but I'm not . . . sure.

JAMES: Well, I can't say I'm happy. But I'm glad you told me you're
going, that it's all out in the open. I'll hope for the best—that
you find him sluggish, materialistic, and not your type. Joy,
no matter what, I'm here.

In an analysis of this transaction, the internal cues of love, respect,
and total honesty made this conversation possible. Joy wanted to tell James
what her intentions were beforehand—not surprise him with the story of
the meeting after it had taken place. In a difficult act of self-disclosure, she
wanted James to know precisely how she felt—that for complex psychological reasons not clear to her, she felt a need to see her former friend and to
check out an old longing. She was willing to risk describing her true inner
state to James, a state of mind that many others in her position might
choose to conceal because they know that their lover's reaction would be
painful or unreasonable or both. In our case, however, Joy knew that James
would attempt to understand how she felt and appreciate her honest effort
at self-disclosure. She had carefully weighed beforehand what she felt was
the most honest way to handle this situation: she truly wanted to see Robert
Ray—for reasons she couldn't quite describe except to say she felt
compelled—and she wanted James to know how she felt and to understand
her dilemma. In her communication she displayed admirable honesty;
James reacted with total trust.

The final meaning we'd like to discuss is one that too often is a regret-
table outcome of interpersonal communication—anxiety.

Anxiety

In a sense we've already talked about anxiety. Anxiety may arise if one is not found attractive, or if one is not understood, or if one is not trusted. Since it's a factor that can play havoc in interpersonal encounters, let's examine anxiety in its own right.

Anxiety has been variously defined. It's been likened to fear. We may have real and legitimate fears of possible dangers. We may have imaginary fears: someone may be anxious about cancer, heights, or enclosed spaces. Anxiety may also refer to general and vague feelings of tension, of uneasiness, and of uncertainty. Feelings of psychological imbalance, discussed in Chapter 7, also bring on anxiety states. Even our tendency to worry has been called anxiety. Although a tight unequivocal definition is difficult to find, anxiety is a term that we all seem to understand. Thus we understand when someone says she's anxious over her final grades or her relationship with her boyfriend or whatever. Let's now examine the significant internal and external cues contributing to meanings of anxiety.

Anxiety: Internal System   Of all the internal elements that have a possible bearing upon anxiety, one seems to be present consistently—the personality element of *self-esteem*.

We've already talked about self-esteem as a person's evaluation of his own self-worth. It's an element of the Internal System that we all bring to any interpersonal communication situation. Individuals high in self-esteem are more confident of their behavior, see themselves as more competent, and are more optimistic of favorable results from situations in which they find themselves. Low self-esteem is probably the most important single element leading to anxiety in an interpersonal communicating situation. Self-esteem varies in individuals—from very low to very high levels. Most people aren't on either end of the spectrum but fall somewhere in the middle. Let's now examine factors of the External System bearing on anxiety.

Anxiety: External System   In general all verbal and nonverbal cues showing or implying *threat* are related to anxiety. For instance verbal messages may refer to threats of physical injury, pain, or even death. We typically see messages of this type in campaigns promoting the use of seat belts and discouraging the use of cigarettes. In interpersonal situations threats may also be used: a typical example is the employer who threatens to lay off a worker if his level of production doesn't improve. But more commonly the threats will imply psychological injury or pain. Any verbal or nonverbal cues signaling disapproval, rejection, or lack of attraction may be interpreted as threatening and consequently may lead to anxiety.

Closely associated with threatening stimuli are all cues serving to maintain *psychological distance* between two communicators. For example Jeanette's formality toward Jim, when they're on a casual date, can arouse anxiety on Jim's part. To indicate displeasure, husbands and wives may act at times excessively cool, courteous, and formal—without any trace of their usual warmth and affection. Such tactics keep them psychologically distant. External cues of this type create an electrifying atmosphere—of anxiety. The anxiety is heightened even more if someone asks: "What's wrong? What are you so upset about?" And the response "nothing is wrong" is followed by a continuation of the cool formal behavior.

Anxiety often results from one individual asserting his *status* or *power* over another. The status and power one person holds over another can be made perfectly clear during a conversation: one communicator can refer overtly to the fact that he holds a superior position—hardly a subtle approach. Power and status differences are frequently conveyed more indirectly. Typically placement of chairs around a table or a desk can be a clear signal of who is boss. Use of formal titles in place of first names is another means of maintaining differences in position. By speaking down to someone with a very subtle use of condescension, the person in a higher position maintains power and status differences. And the sum total of this maintenance of distance is to increase anxiety in the person of lower status.

A final external cue creating anxiety is *unresolved psychological inconsistencies*. This cue is picked up only by one communicator; there may be no direct intent on the part of one of the communicators to create anxiety for the other. So in this situation, meaning is not shared by both. Anxiety, in this case, arises from the creation of unresolved psychological inconsistencies for one communicator. For instance let's say that Bob likes both Ava and Alice. If Alice makes distasteful remarks about Ava's conduct to Bob, Bob will probably begin to feel uncomfortable and anxious. We've seen this type of situation illustrated in Heider's model, discussed in the last chapter. Bob has become anxious from the psychological tension created by having someone whom he likes dislike another person whom he likes also. In the same way, whenever another person whom we respect and like expresses a viewpoint that directly opposes our own, we may experience anxiety.

Let's now consider how internal and external stimuli operate dynamically in interpersonal contexts to bring about meanings of anxiety.

Anxiety: Trans-Per   Steve is a middle-level administrator in the personnel department of a large national firm. He has been working for the company for several years and has done fairly well. Since his completion of the
firm's executive trainee program, his progress within the firm has been faster than even he expected. Although he's relatively successful, he does not
have a high level of self-esteem; he is not all that sure of himself. For one
thing, he majored in English in college and had no basic training or education in business or organizational management. He initially took the position because he had difficulty finding work as an English major. In their
leisure time, Steve and his wife Lisa are outdoor, athletic types. They are
not especially fond of cultural activities, dinner parties, or night life. Mr.
Gibbs, the other individual in our transaction, is head of personnel for the
entire company. As an executive vice-president, he has high power and
status and, needless to say, high self-esteem. One afternoon Mr. Gibbs
runs into Steve in the elevator.

MR. GIBBS: Steve. Nice to see you. How're you doing?

STEVE: Very well, Mr. Gibbs. Thanks.

MR. GIBBS: Fine. Say, Steve, I liked the way you suggested we handle
the problem of recruiting for our new plant in Texas. You've
been suggesting—right along—many workable ideas. I must
say that while you still have a lot to learn, I see a strong future
for you in this organization.

STEVE: Well, thank you. It was an interesting problem, and I en-
joyed working on it.

MR. GIBBS: By the way, Steve, a few of us are getting together this
Saturday, and I'd like to have you join us. Allen and
Lois—he's a vice-president of the company—and Marge and
I are having dinner at the country club and then taking in
Swan Lake at the City Center. An English ballet company is
in town that Marge says is very good. I'd really like to have
you and Lisa—you wife's name is Lisa, isnt't it?—join us. I
think it would be helpful for you to meet some of the other
people who are in management here.

STEVE: Thanks, Mr. Gibbs. It sounds good. I'd love to come. But
I'd like to check with Lisa first to see if she had anything planned for Saturday.

MR. GIBBS: Hope to see you there, Steve. As I've said, you have a good
future with this company.

Let's look at this conversation to analyze how internal and external
stimuli brought about anxiety in Steve. First, consider the internal cues

that Steve and Gibbs brought with them to the conversation. Steve has a negative attitude toward ballet, formal dinner parties, and the formal social scene. He's a little unsure of himself; his self-esteem is lower than it should be. Gibbs, on the other hand, likes ballet and formal dinners; he has self-assurance and high self-esteem—and is conscious of and enjoys his power and status.

How did these internal cues affect external behavior? And how did these behaviors affect anxiety? In this episode Gibbs unintentionally created anxiety for Steve. To begin with, Gibbs clearly expressed his positive attitudes toward dinner at the country club and the ballet. When Gibbs expressed positive attitudes toward activities that Steve disliked—and then put pressure on Steve to join him—he immediately created psychological inconsistency and tension in Steve. How should he handle this tension? Should he tell Gibbs—putting honesty before discretion—that he didn't care for ballet or the country club? But Gibbs had put additional pressure on Steve by implying that his participation in social activities might help him get ahead in the company. Gibbs added further pressure by subtly stressing the difference in status and power between the two of them. The consequence of Gibbs's strategy was increased anxiety for Steve. Can you determine which of the internal and external elements operating in this transaction led to increased anxiety for Steve, as he walked away from Gibbs?

One means of alleviating tension and anxiety is for the person in the higher position to use techniques which lessen power and status differences. For instance there's the story of the military commander who wanted honest reactions from his aides on an important strategy decision. At the beginning of the meeting, the commander put his hat, with its gold braid indicating rank, on the hatrack and said, "Gentlemen, I'm putting my rank aside. I want some honest reactions to what I've been considering because a lot of people's lives are at stake here." If the person of higher status is aware that differences in self-esteem exist, he can take actions to assure the person of lower status that he respects his ideas and feelings —and doesn't take offense if a subordinate's ideas are not identical to his own. Indeed all of the means we've discussed for fostering attraction, understanding, and trust may be used to lessen the development of anxiety.

In our illustrations of internal and external elements related to attraction, understanding, trust, and anxiety, we were, of necessity, forced to make the transactions simplistic in order to make them manageable. Reality, however, involves the simultaneous interchange of countless numbers of internal and external cues—myriad cues that affect the subjective and

unique meanings people actively create. If we've conveyed in our illustrations something of the dynamic way in which individuals blend internal and external cues to create the meanings of attraction, understanding, trust, and anxiety, then we've accomplished our goal. The further development of this chapter is up to you.

Summary

Interpersonal communication is what we do when we speak informally with someone in a face-to-face setting. We began our analysis of interpersonal communication by considering various theoretical approaches that have been taken to explain and account for some of the important things that happen when people communicate informally. We looked at Attribution Theory, Social Comparison Theory, Game Theory, and Newcomb's Balance Theory. These theories helped us explain how we interpret messages, why we seek to communicate with others, what we tend to discuss, tactics or approaches we might take, and how feelings we have toward the other person and the topic operate within a total context. In the last portion of the chapter we looked at four major factors of interpersonal communication: attraction, understanding, trust, and anxiety. We examined some of the more important internal and external cues related to each of these factors, and tried to illustrate through Trans-Per the dynamic relationship existing between these stimuli and the communication factor being discussed.

Additional Readings

Barnlund, D. *Interpersonal Communication*. Boston: Houghton Mifflin, 1968.

The chapter "Communicator Choice" focuses on attraction and the many variables related to attraction. "Therapeutic Communication" examines communication variables that affect the development of genuine, accepting, and empathic interpersonal communication. These chapters contain excellent research summaries and bibliographic sources.

Benjamin, A. *The Helping Interview*. 2nd ed. Boston: Houghton Mifflin, 1975.

Although written for the therapeutic counselor, this compact book has direct applications to everyday interpersonal communication. The author suggests practical, well-tested means of establishing open, trusting, and helpful relationships.

Heider, F. "Social Perception and Phenomenal Causality." In *Person Perception and Interpersonal Behavior*, edited by R. Tagiuri and L. Petrullo. Stanford: Stanford University Press, 1958.

A condensed, sophisticated account of attribution theory and variables affecting the attribution process.

Newcomb, T. "An Approach to the Study of Communicative Acts." *Psychological Review* 60 (1953):393-404.

Newcomb's classic presentation of his interpersonal balance theory. A somewhat technical and complex article, it should only be read after an examination of Heider's intrapersonal balance theory.

Rapoport, A. *Fights, Games, and Debates.* Ann Arbor: University of Michigan Press, 1961.

A semitechnical account of game theory, Rapoport's considerations of the social implications of game theory should be of interest to students of interpersonal communication.

Rubin, Z. *Liking and Loving.* New York: Holt, Rinehart and Winston, 1973.

A lively, yet sound treatment of interpersonal attraction. This very readable text is one of the few which treats the topic of love from a scientific perspective.

Applications

Exercise 1

As an outside observer, analyze the following situations and decide what motives the second person would probably attribute to the first. Give reasons for your choices.

TRANSACTION 1

Ben: A Mercedes-Benz salesman in Beverly Hills, in coat and tie
Frank: A college student, twenty-one years old, in ragged jeans and T-shirt

Frank has passed by the Mercedes dealer many times looking longingly at the cars in the window. He needs a new car—his 1960 Volkswagen has just "died" for the last time—and he wonders if he might be able to afford an older Mercedes. As he enters the showroom, he is approached by Ben.

BEN: Hello, sir. May I help you? (*eyeing the patches on Frank's jeans*)

FRANK: Well, I'm in the market for a new car. I thought I'd ask if you had any used Mercedes—say 1964 or 1965?

BEN: Well, we don't get those in too often, and they're gone pretty quickly when we do. But we do have a couple you might want to look at.

FRANK: Could you give me an idea of the price range?

BEN: I wouldn't count on spending less than $3,000 for one in good shape. Are you a student?

FRANK: Yes.

BEN: You know, I have a son about your age. A year ago he needed a new car and wanted to buy an older Mercedes, I was against it—too much money for an old car. They can be a real drain on the pocketbook, you know.

FRANK: *(puzzled)* Really? I thought they were one of the best sturdy cars.

BEN: Oh, they are, they are. It's just that when something does go wrong, the parts are expensive . . . you sure you want to get yourself into that?

FRANK: Hmmm . . . I don't know.

TRANSACTION 2

Arnie: A waiter in the Corner Cafe with a reputation for giving very fast and efficient service; he's also known to be quite disagreeable when he's had a bad day

Elaine: A frequent customer of the Corner Cafe

ELAINE: Hello, Arnie, what's the special tonight? Anything good?

ARNIE: It's beef stew, and it's absolutely terrible. That stupid new cook can't do anything right!

ELAINE: Oh, well, I'll try it anyway.

ARNIE: All right, but it's your stomach. Don't say I didn't warn you.

Exercise 2

Consider this hypothetical situation:

Bill, a middle-aged person of average intelligence, is inclined to be very dogmatic. He recently made a visit to the family doctor for his yearly checkup. He has been going to the same doctor for twenty years, appreciates his continued medical help, admires him greatly, and sometimes goes hunting and fishing with him.

During the visit, the doctor tells Bill in no uncertain terms that he must lose forty pounds to protect his health. The doctor reminds Bill that Bill's father died from a heart attack—probably the result of being overweight. He also quotes him some alarming statistics linking obesity to heart failure.

Bill is very upset. He has known for some time that he should lose weight, yet he loves to eat. A gourmet cook, his favorite activities are trying out new recipes for his friends and enjoying elaborate meals at many different restaurants.

a. What decision do you think Bill will make about starting to diet and attempting to lose weight?

b. How do you think he will feel after he has made this decision?

c. What theories we have discussed explain your answers to the above questions?

CHAPTER • 9

The Purposes Served by Groups
Groups for Sharing Information
Groups for Socialization
Groups for Solving Problems
Conformity—A Group Communication Factor
Conformity: Internal System
Conformity: External System
Conformity: Trans-Per
Roles—A Group Communication Factor
Roles: Internal System
Roles: External System
Roles: Trans-Per
Leadership—A Group Communication Factor
Leadership: Internal System
Leadership: External System
Leadership: Trans-Per
Summary
Additional Readings
Applications

Communication
in the
Group
Context

Our life is filled with communicating experiences within groups formed for widely different purposes. Family groups, neighborhood associations, volunteer groups, graduate seminars, sensitivity groups, and work task forces are just a few of the groups in which we participate. It has been said—by one of your authors—that "from the womb to the tomb" we are all engaged in group activity of one type or another—for example, the family group in which we were a child, the new family we form as adults, and the family with whom we live in our old age. But for all our activity with the various groups to which we belong, very little time is spent analyzing the nature of our group communication. In this chapter we'll concentrate on analyzing group communication.

In Chapter 6 we called attention to some basic assumptions underlying group experience: we noted then that *norms*, *roles*, and *duration* of the group serve as important criteria for an analysis of any particular group. We also said that it was useful to determine whether the orientation of the group was primarily a *task orientation* or a *social-emotional orientation*. In addition to developing these criteria, we want to spend our time in the present chapter on *group communication factors or meanings* that are created when elements of the Internal and External Systems are combined. By now you know that internal elements are those cues which individuals bring with them to any communication and that there are as many Internal Systems in a communicating context as there are individuals. We also want to remind you that it's the individual's perceptual mix of elements from these two systems that leads to the assignment of meaning or to that transaction we call communication.

We want to examine first the question of why groups exist and then to consider the various meanings or communication factors that develop in a group transaction. Since there are an infinite number of specific communication factors or meanings that are developed in the course of a group transaction, any selection that we choose for discussion must be arbitrary. We've chosen three group communication factors that we consider most useful and inclusive: *conformity*, *roles*, and *leadership*. We think that an analysis of how these result from the perceptual blending of Internal and External Systems will help us explain most of what is taking place in group communication. So for each of these communication factors or meanings we want to suggest how they probably come into being or are created and how they lead in turn to the creation of other group communication meanings. Before we can describe meanings that evolve in a group setting, we must consider the purposes that a typical group serves.

The Purposes Served by Groups

We do not pick and choose all of our groups: some we have had little choice about joining, such as the family, religious, or ethnic group into which we were born. Other groups we join voluntarily—the political activist group or the swimming club or the amateur orchestra. If you were asked to list the groups to which you voluntarily belong, it's fairly certain that the first ones listed would be those whose stated purposes or goals you most strongly subscribe to or support. As you look at the list of your groups, you would probably have little difficulty in identifying the major goal of each. For your work group, that goal might be the weekly paycheck of each member, or the increase in profits that the company hopes to report for its next quarter. You might list a hospital volunteer group and think immediately of the movie equipment it bought for entertaining the patients or of the parties that it sponsors. Or you might think of your union group and be pleased about its repeated and successful negotiations for cost-of-living increases.

Whatever your quick assessment of the goals or purposes of your particular groups, you can think of any group as generally serving one of three different purposes. A group may have as its primary purpose *sharing of information*, *socialization*, or *solving of problems*. Although these purposes may all exist to varying degrees in any group to which we belong, a group typically has only one primary purpose. When we say that the original, intended purpose of the group is directly related to group outcomes, we mean that the purpose of a group indicates what a given group eventually aims to achieve.

Groups for Sharing Information

Groups that exist to share information have as their primary purpose the *acquiring* and *the sharing of knowledge*. All classes from the formal study of applied math to the informal study of contract bridge exist for such a purpose. The precise outcomes associated with this group purpose are not always easy to identify. For example, if you think of this class as an information-sharing group, the passing grade you receive may be the single most important outcome you foresee from the class. Or the information might turn out to be helpful to you in ways you cannot now anticipate —such as helping you understand communication problems at some future job. Or if the class is one in your major, you may see it as fulfilling a requirement in your degree program. In addition to formally or informally structured classes, other types of information-sharing groups are political clubs, religious organizations, book study clubs, and debate groups. The common thread joining these different groups is that members participate for the primary purpose of acquiring or sharing knowledge or information. Members are *task-oriented* to gain new knowledge.

Groups for Socialization

Whereas people involved in information-sharing groups are primarily concerned with knowledge, information, or issues, members of *socialization* groups focus their attention on being together and on each other as individuals. This group purpose is more one of social-emotional orientation than of task orientation. These groups emphasize the social relationship between members: the most desirable outcome for such groups is that the members recognize each other as social beings and unique personalities. Do you belong to any socializing groups? The typical country club, sorority, bowling team, or coffee group has many members who meet first and foremost for the purpose of being together. Other peripheral activities such as sports, volunteer work, or fund-raising are secondary interests of these primarily social groups.

We suspect that most people continue many of their memberships in socialization groups to help themselves: there's nothing wrong with it or with admitting to it. Most of us need others, and a group, meeting regularly and frequently, provides us with the means of satisfying that need.

Have you ever participated in a sensitivity group? In this type of socialization group, some people have found the atmosphere useful for understanding the needs and motivations of others; others have found it threatening and unsettling. Why these different reactions? Generally this particular kind of group has clear norms that define the standards of behavior for participants. These norms indicate that it is desirable, and expected of everyone, to be open and honest—and for each individual to say what he feels deeply within him. Many people find this intimate atmosphere comfortable: they reason that self-disclosure holds for everyone, and so they don't mind participating as well. On the other hand, certain people need some time to warm up to the effort of disclosing their deeply felt opinions, attitudes, and emotions to others. The norms of a sensitivity group might frustrate these individuals and prevent them from satisfying their need to socialize comfortably with others—since the group demands more self-disclosure than they are willing to make and at a rate faster than they find natural.

Groups for Solving Problems

Whenever we participate in groups seeking to carry out a particular job, resolve a problem, or accomplish a given task, we are members of a *problem-solving group*. Keep in mind that we are talking about determining the purposes of groups by means of establishing priorities. Therefore problem-solving groups, in addition to their major task, may also carry on information-sharing or socializing activities. Typical problem-solving groups include temporary political committees, which seek to elect a specific candidate; Alcoholics Anonymous groups, which attempt to support individuals suffering from a serious problem; and Weight Watchers for those who seek happiness in slim bodies. Generally the jobs that most people hold place them automatically in problem-solving groups. On the job, an individual typically finds himself communicating daily with several different groups who are attempting to find some techniques of increasing productivity. Various *ad hoc* committees of faculty and students are formed to make plans for a class project or to solve a campus parking problem. In all these associations, something has to be done and that something explains the purpose for existence—and the goal—of a problem-solving group.

What we want to suggest is that, anytime you think of your own memberships, one of the first things you should pay attention to is the purpose of the group—what does it hope to accomplish? Are your groups primarily aimed at sharing information, at fostering socialization, or at solving problems? As we'll demonstrate, your perception of group purpose directly influences your judgments about communication factors or meanings in group contexts.

We have attempted to suggest the many diverse reasons that groups come into being and for what typical purposes they maintain their existence—as background to our analysis of specific communication factors or meanings that arise in group contexts. Now we want to consider, one by one, the communication factors that will help us analyze and understand the behavior that results from group communication. As we said previously, analysis of these major communication factors of conformity

roles, and leadership—how they result from the perceptual blend of Internal and External Systems—will help us deal with the complexity of group contexts.

Conformity—A Group Communication Factor

If there is one term that typifies group behavior, it's that of *conformity*. Essentially conformity is *behavior that is consistent with group standards or norms*. These standards or norms can be recognized or identified depending on the specific group that we're describing. We think an understanding of conformity behavior requires some consideration of this notion of group norms.

Norms can be defined as group rules that govern member behavior or as *standards of acceptable group behavior*. We shouldn't be so naive as to think that group norms must be written or formally announced. What do you call your instructor—by his first name or by his title? How do you dress at a wedding or a graduation? How do you behave in church? Can you find any written rule or regulation dictating any of these behaviors? Hardly. Yet we sense or pick up very quickly the norms of those groups to which we belong, and we learn just as quickly the standards of behavior of those groups to which we do *not* want to belong.

It should be clear by now that adherence to group norms represents *conformity* behavior. For example, as much as you may dislike examinations, you understand that when you're given one, you are expected to complete it. To stay in college and complete your degree, you conform to class norms. You may sense certain norms in operation at your job —norms that mean you wear a particular type of more formal clothing than you generally wear. To keep your job, you conform to the group norms.

Every member of a group conforms to some extent, even the rebel or devil's advocate of the group. Simply by having joined a group, a member has signaled his intention to live by the rules of the group—if not by all the rules, at least by a significant portion of them. Even those people who are forced by certain personal ambitions to join groups they would otherwise easily forgo must conform to some degree: the student who takes a required course may not attend classes regularly but probably takes the exams to obtain the desired credits.

Norms are necessary for effective group operations: at best, group norms operate to provide a high level of group productivity. To work effectively with one another, people do not "do their own thing"; they subordinate their own wishes to the group's best interests. It is a norm in some industries that people go to work at certain times and quit at certain times since the performance of their specific tasks requires mutual cooperation and assistance. In other cultures, and for tasks not requiring coordination, the times that people go to or leave work may be unimportant, the driving force is to get some particular job done.

At the worst, norms operate to remove differences of opinion from a group when these differences might provide creative or innovative thinking. For example certain students are able to get more out of particular courses by studying at home and missing classes; however, if the requirement or the norm is to attend each class, these students will probably not do their best work—they'll be distracted. The term *misfit* is given to someone whose life-style or behavior deviates from the norm. But all things considered, without group norms and with individuals operating almost randomly, there could be no predictable group activity or accomplishment. The whole idea of group activity for cooperative performance of given tasks would be undermined. Even groups that exist primarily for socializing would be torn apart by dissent if members were unable to agree on norms satisfactory to the majority of members.

Researchers in this area identify some characteristics of group norms which have significant implications for our discussion of conformity behavior. Shaw (1971) points out four characteristics: (1) Groups evolve norms only for those things which have some significance for the group. An example of his point might be that a group of mineworkers adheres to certain safety standards (norms) of particular concern to them. (2) Norms may apply to all members of a particular group or to a select number. For an example, we may think of hospital workers who dress according to the group to which they belong; surgeons wear sterile clothing appropriate for the operating room; nurses wear uniforms that distinguish them as a group from all others; and orderlies wear still a different uniform that distinguishes their activities. (3) There is some difference in amount of acceptance of norms by group members—some group norms may be accepted by all while other norms may be accepted by only a few. Individuals interpret and reinterpret norms. Our example of Shaw's point might be that a fraternity member may see the norms for behavior at meetings as inflexible but the norms for parties as more flexible, that is, allowing greater freedom of expression. (4) Groups vary in the amount of permissible deviation from norms that will be tolerated. An illustration of Shaw's point might be that some religions accept a wide range of personal beliefs; others accept a relatively narrow range.

When we think of accepting norms or of such requirements "applying" to us, we're speaking of the conformity behavior imposed by the group. But if we look at this idea the other way around, what possible internal elements lead individuals to accept conformity behavior required by the group? Let us now take a look at these internal elements as they're classified and described in the Trans-Per model.

Conformity: Internal System

You will recall from our ongoing discussion of internal elements that they include attitude and personality (self-esteem and dogmatism), IQ, sex, knowledge, intelligence, and needs. We now will consider which of these internal elements contributes most directly to conformity. What we're interested in here are those in-the-head variables that a person brings to a group and that lead him to conform to group norms.

Involvement   A primary internal element that affects an individual's level of conformity concerns his perception of the group's significance to him. Stated another way, this element deals with the member's level of *involvement* with the group and its purposes; ego-involvement was one of the first internal elements we introduced in Chapter 4. People like to think that they're highly selective in their commitments and that they concentrate on those things in which they're ego-involved. The extent to which a person perceives the group to be significant to him will affect his desire to conform to the group's standards for behavior or operation—its norms.

We bring to any group to which we belong a feeling or intuition of how important that group is to our life. The nature of our conformity to certain group standards will depend on the nature and degree of the involvement that we feel with that group or its members. For example, as a political science major, you may be very interested in the political campaign process. Considering your membership in the Young Democrats Club as very significant to you, you attend meetings, serve on subcommittees, talk with precinct workers, and campaign for local and national candidates. In other words, you conform as much as possible to the group's norms. At the same time, you may be a member as well of a poorly organized student political association, in which your level of involvement ranges from moderate to weak. Conforming minimally, you occasionally attend meetings, pay your dues, but generally decline to volunteer for any committee work. Thus the level of involvement you have in the group directly affects your conformity behavior.

We tend to conform willingly to group norms for which there is some premium to be gained for our involvement in the particular group. What we usually want in a group to which we belong is some reward or satisfaction for our commitment. To extend our previous example, we can say that you, as a political science major, want to gain experience in the "real world" of politics. You see that participation in the Young Democrats Club has practical rewards and long-range value: your membership gives you a concrete opportunity to work in campaigns, to meet candidates, and, quite possibly, to help you make personal contacts for some type of government job. On the contrary the student political club, as a discussion group, has little to offer you directly by way of personal contacts, practical campaigning experience, and so forth.

What's important to remember is that the significance that an individual attaches to a group—or his ego-involvement in it—is one of the internal elements affecting his conformity to the group's norms.

Self-esteem   A second internal element affecting an individual's willingness to conform is his *self-esteem*. Individuals who have a low opinion of themselves will probably give in to pressure to conform more frequently than those who have high self-esteem. Yet the element of self-esteem, discussed previously in Chapter 4, has particular bearing on conformity behavior in group communicating environments. Perhaps a brief example will help us better understand this internal element as it affects the individual's willingness or unwillingness to conform.

Think for a moment of your first days in this class. Other members of the class were for the most part strangers to you, and of course you were a stranger to them. During the course of the term you've probably developed some significant relationships with at least one or two members of the class; these relationships should have helped raise your level of self-esteem and self-confidence. What was your perception of yourself as a student prior to these relationships? Hard to define? Well, that's exactly the point. In any circumstance in which we're unsure of ourselves or somewhat insecure, we're ripe for conformity behavior. The initial internal state that you brought with you to this class was probably one of some confusion — which probably prompted you to get together with others.

Lack of personal relationships and ambiguous or uncertain situations frequently lead an individual to conform. A newcomer to the class, placed in a situation that is unfamiliar to him—new course material, new instructor, new students—is more likely to conform to class norms than the rest of the students, who are already more "at home" in the setting. The stranger's level of self-esteem may be affected or lowered by the uncertainty of the setting and the strangers around him. However these feelings of ambiguous self-esteem are very much dependent on the particular situation, or are *situation-specific*. As we said previously, levels of self-esteem change with an individual's ongoing experience.

The feelings of ambiguity caused by a new situation account for much of a student's conforming behavior throughout the first year of college or university life. A freshman's desire to join and participate in social groups, study groups, and religious centers provides some evidence of an individual's need to conform when in new and unfamiliar situations. Several years ago, when fraternity and sorority groups were powerful forces on American campuses, an interesting phenomenon took place that illustrates the interrelationship between conformity and ambiguous self-esteem.

During that period individuals who were rejected from such groups or who were opposed to them struck out at the "nonindividualistic" behavior of people who participated in fraternities. Essentially opponents of fraternity life argued that members of this type of college society were all unthinking conformists. In an attempt to fight these conformists, the "independents" banded together, wore matching sweatshirts, had similar lively parties, and by their conduct attempted to point out the foolishness of such societies. But by their own behavior the "independents" were conforming in very similar ways to those they were criticizing; the independents had the same need as the fraternity members to shore up their ambiguous or low self-esteem by group conformity.

Our point is that we all carry with us certain evaluations of ourselves; this evaluation or self-esteem affects the extent to which we conform to group norms. In our example of "independents," we can see that those people were no more independent than the fraternity members they criticized. And we can assume that they had similar needs to conform and to reinforce their self-esteem by relating to others who shared their ideas about the immaturity of traditional fraternity members.

Needs   So far we've said that an individual brings certain internal elements into the group context that affect the extent to which he'll conform to the group's norms. The internal element of involvement represents a person's evaluation of the group's significance to him; the internal element of self-esteem represents his evaluation of his own self-worth. The next internal element we will look at is just as important as the two already mentioned; we will investigate the *needs* that an individual brings to the group. How do needs relate to conformity behavior in group communicating contexts?

In a very simple sense we may think of a need as a *demand* or a *requirement* that a person carries within him. We may say that a child has a need for attention if he behaves in a fussy manner that is different from his normal cheerfulness. Someone who slaves at his desk, takes no coffee breaks, and does far more than the job requires may have a need for recognition that he's trying to satisfy. If we know that someone makes great efforts to be alone—for example imitating Thoreau by camping out alone at a pond—we may say that that individual has a need to find himself. In other words a need motivates certain behaviors; it drives us to act in a specific manner; it explains why we acted as we did. We've given you a few examples; you can think of many more.

Furthermore, when we speak of a person's needs, we are implying that his needs will be met or satisfied by whatever means are available to him. When we communicate our needs to others, we assume that such needs can be satisfied and hope that the psychic pressures can be relieved.

Abraham Maslow (1954) categorized five types of human need: needs of physiology, safety, love, esteem and self-actualization. We are to think of these needs in a definite order or hierarchy; each level must be taken care of before the next can be satisfied. As we describe each of Maslow's types, keep in mind that—in our Trans-Per approach—we're conceiving of each one as part of the internal element we've called *needs*, which are brought to the group context by a person as part of his Internal System. In our development of this internal element, we have used Maslow's basic concept of hierarchy or levels of needs but have provided our own interpretation and examples.

Although it's quite true that the satisfaction of any need lies outside the person, the need itself comes from within. In Maslow's hierarchy of needs, the physiological needs, the most basic of all, involve our very survival and include the demand for adequate food, shelter, and water. Freedom from fatigue and protection from excessive heat or cold are also typical physiological demands that must be met before any other needs can be satisfied. This level of need dictates that, rather than seek pleasure all day long, an individual must work full time in order to feed, clothe, and shelter himself. Certain individuals, who prefer to avoid legitimate work, join deviating underworld groups to satisfy basic needs by the illicit means of stealing or selling drugs. The physiological demands are the strongest in our hierarchy of needs. Without satisfaction of these needs, we can pay little attention to the other needs in the Internal System.

Once physiological needs are satisfied, a person's demand for safety within his environment represents his next most basic need. An individual's need for order and safety in his environment reflects a desire for basic security. We may subscribe to *Consumer Reports* or enroll in insurance programs as part of our effort to fill this need. Regardless of the elements from the External System which may satisfy these needs, we should think of this type of need as an internal demand for order and structure in our lives.

The next level of need is that dealing with love—love needs that are satisfied by family love and love needs that are satisfied by membership in a group such as the priesthood. Marriage, close friendships, communes, and other such associations provide satisfaction for these internal needs.

We've already partially touched on Maslow's next level of need—the need that individuals have for esteem—in our previous discussions of self-esteem as an internal element. But we're more concerned here with an individual's desire for a wide reputation and high attainment or status in some field—that is, for the esteem of others. For example an individual who's preoccupied with satisfying his need for status will be attracted to those groups that will provide strong support for his advancement and promotion. He may typically join the most prestigious country club in town, move into the finest neighborhood, or join an exclusive social club. Since his motivation or need is to achieve improved status, his behavior will conform very much to group standards. In addition election to office in professional associations, awards from one's company, compliments by people one respects, admission to professional societies as a "fellow," and even admission to a prestigious professional school—say a medical or a law school—are typical examples of esteem needs.

Finally, when more pressing requirements are satisfied, people have the need for and can move toward self-actualization. This notion suggests that a person strives to achieve his maximum potential. Some examples of groups that reward high individual attainment include honorary societies (Phi Beta Kappa), professional societies (Million-Seller's Club), and the elite teams of professional sports. The point here is that a person, after having satisfied needs at all other levels, strives to reach his full potential.

Generally it's very difficult to think of Maslow's hierarchy of needs as internal elements alone: there's a natural tendency to think of the external satisfaction of the need as inseparable from the internal need itself. Yet we must try to think of these internal needs as strong motivations in analyzing a person's conformity behavior. How do needs explain an individual's conformity behavior in group communication contexts? The type of needs that drive and stimulate an individual provides reasonable explanations of why he joins particular groups and why, in turn, he willingly adheres to their norms.

So far we've discussed those three elements in the Internal System that we think contribute to a group member's conformity behavior. The element of involvement is a measure of the amount of significance an individual attaches to his membership in a particular group. Knowing his degree of involvement in the group gives us a great deal of insight into predicting the degree of his conformity to the group's standards.

Another internal element that indicates a group member's susceptibility to conformity is self-esteem—or whether he holds himself in high or low regard. Generally those who hold a low opinion of themselves conform the most.

The third internal element, an individual's hierarchy of needs, clearly points to the type of groups to which he will be attracted.

As we have stated so often, an analysis of internal elements is only half the picture; for these internal stimuli describe only what the person brings to the group context—not what resides in the external environment. Let's turn now to a description of pertinent external elements that contribute to the communication factor or meaning of conformity.

Conformity: External System

Group Membership A person's tendency to conform—or not to conform—will be strongly influenced by his respect for the other members who compose the group. The external element of *existing group membership* is the first we will take up. Such groups as fraternities, political groups, and social organizations all have as members individuals whom we respect and like—and who, we hope, return our respect and affection. Conformity to the group's norms is easy for us when we hold its members, individually or collectively, in high esteem. Our desire to enroll in honors sections of certain courses or to be assigned to work in certain class projects with people known to be excellent students are additional examples of our willingness—even eagerness—to conform to certain group norms.

Also the availability of people with special expertise within group contexts cannot be overemphasized. For example you may be attracted to a specific group for what you consider an opportunity to learn from a professional in his field—to learn tennis from a coach who can help you with your game. Or you may join a special intensive tutorial group to help you prepare for the law boards. Regardless of its particular direction, the group possesses some expertise you hope to gain. And again you are willing to conform to group standards of behavior to avail yourself of the expertise available in the group.

Group Sanctions   A second external element, which helps to explain group conformity behavior, is the nature of the group's sanctions, that is, the rewards that the group applies to those conforming and the punishments that the group deals to those not conforming to group norms. We're referring to the measures the group takes against those who don't behave in acceptable ways and the honors the group bestows on its respected members.

For example this class probably has a very structured set of rewards or sanctions for conformity. If you do well in the exam, write all the papers, and generally do what's expected of you, your grade will reflect the instructor's evaluation of your conformity behavior. On the other hand, miss a lot of classes, fail an exam or two, and you know the unpleasantness that follows. The grading system simply enforces the imposed standards of acceptable behavior. Often we'll see in a group an atmosphere in which conformity encourages and motivates the individual, an atmosphere directly related to the way that norms are enforced. The norms established for admission to honorary scholarship groups—Phi Beta Kappa, Phi Kappa Phi, and others—are examples of this encouragement of productive conformity. Students are encouraged to maintain high grades and to be active in university service to be eligible for membership. Similarly independent study programs and a flexible curriculum motivate students to gain admission to certain honors programs.

Other groups—outside the classroom—provide a different set of sanctions for those who conform or fail to conform to the group's norms. Take the wrong entrance to a highway, drive your Triumph beyond the speed limit, or thumb your nose at a policeman—and a different set of sanctions are imposed. The point is that the sanctions imposed by the group, its *mode of norm-enforcement*, strongly affect our tendency to conform. Whether we are voluntary or involuntary members of a group, we generally abide by the mode of norm-enforcement. Often we have no choice about conforming; that is, our family has a set of sanctions that were imposed upon us from birth and that we've learned to live with.

Instrumental Utility   A third external element is the group's *instrumental utility*, or its potential to act as the means by which an individual will accomplish some end. This class, for example, may be a means to an end or a goal that you consider well worth achieving: by satisfying one of the requirements in your field, you move closer to the larger goal of your degree. In other words there is a pragmatic usefulness to be gained from group memberships—the satisfaction of personal, long-range objectives. For example norms may have been established when you were younger that governed your dating behavior: you were expected to be home by a reasonable time and to stay away from certain unhealthy places. Failure to conform may have led to your being "grounded" or punished in some other way. Even now certain conforming behaviors may be expected of you: you may be expected to come home for the holidays, to call home regularly, and so forth. In sum the sanctions—rewards or punishments—of certain groups affect the meaning you attach to conformity.

Finally we mention, as external elements, the activities associated with specific groups which, in and of themselves, are satisfying to us. The Young Democrats Club, the crew club, the church choir, the foreign students' association are all examples of groups whose activities are more attractive than utilitarian. It's reasonable to assume that the conformity behavior is strong for individuals joining groups whose activities have such a strong appeal.

We would like now to review briefly our analysis of conformity in group contexts: (1) Each person brings to his group activity an infinite number of internal elements. (2) Out of all these internal elements, the individual's ego-involvement, his level of self-esteem, and his hierarchy of needs affect his tendency to conform to group norms. (3) Each group environment contains an infinite number of external elements. (4) Out of all these external elements, the group's existing membership, its system of sanctions, its instrumental utility, and the attractiveness of its activities and purpose affect an individual's tendency to conform. (5) The degree of conformity is the result of the individual's perceptual mix of pertinent internal and external elements within a specific group communication context.

In the following section we want to use Trans-Per in an analysis of conformity behavior in group settings.

Conformity: Trans-Per

Let's assume that our group transaction is one involving three individuals, a very small group, meeting for a specific purpose—one of problem-solving. Remember that individuals who communicate for problem-solving purposes are attempting to accomplish a task, handle a problem, or alleviate some perceived difficulty. The group consists of three sociology students who are working together on a class project, the purpose of which is to analyze communicating patterns among faculty and students at their particular university.

Keep in mind that our primary purpose in studying this small group is to analyze how each individual's perceptual blending of public and private stimuli determines his own level of conformity to group norms. First let's look at the Internal System of each participant. What internal elements does each bring to the series of discussions that they will have during the course of the project?

Our first participant, Harry, is a senior, who's taking the course as a requirement in his last semester. A confident individual, with strong self-esteem, he views the task as one more relatively useless obstacle to hurdle before graduation. His personal experience with student-faculty committees—and particularly with some indifferent faculty members—has led him to the conclusion that it doesn't make a bit of difference whether students and faculty communicate with each other or not. Eager to graduate, he doesn't want at this time to be a member of any group or class; a good athlete, his main interests are basketball, ping pong, and golf. His strong level of self-esteem and a negative attitude toward the project are the most dominant internal elements that Harry brings to the situation.

On the other hand, Helen, interested in collecting her first research data, is quite excited about the task. A sophomore sociology major, she sees this project as teaching her necessary techniques for further undergraduate and graduate study. The class instructor is also Helen's advisor; Helen knows that this project may provide useful results for the instructor's own dissertation. In fact she's pretty sure she was assigned to this class because she had once asked her advisor how a sociologist sets up a research project. For Helen the internal elements of involvement and the need for self-esteem will determine her level of conformity.

The third member of the team is John—a first-semester transfer student, who's still trying to feel his way around his new surroundings. John, quiet and withdrawn by nature, is intimidated by the instructor as well as by most of the other students in the class, especially Harry. Although somewhat interested in the project—the work appeals more to him than the other workers—he is a person of low self-esteem. He sees this project as a "make or break" assignment for him—an indication of his ability to survive in a more competitive setting than that of his previous college. He has a strong need for closure, organization, and safety—and is willing to do almost any task assigned him to get along with the group.

We must also analyze carefully the External System available to the three communicators. Among the elements existing in this system are the expertise of the members, the desire to be liked by other group members, the various rewards or sanctions for completing the work, and the instrumental utility of the group for each individual's future. Can we now determine how each individual's perceptual blending brings about the conforming behavior observable in each of the three group participants?

An analysis by our Trans-Per model suggests that, while all three participants will demonstrate some degree of conformity during their frequent discussions and will achieve a limited amount of shared meaning, more significant communication will take place between Helen and John. Why? One reason may be that these individuals are closer to each other than to Harry—since they select more of the same stimuli from the External System than he does. Harry, on his part, sees little to be gained by more than perfunctory attempts to work on the project. He is not particularly concerned with learning from the expertise of the other members. Nor does he particularly desire to win their respect or friendship. Therefore these external elements are not crucial to his perceptual blend.

On the other hand Helen and John want to learn what they can from each other, and the instructor, and want to be liked. Even more significant is the level of involvement that Helen and John bring to the situation. As we indicated earlier when we discussed problems with modeling, there's always the danger that we might have made incorrect choices of significant and pertinent elements. Nevertheless we know that differences in internal elements that communicators bring to the transaction affect the level of conformity. We also know that, although all conformed somewhat to the group norms, their different levels of conformity resulted from each assigning different meanings to their perceptual blends.

What can we conclude from our brief examination of conformity by our Trans-Per analysis? First, we can say that people conform to group norms—either partially or fully—because of internal elements that they bring to the situation and external elements that exist in the situation. Second, we can say that in this instance one of our participants—John—was probably the most persuasible and most conforming due to his need for safety and his low self-esteem.

Finally we can say with some confidence that *the extent to which an individual conforms to group norms is directly related to the level of involvement that he brings to the communicating context*. In this case, since Harry was not deeply involved in the project or the group, he was least susceptible to group norms.

Up to this point we've been discussing the nature of a person's adherence to group norms—his level of conformity—and the impact of this type of behavior on group communication transactions.

Roles—A Group Communication Factor

For a moment or two think about the groups to which you belong; then decide on your favorite among these groups, and specifically call to mind each of its members. Probably you can categorize each member in a few words: one may be the organizer or dictator, another may be the group comedian or sophisticated wit, and still another the willing volunteer or hard worker. Regardless of the specific term you have chosen, you've labeled each member in your group by the role that he or she plays.

We can think of a role as a *set of behaviors expected of each member of an established group.* In fact we can say that the role we occupy is formed by the expectation others have of us—and those we have of ourselves. To return to your most significant group and its members, think of the person whom you have labeled the comedian or wit—the one who helps put the group at ease. When things seem at an impasse, he relieves the accumulated tension and helps the others in the group look at the hopeful side of a discouraging problem. The group may be surprised when a member acts contrary to the group's expectation of him. After it has come to expect a member to behave in a certain way, the group notices immediately when he violates that expectation.

Think of the role that you are expected to play in your favorite group. Are you comfortable with it? Of course you're just deluding yourself if you say that you don't quite know what role you occupy. It may be true that you haven't thought about your role before, or you aren't happy with it, but the fact remains that you have come to understand what behavior is expected of you.

We now want to look at some of the internal and external elements that contribute to our perception of the role that we assume within the group. As we move through our discussion, we'll point out some of the relationships that exist between the communication factors of role and conformity. Performance of a role is essentially a conforming behavior; we mention such an overlapping of role and conformity only to reinforce our contention that these communication factors are interrelated. Let's now consider the internal elements that contribute to our understanding of the meaning or communication factor of roles.

Roles: Internal System

Self-expectation The first internal element that we'll discuss pertains to one's self-expectation of role. Each person brings with him certain expectations of the role behaviors he will perform in a given group. When you entered this class, you had in mind a role for yourself—that of a student. Your self-expectation might have been that you would remain very quiet; it might have been that you would try to enter discussions and be very active. Generally our self-expectation is our *preferred* role—or our ideas or conceptions of the roles and behaviors we *wish* to perform.

When you first entered this class, your preferred role might have been to take a "wait and see" approach and to find out what the class was like before deciding on your behavior—often the case in experiences with a new group. On the other hand, if you already had had prior information about the class or prior experience with the instructor, you might have decided upon a clear preferred role from the start. Often your preferred role—your self-expectation of the role you wish to perform—will be very closely tied to one of the needs we discussed earlier. For example if your need for esteem of status is predominant, you may wish to play a preferred role that fulfills your need for status. As a hypothetical case, a fraternity member with a strong need for status may see that need satisfied with his winning the election for house president. He has observed in his experience that house presidents are usually dynamic, resourceful, and popular. Therefore his preferred role will be consistent with these past favorable observations: he sees himself about to perform a role in which he too will be outgoing, innovative, friendly, and popular. In other words he has a self-expectation of the role that he prefers to perform in a group, and he behaves accordingly. The internal element of self-expectation is the preferred role an individual desires to play in a group.

Self-esteem   Another pertinent internal element for the analysis of role is a person's *self-esteem*, already mentioned as an internal element in other contexts. We can assume that the lower the level of a person's self-esteem, the more persuasible he probably is. The more persuasible members are those who seldom assert themselves in group decision making. Other group members find it difficult to place confidence in weak members who bend with the wind. Individuals who bring low self-esteem into the group context indicate by their weak opinion of themselves that they may be willing to perform virtually any unpleasant or menial role thrust upon them —roles that other members avoid. Those who bring high self-esteem into a particular group have a great deal more confidence in their ability to perform well within the group. Regardless of the level of an individual's self-esteem, this element is one of the most important in an analysis of role behavior.

The role behavior that an individual performs in a group is essentially the result of his own perceptual activity. Neither wholly under the person's control nor wholly under the control of the group to which he belongs, role behavior comes into existence because of the individual's blend of internal and external elements.

Thus we have suggested two internal elements, self-expectation and self-esteem, that an individual brings to the group and that directly affect his attachment of meaning to roles that he performs. Self-expectation and self-esteem are two internal elements. Next let's turn our attention to a consideration of some external elements, chosen arbitrarily, that are useful in explaining the roles we typically adopt within a group.

Roles: External System

Group Expectations   Perhaps the single most important external element affecting an individual's role behavior is the expectation of other group members of his role. This element— group expectation of role—is very closely related to the group's norms, that is, an individual is expected by others to perform in ways that are consistent with stated requirements of the group. We think of this element—group expectation of our role—as external, for it's largely imposed from the outside and beyond our control. Stated another way, we can say that the role required of us by the other members is usually created by the group without our influence. For example in your role as student you are expected to perform certain role behaviors. There are expectations that other members of the group —administration and faculty—have of you. Among the group's (or the college's) expectations of you are such things as registering for classes, paying tuition, and majoring in a discipline.

A group communicates what it requires or expects of members in two basic ways, overtly and covertly. Overt requirements or expectations of members may be written out on documents that outline roles and behaviors of members or may be conveyed by word of mouth at orientation meetings—or may be made known even less formally. Covert methods of the group's expressing its expectation of roles of individual members may take the form of imposed seating arrangements or of delegating specific jobs to favored members. Thus the person given the more menial jobs is subtly informed that his role is significantly less valued by the group than those roles with more responsibility.

Group Purpose   A second external element related to role behavior is the group's stated and explicit purpose: we assume different roles if the group is a serious class in computer technology, a temporary association to build a scholarship fund, or a social group that is planning to revive the tango. (Recall the three main group purposes of sharing information, of solving problems, and of socializing.) An individual's recognition of the purpose of the group's existence definitely stands as an external cue in his perception of the role he will assume within the group. Take the case of the person who is an average student in his medical school courses, which we classify as information-sharing groups. His behavior in the classroom may be subdued and passive—the rest of the group, including professors and peers, expect only average work from him. However during his in-service training in the hospital, when he is expected to assist doctors in emergency duties and regular rounds, he may be a superior performer. In this type of problem-solving group he performs very well. In other words the role he occupies depends on the group purpose.

Group Norms   Finally the group norms or standards, whether expressed or implied, exist as crucial external elements generally available to any attentive group member; he will gladly comply if the group serves a utilitarian purpose for him. A well-motivated graduate student will become informed of and willingly adopt group norms; that is, he develops by his unique blend of elements a meaning for the role that he intends to perform.

No doubt you have noticed that, as we move through our discussions of communication factors related to group contexts, our analysis has become more concise. We are assuming that you have gradually become more familiar with the major elements—and their operation—in Trans-Per. We might say that, as you have progressed through these pages, your Internal System has become more adept at recognizing the terms of this book—the present External System; in the process you have become quicker at attaching meaning to our terms or the written verbal stimuli. Now we will look at a specific application of the Trans-Per model to group roles.

Roles: Trans-Per

The role that we assume in any group is the effect of a complex interplay of internal and external elements. To help us in the analysis of how our role behavior comes about, we'll return to the small group of three communicators—Harry, Helen, and John—who are still trying to complete their study of student-faculty communication. Earlier we tried to determine the various levels of conformity that the three demonstrated; now we want to gain some insight into the development of the roles that they have each assumed. To help us do so, we'll compare one internal element that each of these three students brings to the scene; and we will look at one common external element, as interpreted by each.

We're interested here in the individual blend of self-expectation of role (internal element) and group expectation of role (external element). To the first meeting each member brings a certain initial evaluation of the part that he's to play in the project. Harry, the senior, is confident that his role should be one of very relaxed performance. After all he's just trying to "get the thing over with, one way or another." Helen, who hopes to be a leader in organizing and running the project, thinks she holds a slight edge over the others—her background in sociology is stronger than theirs. Thus her intention is to work as hard as possible to make this project the best and most original in the class. John senses his role in this project is that of a follower: his preferred role is to do whatever the others want him to do.

The external element of *group expectation* is very interesting to examine in this example. For what we're soon to see is that there must be some modifications made in the internal and external elements that each blends. It soon becomes clear that Harry will not be able to relax completely and that even timid John can't be allowed to take a passive role. Why the change? For one thing, the group decides that, with the time pressure and the enormity of the task, the work will have to be divided equally. Thus the preferred roles or self-expectation that each had initially is affected by other elements. The point to keep in mind is that the meaning that each eventually assigns to his or her role is affected by the expectations of the other group members.

In terms of Trans-Per, the meaning created by each was an outcome of the perceptual blending of the internal element of preferred role and the external element of group expectation. Not one of the three students was able to perform role behaviors that each originally had expected to perform. Harry could not relax in quite the way he had planned; Helen had to share some of her control and direction; and John could not be as quiet and reserved as usual. As you can see, the expectations of each were modified by communication transactions of the group. Of great importance is the notion that this mixing of internal (preferred role) and external (group expectations) elements affected role meanings and ultimately role behaviors that the individuals were to perform. Although we didn't analyze any other internal and external elements, think for a moment how the elements of involvement, norms, self-esteem, and group purpose were also simultaneously blending to affect role behaviors eventually performed by each of our students.

In the next section we will take a look at another group communication factor closely connected to role behavior—leadership.

Leadership—A Group Communication Factor

Virtually every book in the area of group communication deals with leadership. Researchers have spent more time analyzing leadership than any other group communication factor. In fact you can probably look around at members of your class and easily identify any number of people as group leaders. Yet for all of our interest in leadership, we know relatively little about it. And it seems that each additional investigation has demonstrated that this meaning or communication factor is one of the most complicated of all. What is leadership? What's a leader? What are the more prominent internal and external elements contributing to a person's perception of leadership?

First of all we should think of leadership as a set of behaviors—certain activities that are performed by certain members of a group. Researchers describe leadership in several different ways: some describe leadership as a position in a group. Thus we can think of an instructor as the leader of the class, a valedictorian as the leader of his classmates, and the captain as the leader of a football team.

Other researchers describe leadership in terms of personal characteristics: people often speak of a "born leader." The person who's bright, witty, and generally popular is often termed a leader. And the individual who takes charge during times of crisis is often said to possess personal qualities or characteristics of leadership.

A third way of describing leadership, as an enduring trait or group of enduring traits, seems unacceptable to us; essentially this describes leadership as a role performed by certain individuals who are always leaders, no matter what the situation. We can think of many examples contradicting this idea of leadership as a constant trait: the person who's a leader in one circumstance is not necessarily influential in another.

We feel that it is more accurate to describe leadership as a set of behaviors or activities than as a group of enduring traits. Such a definition allows us to treat leadership as a behavior arising out of a specific situation; that is, the emergence of leadership behavior depends on the particular circumstance or situation. Therefore we will define leadership as a *set of behaviors arising out of a specific situation performed by the individual to assist the group in its operations.*

Leadership: Internal System

It should be clear by now, but it bears repeating, that our choice of internal elements is not an exhaustive selection. One could logically argue that, in addition to those we mention, an individual's level of involvement, self-esteem and attitude, just to name a few, are other internal elements that contribute to the emergence of leadership behavior.

Capability   The internal element we will term *capability* refers to the individual's assessment of his own intelligence, alertness, speaking ability, confidence, and sound judgment. This particular element is concerned with the person's evaluation of what the task involves and of his ability to perform it. In essence each individual brings to a group task a feeling about his ability to do the job. This estimate of ability depends on the way that an individual evaluates himself in terms of personal capability. In general this internal element includes an individual's self-evaluation of his ability to influence the group.

   As you can see, notions of capability relate quite directly to our earlier comments on self-esteem and preferred role. An individual's assessment of his possible contributions to a group directly affects his potential leadership behavior.

Self-perceived Status   The second internal element we will single out is *self-perceived status*. A person's evaluation of his status within the group signifies to him how influential he may be. For example, if he sees himself fitting in comfortably with his established group—or even with a new group—this intuition might suggest to him that he has a strong potential for leadership behavior. On the other hand, if his initial feeling is one of fear, of indifference, or of low status, chances of his leading the group or affecting its outcomes are limited. These inner judgments of status are affected, for one thing, by an individual's evaluation of his socio-economic position in relation to other members of the group: he may expect himself to have little influence on a group when his income is significantly lower than that of the other members. Why? It may be that he simply doesn't feel comfortable communicating with group members who have nothing in common with his economic needs. Also contributing to a person's self-evaluation of status within the group is his estimate of his personal popularity among group members.

   In general these internal elements—a person's estimate of his capability and status—probably affect an individual's evaluation of his own leadership behavior the most. In addition, his attitude toward the task, his open-mindedness or level of dogmatism, his tendencies toward conformity, his preferred role—all these may exist as internal elements affecting his leadership behavior. Since leadership behavior arises out of the particular situation, various internal elements that may affect an individual's leadership may or may not operate as a result of the external cues operating in a particular situation—the particular task, the particular group norms, and the specific group expectations of the individual's role. Let's turn now to a consideration of these external elements as they may affect the assignment of the meaning of leadership.

Leadership: External System

Assigned Task   The group's *assigned task* affects the determination of leadership within that group. This external element, the specific nature of the task, is directly related to a group's primary purpose, whether it be sharing information, solving problems, or socializing. (As we've said previously, any group serves one of these primary purposes and may serve either or both of the others in a secondary way.) In its attempts to serve its primary purpose, a group undertakes specific tasks. For example this class exists for the general purpose of sharing information on the communication process. At the same time, in order to carry out its general purpose of sharing knowledge about human communication, it has several assigned tasks —each presumably consistent with the general purpose. Group members are assigned examinations, term papers, projects, reports, and so forth. These tasks are external elements which combine with particular internal stimuli to create the various meanings that members assign for this course. An individual evaluates his potential leadership ability by assessing his capabilities and status within the group and blending these with the major external cue of the assigned task. As we said, leadership arises out of the situation. The apathetic medical student is stimulated by his assigned task in the emergency room: he sees a genuine need for his leadership and performance.

Group Expectations   Another external element that crucially affects a person's perceptions of his own leadership potential is the *group expectation* of his role or the expectation that other members share of his role in the group—an idea discussed earlier when we described the communication factor or meaning of roles. In a way we may think of this external element—group expectation—as the most critical cue affecting an individual's perceptions of leadership; that is, group expectations of the possible contribution of a particular member may be such that he is singled out by the others as a highly influential group member.

As we've moved through this chapter, we've been concerned with three group communication factors or meanings that are, of course, highly interrelated. It is difficult to talk about roles or role behavior without introducing conformity, it is difficult to analyze leadership behavior without introducing role behavior. Our previous discussion of conformity and role has already given us much of the necessary information on the external elements affecting leadership that we will use in our Trans-Per analysis.

Leadership: Trans-Per

Recall that we've been discussing two internal elements—capability and self-perceived status—and two external elements—assigned task and group expectations. In this section we want to illustrate how the meanings a person creates of leadership evolve from the perceptual blending of these internal and external stimuli. When we last checked our three students —Harry, Helen, and John—they were still trying to organize their class project. Let's see what internal cues each of the members has processed and what meanings of leadership each has assigned.

There is little doubt in Harry's mind that he can perform the task. Harry has a high evaluation of his own capabilities—he is confident, intelligent, alert—and in general sees himself quite capable of getting the job done. Yet keep in mind that Harry isn't really too excited about working with this project. Since he really doesn't see himself fitting in too well with this group, he sees his potential to influence this group as questionable. He is initially indifferent to the group's activity.

Helen, on the other hand, sees herself as a natural part of this group. With some training in this area, she thinks that her potential for influencing this group is fairly high. As far as her personal estimation of her capabilities, she sees herself as articulate and sound of judgment. Helen has both a high level of self-perceived status and a high regard for her own capabilities.

Finally, John's estimate of his own capabilities and his self-perceived status in the group are both quite low. He does not see himself as being very articulate or very effective in persuading anyone to his method of handling the task. In terms of his own self-perceived status, he sees himself as "low man on the totem pole," with very little if anything to contribute to the group. As such he doesn't consider himself as a leader within this or any other group.

The external elements of task and group expectation have been al-luded to in our earlier discussions of conformity and role. The task is for the group to produce a report analyzing the communicating behavior of fac-ulty and students. In terms of group expectations, we've already seen that Harry is expected to participate actively. Similarly Helen is expected to share her leadership with Harry. Although she has expertise in this field, he has had previous experience in administration and coordination of proj-ects. He also is effective at making the group work together as a unit —since the others admire his air of ease and sophistication and are willing to work under his guidance. How do these internal and external elements blend to create the meaning that each of our members assigns of leadership within the group? Let's take each member and examine the individual meanings each has evolved. For Harry the early discussions and disor-ganized approach of the group lead him to conclude that, if the project is to be completed at all, he had better actively participate—even take charge of assigning and coordinating specific tasks. He tells himself the task isn't that arduous or time-consuming and that, as a senior, he has more experience at independent group projects than the others. For Helen the group discus-sions indicate that, although she has the best background in sociology, Harry has had previous administrating experiences and has obvious leader-ship abilities that could be of great benefit to the successful completion of the project. John is willing to do his share of the work, but prefers not to be placed in a position of making any decisions. The opposite of a born leader, he prefers, under any circumstances, to follow.

In terms of shared meaning, Harry and Helen develop similar mean-ings: the group should take advantage of Harry's administrative strengths and Helen's intellectual expertise. Helen has succeeded in communicat-ing to Harry that it is necessary for him to cooperate if the job is to be com-pleted within the required time limit. All of them come to the conclusion that John should be assigned, and is quite willing to perform, the routine work. Essentially the three agree that leadership will be shared by Helen and Harry. For these two, the combination of internal elements (indi-vidual capability and self-perceived status) and of external elements (group task and group expectations) combine to affect their mutual assignment of the meaning of leadership.

Summary

In this chapter we've tried to demonstrate just what happens when we speak of conformity, roles, or leadership as having *meaning*. The private internal and public external elements perceptually blend to allow us to attach these meanings; each of the elements that we discussed can be viewed as a group communication factor that comes to have meaning because of our perceptual process of linking internal and external elements. Of course there are other group communication factors, such as cohesiveness and conflict, that may apply to a particular group context.

We think this method of analyzing communication is useful and appropriate, for it calls attention to the ever-changing nature of a communication factor. Hopefully you will apply some of our Trans-Per methods to attempt to understand more clearly the complexity of your own ongoing group communication transactions.

Additional Readings

Aronson, E. *The Social Animal*. San Francisco: W. H. Freeman, 1972.

Included is one of the clearest chapters on conformity that we've seen, Aronson's handling of the earlier research in the area is excellent. His discussion of the variables affecting conformity provides useful information for our Trans-Per analysis.

Rosenfeld, L. *Human Interaction in the Small Group Setting*. Columbus: Merrill, 1973.

Rosenfeld's thorough analysis of leadership behavior provides helpful insights in this area. He traces the different approaches to leadership and furnishes some very useful exercises. In fact some of his exercises demonstrate beautifully the perceptual blending of internal and external elements that form group communication factors. His discussion of role behavior is also very useful.

Shaw, M. *Group Dynamics: The Psychology of Small Group Behavior*. New York: McGraw-Hill, 1971.

Perhaps the greatest strength of Shaw's work is his ability to place ideas and concepts in perspective and to provide a general framework. His work with role and role effects demonstrates this strength. By considering variables relevant to the development of a role and to the performance of role behaviors, Shaw provides us with material that can be adapted to Trans-Per.

Applications

Exercise 1

Make a list of all the groups to which you belong. (If you do this thoroughly, your list is likely to be quite long.) Beside each group, make a column in which you try to state the primary purpose for its existence. Think about how well that purpose is being fulfilled. Does the success of the group in fulfilling its purpose have anything to do with your satisfaction as a member? Compare your list with those of other class members. Did you state the same purposes for similar groups?

Exercise 2

Now go back to the list of groups you made and add another column; try to state for each group the primary need or needs that it fulfills for you.

Exercise 3

How does commercial advertising appeal to our needs to belong and conform to various groups? Go through several magazines representing different large groups of people *(Seventeen, Playboy, Fortune, Esquire, Ladies' Home Journal)* and clip ads which you think appeal to these needs, identifying the following:

a. At what group is the appeal aimed?
b. What is the purpose of the group?
c. What needs does the group fulfill?.
d. What sanctions for conformity are applied by the group?

Exercise 4

Divide the class into groups of four members. Each group should decide on some kind of project to present to the class in three to six weeks. Each group should work together both in and outside of class during this time.
    Suggestions for projects:

a. Read and report on some major theorists' ideas about group communication. See Additional Readings at the end of each chapter.
b. Work together on the advertising project suggested in Exercise 3.
c. Make up an exercise, in which the class will participate, to demonstrate the nature of conformity in groups; then lead the exercise.

    During the course of your project, notice what kinds of norms and sanctions for conforming and nonconforming behavior develop within your group. Report your findings to the class.

Exercise 5

Pick a group of which you are a regular member (another class, your family, your team); identify your primary role as perceived by yourself and as perceived by others. Next time you meet with this group, purposely violate your role expectations for the duration of the meeting. See what happens; report findings to the class.

Exercise 6

Alternate with a friend at playing these roles:

a. employer and job applicant discussing salary

b.   parent and teenager discussing sexual freedom
c.   boyfriend and girlfriend discussing jealousy
d.   one friend selling a stereo set to another friend
e.   a dissatisfied customer taking back his purchase to a store clerk
f.   a conscientious citizen trying to persuade an apathetic citizen to vote

As you play these roles, try to note at what point you break out of them—when you start laughing or when you say something a person in the role wouldn't say. Compare your "breaking points" with your friend's. Then decide the "limits" of each role.

CHAPTER • 10

Communication in the Organizational Context

In Chapter 6, we briefly outlined communicating behavior as it occurs in the organizational context. You may remember we said that in many respects organizational communication shares elements in common with interpersonal and group contexts. In fact we should point out that only in the organizational context can we observe the ongoing simultaneous processes of intrapersonal, interpersonal, and group communication.

As we said earlier, intrapersonal communication is the foundation of *all* our communicating behavior. We built upon what we concluded about the intrapersonal context to explain the next level of complexity—interpersonal communication. In interpersonal contexts, we noted an informality, a spontaneity, and an intimacy not experienced in any of the other contexts. In Chapter 9, we saw that communication in group contexts, although more structured, contains many of the characteristics of the more fundamental intrapersonal and interpersonal contexts. In the present chapter, we will use all our previous analyses to help us explain the most complex type of communication—that which occurs in a typical organization.

We'll begin by detailing those specific assumptions we will make when we call a particular context an "organization" instead of a group. Specifically we will describe conflict, decision making, and power as three representative communication factors or meanings that are useful in our analysis. Although they are not the only communication factors or meanings which are significant in an organizational context, they seem to us to be among the most pertinent.

Describing the Organization

It's unnecessary to go into too much detail about the impact or the importance of organizations on our lives. Most of us spend most of our waking hours involved with or working for a wide range of organizations. You've probably had some experience with quasi-organizations: the student government, a sorority, the school newspaper—or perhaps a full-scale organization, such as a labor union. It's been said that some fortunate preschool children and housewives are the only ones to escape organizational pressures. But with the current popularity of nursery schools, we seem to have successfully "organized" our toddlers. And with Women's Liberation, some housewives no longer wish to escape organizational pressures.

It's a fact that organizations influence our lives: we're all, in one way or another, "company people." Executives, sales clerks, students, and even professors are responsible to organizational structures of one type or another. What's an organization? How can we define organizational communication? You can think of an organization as *a system with a definite structure in which people perform roles that are interdependent and coordinated.*

An organizational system is sensitive to influences outside its formal structure and interacts with its surrounding environment, whether it be political, social, economic, or cultural in nature. If there's any one group that has been significant in showing the sensitivity of the organization to its environment, it would be Ralph Nader's "raiders." Beginning with the Corvair issue of the 1960s and moving on to more current issues, such as food additives, this group has constantly demanded some response from formal organizations. Other consumer movements, which have ranged from meat boycotts to truth-in-lending laws, have demonstrated the impact of economic and legal pressures on formal organizations. Thus an organization depends not only on the purchases but also on the attitude of its customers.

Any organization, regardless of its size, contains a number of other units—subsystems. If you've been to a hospital lately for medical help, you've experienced this fact of organization life. Your first appointment is with the admissions office; after that, you go to another section of the hospital and to other personnel for medical care; last, before you leave the hospital you pay a cashier, a totally separate department. Although the admissions office and the doctors may never work together, both subsystems are necessary to the organization's functioning. Thus we have first characterized an organization as a *system* with a number of interrelated subsystems, and we have implied that the organization is responsive to the external environment or systems that surround it.

Next we will describe an organization as a *structure* represented by a chain of command. Any organization requires an ordering of its authority structure with well-established lines of duty and responsibility known to all. Titles typical of hierachical structure are "staff," "management," "administration," and "training." When formal channels of communication are established, the assembly line worker knows that he's to communicate any work information or problems to his foreman, the foreman speaks to his supervisor, and so on, up the line of command. Obviously this type of linear structure makes clear the necessity of sending and spreading information efficiently throughout the organization. The same linear structure exists for those working in universities: students tell their problems to their instructor, the instructor speaks to the chairman, and the chairman of the department speaks to an official in the administration. The hierarchical structure formally specifies the organization's chain of command and identifies the available channels of communication.

Performance of *roles* is a third characteristic of an organization. In our discussion in Chapter 9, on the development of roles, we said that a group role implies expectations that we have of our own behavior as well as expectations of other group members of our role. For organizational roles, there's a great deal more formality in describing role behaviors that individuals are required to perform. For example roles that workers are assigned are usually defined in terms of printed job descriptions. Not only are we told what our role in the organization will be, but also everyone else knows what we're supposed to do. For example a college professor who steps outside of his role and who participates in a protest with a group of his students violates a role expectation. The young staff accountant with a large CPA firm who decides on his own to take over the account of one of the senior partner's clients is not following the job description. Why would the professor and the young accountant be in some trouble? They were given clear directions concerning their specific roles, and they seemed to violate these directions. The point is that the organization spells out what is expected of its members much more clearly than more informal and less organized groups.

Fourth, we want to discuss what's perhaps the most distinguishing characteristic of the organization—the notion that organizational roles are *interdependent and coordinated.* Role behaviors are interdependent when the duties that some people are to perform are closely connected to those that others are to perform. When members of an organization begin to act independently, their behavior challenges or opposes expected norms. The idea of interdependence means that the behavior of one person influences the behavior of the others. Actually it suggests that people in the organization need each other to get the job done.

Along with the notion of interdependence is the requirement of coordination. Regardless of how well the roles are specified or of how interdependent people acknowledge themselves to be, without careful coordination of performance a lot of "wheel spinning" will take place. This pulling together and planning of schedules is usually carried out in an organization by those whose roles are specifically defined as coordinators—otherwise called managers, supervisors, foremen, or deans. Of course it might be assumed that, with specific and clear role descriptions, coordination is unnecessary: if people do what they're supposed to do, coordination will follow. This assumption is a fairly unrealistic assessment of human nature. It remains necessary to integrate as precisely as possible all units of an organization. The grocery store manager knows that his produce people will take care of their lettuce, the butchers their roasts, the purchasing people their orders, and so forth. His primary role is to coordinate each department so that all parts of the system work together as productively as possible.

Many researchers have analyzed organizational behavior in terms of participants, goals, roles, and environment. To think of an organization as we have certainly takes these four factors into account. One really gets the feel of a systemic approach to communication behavior by studying the organization. In fact our Trans-Per system is much like the organizational system we've been describing. For just as our model relies on the mixing of internal and external elements, we can imagine that the decisions of an organization are dependent on the mixing of elements both inside and outside its system. Up to this point we have been dealing with the organization only; we haven't said much about the communication within it. What characterizes organizational communication?

Communication in the Organization

We're troubled by the many theorists who define organizational communication as the transmission of information. Communication is much more than movement of information—memos, phone calls, policy statements—through certain channels. We feel that this view of the process as a one-way act is often responsible for the communication breakdowns that occur.

When individuals communicate in an organization, they're still attaching significance or giving meaning through their individual perceptual processes. For perception is no different in this context; it is still the selection, organization, and evaluation of stimuli. Communication as transaction describes much more accurately what is taking place in the organization context than communication as one-way action.

What distinguishes the organizational from the other contexts that we previously discussed is its complexity. The interrelationships among subsystems, predictable performance of tasks, and the chain of command of authority and responsibility provide a more formal and complex structure than the one we observed in the group context.

It's the organization's demand for homogeneity—or sameness—that affects the way that we occasionally assign unfavorable meanings to it. The organization requires that we use certain channels, that we perform very stable roles, and that we coordinate our work with others. Although the individual operates under certain restraints within organizations, organizations should not be looked at as negative—institutions to be avoided at all costs. It is a common tendency to underestimate the positive contributions of organizations in many areas of our lives—products organizations achieve that we would be very reluctant to do without. Try to think of some of these positive products of organizational activity as you move through the chapter.

Now that we have a general understanding of the organization, let's discuss conflict, decision making, and power as three significant communication factors or meanings in organizational contexts: you may want to think of the three as outcomes of Trans-Per. They represent the outcome of the perceptual blending of internal and external elements by people involved in organizations.

Just as some of the other communication factors that we've discussed are interrelated, conflict, decision making, and power are closely tied to or dependent upon one another. In fact it's difficult for us to think of examples of decision making in which considerations of power and conflict do not enter into the transaction. The point is that we wanted to forewarn you about the extent of their interrelationship.

What we want to do in this section is much like what we've already done in previous discussions of communication factors. First, we'll look at general characteristics; next we'll talk about relevant internal and external elements; and finally, we'll use Trans-Per to analyze the perceptual activity leading to the development of the meaning or the communication factor.

We feel that what makes our approach to communication in the organizational context useful is its ability to account for the individual's continuous moving in and out of subgroups or subsystems within the overall system. When we spoke of the group context in Chapter 9, we had no subgroups or subsystems to concern us; in comparison to the organization context, there was much less rigid definition of roles. By contrast, in the formal organization, we are constantly moving in and out of various subsystems within the broad organizational framework. We work with one group; we

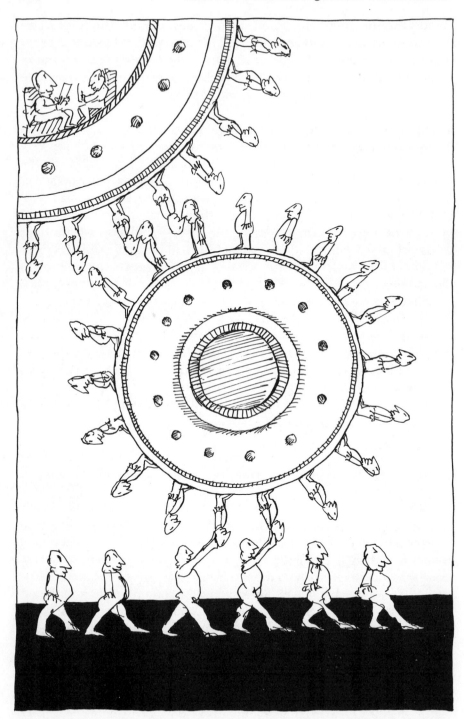

compete against another; we may bowl with yet another. The point is that each subsystem or subgroup is different from the other subgroups in terms of conformity, norms, and roles. But it is similar to the other subgroups in that they all exist in and share the rules of the same general overall system.

Conflict—An Organizational Communication Factor

It's probably true that for most people the term *conflict* has bad, destructive connotations. Some people have had enough disagreements in their lifetime to leave them with a permanent distaste for such situations. Many of us do have negative feelings toward the term conflict and can see little positive about it.

Some researchers feel that conflict is helpful in a group context since it allows members to define problems of the group. Conflict helps a small group (1) by allowing individuals to express underlying hostilities, (2) by providing members with a certain amount of trust—after allowing them to take communicating risks, (3) by allowing for the airing of multiple approaches to problems, and (4) by bringing into the open power relationships existing within the group.

These positive aspects of conflict can be extended to the organizational context. First, conflict behavior can be helpful when members of an organization are allowed to air their grievances. Forced to remain below the surface, these hostilities or negative attitudes can gnaw at individuals (or at subgroups) until open hostility breaks out. Perhaps the most well-known illustration of the productive aspect of conflict has been the rise of the union system. Recognition of unions by management has provided a setting in which superiors and subordinates can operate on equal footing. Of course the most dramatic example of open expression of conflict is the strike. Fortunately many of the disagreements between union and management are resolved without such a measure. Rather than being expressed in a potentially harmful strike, conflicts between two such groups are most productive when each has the opportunity to hear the other's position.

Similarly conflict is productive and functional when people can feel free to disagree openly without fear of punishment. Such an atmosphere leads to increasing trust among interested parties. For example an instructor, by creating an atmosphere in a classroom in which students can openly disagree with each other and enter into conflict, will encourage development of trust within the group that should make learning enjoyable.

On the other hand the instructor who asks for honest feedback from students—only to react defensively when it's offered—faces a great silence the next time he asks for opinions.

A third benefit of conflict is that it allows for the airing and reviewing of different solutions to a problem. The supervisor, for example, who allows each worker to express his opinion—even though it may be at odds with his own opinion—is insuring a wider range of solutions to his problems. Allowing conflict among workers is to a supervisor's advantage if he wants to emphasize that many good approaches to the same problem exist and that his job is to choose among them. Therefore it's important to recognize that conflict among people within an organization can help the organization gain its objectives.

To be sure, conflict does have its dysfunctional or harmful aspects. Destructive, dysfunctional conflict can be identified when organizational goals or objectives are not achieved. Disagreement for the sake of disagreement is a problem for many organizations. If we think of a classroom as an organization (system, subsystems, roles, hierarchical structure), examples of harmful conflict easily come to mind. Those cases in which certain students and the instructor disagree on virtually every issue exemplify unproductive conflict. Here we see individual goals taking precedence over the organization's objectives: both student and instructor need to "win" at the expense of other class members, who must wait out the conflict.

Conflict can also be dysfunctional when the authority to resolve or manage the disagreement does not exist within the group itself. For example the disagreements that people in a secretarial pool typically engage in are hardly productive when the only method of resolving the problem is to call in the department head. Perhaps a more immediate example might help us here. Let's imagine that members of a class have broken into small groups to work on independent projects. Each small group can then be seen to be a subsystem of the organization, in this case the class. Further assume that within one of the groups two members are at each other's throat on virtually every issue. In this instance the other group members soon tire of the bickering and psychologically remove themselves from it—on the assumption that resolution of the conflict is the instructor's problem. Obviously if the group is to be graded for work completed, the conflict must be resolved quickly so that some productive work can be accomplished. But as long as the group has some outside authority, in this case the instructor, to resolve the conflict, members will generally stand back and leave the resolution of the disagreement up to him. In this case conflict is harmful to the group's immediate goals and, in the long run, damages the entire organization.

So we can see that conflict has both its good and bad sides. And that's our point. Conflict, in and of itself, isn't necessarily a harmful behavior. Whether it is productive or unproductive depends on the nature of the conflict and on the group's goals.

Burns (1973) argues that organizations are "fundamentally designed to generate conflict." He points out the necessity of conflict if an organization is going to have the capacity to change and to respond. If one accepts the notion that organizations are open to external influences and are subject to constant pressures to change, his argument makes good sense. However he also agrees that conflict isn't necessarily beneficial and that much conflict is dysfunctional when it draws on the organization's efforts and resources without significant production. Returning for a moment to our example of the disagreement among class members, we can see his reasoning to be obvious. When the conflicting members take class time, the instructor's resources, and time of other group members, some benefits or achievement must result—such as a troublesome point cleared up, a decision made, or a plan of action set up. If not, conflict, no matter how interesting, is harmful to the organization. The assumption that organizations constantly change leads to the conclusion that they must generate conflict. Just as organizations are designed to generate conflict, they must provide strategies or methods of conflict resolution.

Now let's examine some internal and external elements of our Trans-Per system. What are the pertinent private cues that affect an individual's behavior within the organization? What are the public cues existing in the organizational environment that affect the individual's behavior? How do individuals blend these cues perceptually to create conflict behavior?

Conflict: Internal System

In the previous chapter we described Maslow's "hierarchy of needs" as a set of internal elements that influence and affect an individual's conformity behavior. Here we're going to be concerned with the relationship between an individual's needs and his conflict behavior. Many of the conflicts in an organization can be traced to needs that arise from each individual's personality. Each person brings to the organization a potential intrapersonal conflict, based on his need for autonomy (independence) on the one hand and his need for dependence (support) on the other. Thus the first internal element that we want to consider is the *inner need* each person brings to an organization.

A person's *need for independence* has important implications for his choice of an organization as well as for the types of behaviors that he performs on a routine basis. Think for a minute of the type of autonomy or independence that you bring with you to the many organizations to which you belong. Compare the nature of the independence that you feel yourself to have in this class to the independence you feel yourself to have at work. If an individual has a high need for independence, he might have little regard for such concepts as loyalty, dedication or similar values.

A person's *need for support* or dependence, on the other hand, has even greater psychological implications: although an individual feels protected when he is in a dependent position, he is, however, bound to some authority. Yet this need—to be supported—is important, and a person's choice of organization may hinge on it. Our point is that a person often finds himself to have both these needs: while he values independence very highly, he at the same time desires the kind of safety that being a subordinate can provide.

A second internal element is the familiar one of *attitude*, discussed previously and at great length in other communication contexts. Perhaps a convenient way to think of a person's attitude toward his organizational activity is in terms of his cooperative or competitive orientation. Stated another way, we can think of a person bringing with him in his store of private cues an attitude about the organization that makes him want to either work with members or work against them.

When a person is cooperatively oriented, he tends to think of himself as capable of compromise: he thinks of sharing rather than either winning or losing. On the other hand, a person with a competitive orientation looks at himself as either winner or loser; there can be no middle ground for him. We spoke of the individual's cooperative or competitive orientation earlier when we discussed game theory and zero-sum or non-zero-sum games in Chapter 8.

A third internal element is the individual's personal assessment of his *level of information* about the organization's task. In general a person's assessment of his level of information relates most directly to his past experiences; that is, an important criterion for his decision making in the organization is the individual's evaluations of his past experiences with similar situations. It seems reasonable to say that the more the individual's past experience with the particular decision or situation, the less internal conflict that will arise from it.

For what we will utilize as our final internal element, Leavitt (1973) introduced a concept we find useful in terms of explaining potential organizational conflict, the internal element of *conscience*. Leavitt describes the term as "internal control by the person of his own behavior." (We should keep in mind that conscience, as well as all the other elements we have described, must be considered as subjective perceptions—not as objective reality.) In describing an internal element of conscience, we mean a person's feeling he is responsible for and can control his behavior. How important is this internal element for the person existing in the organization? Leavitt speaks of conscience as a source of internal conflict; we agree with his concept and further extend it to apply to organizational conflicts. We have "conscience" to remind us of what is right or wrong —according to some religious or moral standards that we've absorbed along the way. But just as we said that each person's perceptions are subjective and unique, so conscience is personal and unique to each individual. All too often we come to think of a "national science" or a "company conscience." We're told to let our conscience be our guide—as though there were some universal precepts agreed to by all. We know that conscience, rather than being an absolute standard, is directly related to the External System that we experience: we may never consider stealing money from a corporation, but we might add a few dollars to an insurance claim, reasoning that the company will never miss it. The point here is that each person has a conscience that is uniquely his, and he brings it with him to the organizational context.

We have covered only a few of the internal elements bearing upon the development of conflict behavior—the needs a person brings to the system, the cooperative or competitive orientation he follows, the level of information he has, and the subjective nature of his conscience. But alone these internal elements are literally meaningless, for they must be matched with those cues or elements in the External System before meaning can be assigned. Now let's consider some external elements contributing to conflict.

Conflict: External System

The three specific external elements we'll discuss in this section are *task, incentive system,* and *organizational structure.*

The particular *task* of the organization or of any of its subsystems is usually clearly defined. Policy statements or memoranda provide the usual channels for the announcements of task; in addition there are staff meetings, telephone calls, and instructions. Our point here is that the task—the job to be performed—is usually defined with as little ambiguity as possible. Since task is usually the focus of conflict, it's an external element that requires rigorous analysis.

There are basically two types of task requirements. First of all there's the overall requirement that's spelled out by the general organization—to make a product, perform a service, make a profit, and so forth. Second, within this broad requirement are several other secondary requirements, noted earlier in the chapter, of coordination, role specialization, supervision, and so forth. Secondary task specifications include time limits, working conditions, and hierarchy of responsibility.

In the classroom, for example, the instructor requires that papers be prepared by a certain time, following a certain prescribed form and style. Failure to do these tasks usually leads to some punishment—a low or failing grade. Or, in a particular organization, the sales personnel are told by their manager that they must work to increase the division's share of the market by the next fiscal quarter. They are also told that bonuses may be affected if sales are not increased.

A second pertinent external element is the *incentive system* or system of sanctions, used by the organization; the sanctions—rewards or punishments—are usually well defined. People are told what will happen if they're late, if they drink on the job, if they park in the wrong place, or if they're slow on the assembly line.

Some organizations provide clear descriptions of rewards. People who produce four transistors per hour are rewarded if they can step up production to five. People who provide their company with money-saving ideas receive bonuses. Some organizations reward their employees for attendance and productivity with pins for twenty-five years of service or gold watches or some other token of appreciation. But the point is that the sanction system or the incentives are made explicit: the group getting the job done early earns extra rewards; the group finishing the exercise first leaves class early.

A third external element, as important as task requirement and incentive system, is the *organizational structure*. Earlier we discussed the idea that communication moves along formal and informal channels in a hierarchical structure. The formal channels are prescribed, official information lines; the informal channels in the organizational network may be used just as much as the formal lines but are of a more unofficial nature. Both of these, (1) the positions of individuals in an organization and (2) the official and unofficial channels of communication—taken together —make up the hierarchical structure of the organization. It's the existence of this structure probably more than any other single element that distinguishes an organization context from a group context. Development of an organizational structure clarifies a who-talks-to-whom pattern.

The hierarchical structure has sometimes served to frustrate free, open, or spontaneous communication subgroups forming within the organization. Conversely it has provided a mechanism by which the organization can be sensitive to external demands: we mean the various management attempts to tap or monitor the external environment for changes in the surrounding social, political, economic or cultural systems we mentioned earlier. Public affairs divisions and mass media centers are examples of organization subgroups that are primarily concerned with responding to systems outside of the organization.

In addition to showing the pattern of communication, the organizational structure provides its workers with an acceptable procedure for making known their legitimate complaints: employees are informed of the proper things to do when they're unhappy or frustrated over certain tasks or injustices.

Finally, the structure fixes responsibility or accountability. Although there still may be some "passing the buck" in the organization, it is generally possible to determine accountability: the organizational chart points out the responsible people.

The external elements affecting conflict, therefore, are task, the incentive system, and organizational structure. We'll now use Trans-Per to analyze conflict behavior in the formal organization.

Conflict: Trans-Per

Communication comes about when we attach meaning to certain stimuli. *And* we come to attach that meaning through perception. *And* perception is the selection, organization, and evaluation of stimuli. *And* anytime we engage in perception, we communicate, for we're attaching meaning. *And* conflict is a meaning or communication factor created through perception. "And" is pretty useful for conveying the notion of transactional/perceptual communication because it indicates a kind of ongoing process.

We will focus on just one internal and one external element so that we can make our explanation as uncomplicated as possible. Hopefully you will have no trouble applying this example to other examples of conflict involving other internal and external elements. The internal element we will use is the information level that an individual considers himself to have brought into the organization. We will use the organizational structure as the single external element, in this particular example, that affects conflict. Now we want to freeze the communication process again and observe how these two elements blend during a transaction and how the meaning of conflict is assigned by the participants.

Earlier we said we thought the common definition of organizational communication is somewhat simplistic and also limiting. To consider the movement of information through specified lines of authority virtually eliminates any notion of process or transaction. Another reason that we disagree with the traditional framework is that people who think of communication as action or interaction instead of transaction often have the mistaken notion that information is something out there—an easily measured thing. On the contrary we think of information as subjectively perceived by individuals—not as objective data. If our concept is true, then the interpretation of information varies from person to person in an organization. The organization structure often disregards this notion of subjectivity by emphasizing the "sameness" of behavior.

An aim of any organization is to work toward the homogeneity of its members—to make them similar to each other. That's not all bad. After all, organizational behavior can't be unpredictable or random—there must be a predictability about the production levels, number of workers hired, and so forth. When an individual's evaluation of his position in the organizational structure coincides with his evaluation of his information level, conditions are acceptable to him. It becomes much more problematic when two individuals in the same unit of the organization, both described as having comparable levels of information according to the organizational structure, perceive themselves to be at very different levels of expertise or knowledge. Conflict may easily develop between them.

In our example, the organization (the college) has determined that individuals who are at the level of assistant professor belong in one compartment of the structure and that those who are full professors belong in another. Essentially these distinctions are based on a professor's past experience, publications, expertise in research, and teaching skills—all related to what we have called his level of information. Let's say that an individual enters this system who perceives his level of information to be quite high; he is, at the same time, dissatisfied with his entering rank in the organizational structure. He will make known his dissatisfaction in his communications with other faculty members. But the situation becomes even more problematic when this faculty member is grouped at the same level with others who he *knows* have less knowledge, information, and expertise than he does. In this staging of the scene, the possibilities for conflict are fairly self-evident. In a nutshell the disgruntled member sees that when his internal evaluation of his level of information is matched up against the external structure of the organization, he assigns meaning to the transaction that inevitably leads to disagreements. As a recourse, the unhappy member may take a competitive orientation, may withdraw from the situation, or may resort to any number of other alternatives open to him —even another job.

Actually we can see several different levels of conflict in operation in such an example. Intrapersonal conflict is present: "I know more than many men in the department regardless of their higher rank." Interpersonal conflict persists between individuals. Intragroup conflict may develop between members of the same subgroup in the organization. Intergroup conflict between subgroups of the organization may arise. The point is that conflict grows out of the different and subjective perceptions of members. On the one hand the organization expects an individual to carry on contentedly at a certain rank based on its assessment of each individual's information level. On the other hand the individual may not consider his information level to be as low as the organization considers it; he cannot happily exist at the prescribed level.

Of course many other elements come into play—both internal and external. We have chosen organizational structure and information level, one element from each system, to illustrate the dynamics of the transaction. In other situations other internal and external elements will have greater effect on the outcome or assignment of meaning. One proposition seems fairly constant: individuals engage in conflict behavior as a result of their perceptions of incompatible internal and external elements.

Keep in mind that the communication process is an ongoing transaction continuously forcing us to assign meaning to stimuli; conflict is one such meaning created in the organizational context.

Decision Making—An Organizational Communication Factor

The pivotal behavior in any organization is its ability or capacity to make decisions with the most efficiency and least cost. We might define *efficiency* in terms of taking less time or using fewer resources; we might define *cost* in economic or psychological terms. Regardless of the way we define efficiency and cost, they exist as prime criteria for the organization's decision-making functions. And we think of such functions as "pivotal" because they provide the best measurement of an organization's ability to change.

Thus far in our consideration of essential characteristics of an organization, we've generally ignored its policy-making aspect, which controls so much of its day-to-day activity. We think of organizational policies as suggestions for behavior that involve the organization's structure. In other

words a policy is a statement relating to organizational structure and to proposed behavior of the structure.

For example the policy that police organizations may have about use of marijuana offers very specific statements about penalties for its use. An instructor's policy on attendance, which requires everyone to be at every class meeting, is a generalization about his attitudes toward absences. Regardless of the size or purpose of an organization, its type of policy making can be taken as symptomatic of its tendency to change: very general policies indicate a vague notion of change; very specific policies suggest definite directions for change.

Many of our thoughts about policies bear directly on decision making, for it's through a specific decision that we can see support for or rejection of policy statements. As we proceed, keep in mind that the general policy making of an organization affects its specific decision making. One can't describe decision making without also dealing with policy making within the organizational structure.

With these ideas in mind, let's take a brief overview of decision making in the formal organization. What we're trying to determine is how the individual's assignment of meaning affects an organization's decision-making policy.

Although it's convenient to think of decision making as a crucial behavior of an organization, it may be more difficult to look at it in terms of meaning creation. Although we can't imagine a decision without communication, we tend to disregard or overlook the perceptions of individuals—who lie behind the organization's decision.

Assume that Betty and Gloria, elected officers in an organization, are in general agreement about the philosophy of their organizational structure and its behavior. Further assume that they are confronted with an external attack on that organization—it's criticized by people who feel that the organization is not responsive to other social systems. They're told by critics that the organization simply can't continue to pay so little attention to people who put them in office. Betty and Gloria have a choice to make: do they yield to pressure and become more open in their organizational behavior, or do they continue to run a "closed shop"? They decide on the basis of resources available and time pressures that they continue as before. Their latest decision supports the policy that they had started earlier. Of course they may run into trouble if another social system—perhaps a legal one—continues to apply pressure. But through their interpersonal communicating behavior within the organization, they've decided to attach the most significant meaning to keeping things as they are.

Basically we can think of organizational decision making as the organization's commitment to the ideas developed in its general long-range policy. In a very real sense the organization is continually faced with daily problems related to the carrying out of general policies.

In some instances we can conceive of decision making as response to an immediate problem. In other instances decisions are made when there's a discrepancy between what's expected from sales or production and what is actually received. This type of problem is often first on the agenda for the board of directors—particularly when profits don't come up to expected levels. And decisions must be made when people don't perform as expected.

We can point out a direct connection between decision making and the general policy formulation that has preceded it: if an organization states certain generalized policies and if these are made ineffective by people, then some decision must be made concerning either policies or people. For a moment think of a basketball team as an organization: think of its highly paid forward failing to grab rebounds or score baskets. You then get some idea of the problem created for an organizational structure if one subsystem fails to live up to expectations. At this point the interdependence of all subsystems of the organizational system must be taken into account, for people failing to perform up to expectations can't be considered as affecting only themselves. There must be some concern for the effects of their behavior on jobs performed by others. Thus one type of decision making deals with differences between expected levels of performance and actual levels of performance.

Other situations that call for decision-making behavior from members of the formal organization are those dealing with some potential harm coming to the organization. In these instances we can think of the particular problem faced by the decision-makers as unplanned—one that wasn't foreseen by the policy-makers. Yet the problem must be faced, or the policy may be violated. For example California grocery stores were prepared for a strike of meat cutters. The grocers thought they were willing to wait out the strike. Of course decision-making mechanisms had temporarily broken down—with both sides, cutters and grocers, at a stalemate. Yet something new affected the problem that the grocers hadn't anticipated. The new factor in the problem involved the sympathy strikes carried out by truckers, shipping personnel, and so forth. At this point the grocers saw that more harm would be done to them by the strike than they had anticipated or could tolerate. Whereas at first they were only concerned with the loss of cutters, now they had to face the prospect of empty shelves—since nothing at all was being trucked in. Obviously some intense renegotiations took place, and decisions were made to accommodate the cutters.

As so many writers have noted, it's impossible for the organization to constantly monitor all its problems. Organizational decision-makers cannot be watchdogs, and some problems quite obviously are so short-lived that they take care of themselves. Our point through all of this is that decision making is essentially an assignment of meaning. The nature of the decision-making activity of an organization depends on perceptions of individuals in the structure who perceive (select, organize, and evaluate) the particular problem and assign meaning. In other words they participate in the problem—they become involved in the transaction. Before we move on to the internal and external elements that affect the assignment of meaning in the decision-making process, a brief summary may be helpful.

First of all, we should think of decision making as a good indicator of organizational methods of adapting and changing. An organization's policies are essentially blueprints for future change; day-to-day decisions provide for the implementation of these policies.

Second, we should think of decision making as perceptual in nature. Thus we can think of a decision as representing an assignment of significance—a creation of meaning.

Third, decision making is a behavior in which individuals participate; we wish to stress the transactional nature of decision making.

Fourth, situations generally leading to decision making are usually based on problems such as the differences between expected and actual sales performance.

All the problems of an organization can't be settled formally by decision-makers. Many problems either take care of themselves in time or prove to be irrelevant.

We will now discuss the internal and external elements that affect decision making. In Trans-Per we feel it is useful and appropriate to view decision making as an assignment of significance—as creation of meaning. We feel there's hardly any other way to think of it: individuals bring to the decision making certain internal cues, and these blend with elements in the external environment.

Decision Making: Internal System

The first internal element that we want to consider in our discussion of the decision-making elements is that of *individual goal*.

When a woman enters an organization for the first time, her goals and those of the organization—while similar—differ significantly. When she starts her job, she has, as an employee, a conception of what she wants from the organization; and in turn the company, factory, or university has a specific set of objectives in mind for her. As her experience with the organization continues, these differences lessen. Eventually the time comes when there's a great compatibility between her goals and those of the organization. Or she will leave the organization.

Let us consider a person's individual goals in relation to the decisions that he makes on the job—decisions that concern specific organizational problems. For example, when people are called together to solve a high turnover problem in the organization, the individual goal of the person is not a significant element. However if he were meeting with a personnel committee to discuss promotion criteria, his individual goal would probably influence his decision making. But this example is a bit more complex than it appears on the surface. For one thing individual goals differ from one problem to another, while organizational goals generally do not. For the individual, promotion criteria may seem an exception to general policy; for the organization it must be handled in relation to past general policy and future precedents. Thus one thing a person brings to each problem situation is a system of individual goals which he employs in decision making.

A second internal element—and one of a more general nature —concerns the *personality* traits of the decision-maker. A person's level of dogmatism, for example, will dramatically affect the way in which he goes about solving problems and making decisions. In addition to this element, Katz and Kahn (1966) identify four personality dimensions that they argue affect decision making. Of these, the *ideological versus power orientation* is best typified by the idealist and the realist. The fanatic idealist has so thoroughly accepted the ideology of the organization that he can't separate his own ideas from the company's. Moreover he sees no compromise in company policy. On the other hand the realist is more amenable to bargaining within the organization; that is, he sees expediency as a primary means of carrying out his work in the organization. A person with an ideological orientation to decision making within the organization is an idealist; the power-oriented person is pragmatic.

The second personality dimension is *emotionality versus objectivity*. Individuals who bring an emotional personality into the organization's decision making will be impetuous and impulsive. The personality characteristic of objectivity suggests that the person strives for as much information as possible; he is less impulsive.

The third personality dimension is that of *creativity versus common sense*. There are those people in the organization who are known for their innovative contributions to various policy decisions; others are more traditional and less creative in their approach. Of course the ideal person is one bringing both of these dimensions to the organization. But that is an unlikely combination.

Finally there is the action *orientation versus contemplation* personality dimension. Those people who are action-oriented are decisive in a particular situation; those who are given to contemplation of their actions are quite indecisive in their decision making.

It is highly unlikely that any person in an organization is exclusively one or the other of these dimensions. Rather the personality characteristics that people bring with them to the organization probably include infinite combinations of these qualities.

These personality features typically represent value orientations of the individual who exhibits them. Obviously organizational decision-makers bring a varied set of *values* into a problem situation. Moreover these values are not necessarily changed by the existing organizational environment; they imply what type of communicating strategies will be employed by the individual who holds them during decision-making sessions. We're reminded of a television show documenting individual and organizational behavior of one of the world's largest oil corporations. During the program one of the executives called attention to the fact that the corporation couldn't handle many differences or deviations from its norms. For example people who were interviewed for management positions were expected to dress in a certain way, to have hair of a certain length, and to have wives who were interested in the community. His point seemed to be that, when problems had to be solved within the corporation, a small range of personality differences was helpful. In this way, he argued, one could be assured of good decisions that would reinforce the organization's longstanding drive for excellence. He also pointed out that the personality characteristics and values that the company wanted in prospective managers were meant to insure high moral and ethical levels among employees.

In addition to their individual goals and values, organizational personnel bring unique sets of *motivations* into a problem-solving circumstance. Obviously these motivations affect the individual's generation of meaning for a particular group decision.

Although the motivations of some individuals may be humanitarian, it's fair to say the motivations of most individuals are selfish in orientation.

An individual who is taking part in a decision-making situation must be concerned with all pragmatic implications of his behavior. He realizes that his contribution to the situation or discussion will be interpreted as "his best shot"—or representing his best personal interests. These motivations are very closely tied to the needs that we have discussed previously. For example, if a person has a high need for security or esteem, he'll be motivated to make certain decisions that will satisfy those needs. On the other hand there are some organizations in which personal motivation is considered to be a liability, and personnel are provided with a type of "created" motivation. They are told that they will be taken care of—that all they have to worry about is doing their job. Students are often told to do the reading, to study for the exam—and "you'll be all right." We're simply saying that, when individuals are brought into a problem-solving situation, the meaning that they assign to the stimuli may be dependent on their individual motivations.

One other internal element that an individual may bring to the decision-making situation concerns his level of *involvement*—how deeply he cares about the problem. "What does the problem have to do with me or with my unit in the organization? Why should I be concerned? How will it affect me personally?" These may be typical questions that reveal how an individual balances the problem and his own needs and goals simultaneously. An individual's level of involvement may be very high; then again it may not. For example participation on a departmental committee charged with revising the undergraduate curriculum may hold very little interest for a professor whose main interest is graduate instruction and research.

Decision Making: External System

The external elements that we will discuss are the problem, the organizational resources, the time elements, and the leadership norms.

The most obvious external element affecting decision making is the specific *problem* addressed by the individuals. The problem, which is usually clearly set out by the management, may be a departmental reorganization, a new advertising campaign, a decision on hiring a new faculty member, or whatever. Generally the problem is outlined, its history presented, and the significant issues are defined. Let's, for example, talk about several students who've been assigned to a committee that allocates office space for all extracurricular activities. They're told by an official that the students with popular activities are getting better offices, that past procedures have led to favoritism, and that the group's task is to come up with a new set of procedures that will insure fair allocations in the future. In addition the committee is told that it has independence; no decisions on the allocation of space will be made unless this committee makes them. As we said, the problem before the group is generally defined by the management, in this case the administration, of the organization. Of course in cases involving management itself, the problem is defined by a level of the organization higher than management. For the most part the people involved in the decision-making process are reacting to some problem brought to them.

A second external element involves the *resources* of the organization. This element, usually physical in nature, involves the material aspects of an organization—manpower, money, machines, and so forth. For our allocation committee, particular resources would be made available to the group to help it achieve its goal. It would be given a secretarial budget so that its report could be typed up and notices sent to the activity groups affected; it would be given a conference room in which to hold its deliberations; and it would probably be given a budget for mimeographing notices, procedures, supplies, and so forth.

A third external element is the *time* available for the solution of the problem. For how long a period is the group to meet? For how long a period will the decision the group reaches be in effect? If a group is told that it has only two weeks to meet, that time element influences its deliberations. In addition, if a group is told that its decision will affect the organization for three years, that information also has a significant impact. The time element exists as a critical bit of information for the group in its decision making. Think for a moment of the importance you attach to a fifteen-minute quiz in comparison to a sixty-minute test. In our previous example, if the student allocation committee were given one year to make its decisions on procedures, the members would have a very different perception of the problem than if the committee were given six months.

Finally, the external element of *leadership* style strongly affects our decision making. How is leadership determined? Is one person assigned the role of leader, or are members free to choose one? Or are individuals put together and told that there is to be no single leader? Generally we can say that the more people who are involved in the decision making and who influence progress, the more widely distributed are the feelings of satisfaction. On the other hand, if one person is given full control and leadership, others might find it easy to blame group problems on him. Most of what we said about leadership previously applies here; however, in our discussion of group contexts in Chapter 9, we analyzed leadership as a communication factor or meaning growing out of perceptual blending. Here we're talking about leadership as an external element. You will remember we said, when describing attitude, that elements can be a cause or an effect—or a meaning.

Although these four elements are pertinent to the individual, there are many more—organizational structure, roles, and so forth—that are potential external elements. Let's now take a look at Trans-Per and decision making.

Decision Making: Trans-Per

Up to this point we've been concerned with elements of both the Internal and External Systems that affect decision making. We have discussed the internal elements of individual goals, personality traits, motivation, and involvement. External elements we mentioned were: problems, resources, time, and leadership. Now we want to analyze the perceptual blending of these stimuli.

Our hypothetical group is an interfraternity council of an urban university. The council has been directed by the vice-president for student affairs to work out a fraternity-sponsored program that will serve underprivileged children in the area surrounding the university. In our Trans-Per analysis, the working out of a program for the underprivileged children represents the group's problem (external element). The council is told that it will have a budget for this program that allows for the purchase of paper, advertising, wages, and so forth—all those items we classified as resources (external elements). The members were told that they would have the fall semester to work on the program, keeping as their objective the publication of the program by early spring. Finally the vice-president suggested that Jim, one of the group members, should serve as the chairman or leader of the group. The four members or Internal Systems participating in our transaction will represent, in a very simplified form, the decision-makers of a large organization.

Jim, the appointed leader of the group, has a very definite individual goal in these transactions. He intends to be quite forceful in his leadership and to move the group along very quickly in solving the problem before it. A realist rather than an idealist, he is quite pragmatic in most of his dealings with others, modifying his ideas to get the job accomplished expeditiously. He sees himself as objective, cool under pressure, and not inclined to the impulsiveness of more emotional personality types. Yet he prefers to move and to act decisively rather than to delay and prolong decisions. As you can probably tell, Jim is motivated by a deep need for the esteem of others and for high status; he looks at each task or problem as an opportunity to attain reputation and prestige.

Don is quite emotional in his judgments and often quite defensive in his behavior with others. He doesn't like to spend a lot of time weighing ideas; he also doesn't care to take decisive action. His personality tends toward the area of psychological safety; he doesn't care to take chances.

The third member of the council, John, has an individual outlook that is quite different from that of Jim or Don. John's chief goal is to influence the council, and others, with the idealistic principles that he thinks are consistent with a humanitarian perspective. He firmly believes in "good will to all men." Thus one personality characteristic that he brings with him is a very strong ideological commitment. His notion is that the greatest good for any individual is to serve mankind; and no decision should be made independent of that commitment. Although the most emotional person of the group, he has an abundance of innovative and creative ideas for solving any problem he attacks. Yet he is a contemplative sort, demanding that every issue be examined thoroughly and then some. He is motivated by the need to realize his full potential.

Fred is the fourth member of the group. His objective is to be very influential in the group. Like Jim, Fred tends toward the power end of the ideological-power continuum of personality dimensions. He is determined that compromises satisfactory to all members be made and that no one member should force his ideas on the others. Although Fred is emotional and quick to make judgments, he is at the same time one of the more creative members of the group. A man of action, he prefers to move decisively with what might be an only moderately successful approach rather than to continue searching at length for the right solution. Fred grew up in a lower-class section of the city—in fact not far from the university. He is highly committed to the idea of giving the children some opportunities and pleasures that he never had. Like Jim, Fred is also driven by the need for status and prestige; he desires recognition and reputation.

Thus you have some idea of the internal and external elements that will be operational in the transactions of the group. Given this information, we can speculate on the decision making of our council.

Jim and Fred share a significant amount of meaning in terms of their individual goals: both wish to achieve a great deal in a limited amount of time. Since they both have a high need for status and esteem, they probably assess the problem similarly: such a project will give them visibility and attention. Yet the group's decision will be affected by the differences in their personalities—particularly Fred's tendency to be excessively emotional and Jim's tendency to be cool and dispassionate. Jim takes a more traditional and secure approach to decisions; Fred advocates innovative, if more risky, ideas. Jim will probably be in favor of well-tested and conservative programs—such proposals as a summer sports camp or a series of campus tours for the children. Fred will probably favor unusual choices —foster parent programs in which a fraternity adopts several children for a weekend or exchange programs in which the underprivileged and more affluent children trade homes for a brief period of time.

Finally Fred and Jim probably will not regard the external element of leadership in the same manner. Fred's preferred role was to be very influencial in the group; since Jim was appointed the leader, Fred will probably see the appointment as a formality—something that can be changed informally if the group so desires. By contrast Jim sees his appointment as fairly rigid; he plans to assume an authoritarian style of leadership.

Our other two members—Don and John—will also contribute to the group's decisions but probably not as actively as Jim and Fred. Don has fairly low self-esteem; he is easily persuaded, and can be influenced by the more powerful members of the group. John, with his strong ideological orientation, has little practical sense of the economic or social needs of the children. He is much more a theoretical than a practical humanitarian. John is willing to let the others make the practical compromises.

All in all, we can expect the decisions created by this group to reflect primarily the perceptual processes of Jim and Fred—with some minor suggestions from Don. We would expect John to make a minimum contribution to the group's decisions. He moves too slowly and refuses to compromise on what he thinks of as an ideal program for the children—music, art, pottery, crafts. Theoretically fine but beyond the group's resources.

Our example, while admittedly brief, should give you some indication of decision making in terms of Trans-Per. The decision that the group creates is an outgrowth of each member's perceptual blending of particular internal and external stimuli. Decision making is a meaning, and it is reflected in behaviors of the group members. Each person brings with him a unique set of cues or elements that, when mixed with external stimuli, lead him to make particular decisions.

In the final section of this chapter we want to look at power and authority as an outcome of transactional communication in the organization.

Power—An Organizational Communication Factor

Although an instructor may have been assigned a position of power in the classroom, we only recognize him as powerful if he is *perceived* that way by the students, other faculty, the administrators, and others with whom he communicates. Stated another way, one may come to occupy a position of power through some legitimate means—election, assignment, promotion—but, in order to have influence, the holder of power must still be perceived by his employees or students or workers as having authority. We're treating power and authority in the organization as something which is meaningful to individuals—not some absolute that exists independently.

In our society individuals recognize police as wielding legitimate authority or power: we know they have the power to punish us—or to inconvenience us if the alleged offense is minor. Yet for all this acknowledgment of legitimate power, we do see individuals in direct defiance of police. Riots, defiance, abusive language, ambushes, and other behaviors of protesters suggest that obedience to legitimate authority is not second nature to some. Different individuals do have different perceptions of authority or of power figures.

Probably the most popular treatment of power is that presented by French and Raven (1959), who argue that power can be analyzed from two different views: (1) the behavior of the individual who wields power and (2) the reactions of the individual who is subject to the power. Describing power as the potential ability of one person to influence another person within some particular system, they identify five "bases" of power. *Reward* power is based on the ability of one person to provide some benefits or rewards for another. *Coercive* power, rather than providing rewards, depends on an individual's ability to punish another within a particular system. *Legitimate* power or authority is legal power given to an individual that enables him to exercise certain lawful rights over another. *Referent* power is based on a person's identification with another; influence comes about because the powerful figure is much admired. *Expert* power is based on a person's perception of another's knowledge or expertise. As we look at these bases of power, we can see very clearly that the exercise of power depends on one person's perception of another's potential to influence.

Let's now consider some of those elements in the Internal and External Systems that influence our perceptions of power.

Power: Internal System

An individual's *self-esteem* is a very critical internal element, strongly affecting the way that he comes to think of and communicate with people in positions of power. We've frequently discussed what we mean by self-esteem and how it affects the meanings we assign, beginning in Chapter 4 when we first talked about selected internal elements.

People with low self-esteem—self-perceptions that "they're not much good"—will tend to assign power to virtually any individual in the organization, regardless of his level in the organization's hierarchy. In other words those with low self-esteem—"yes persons"—can be the most persuasible in the group. Their feelings of inadequacy as members of the organization make them highly compliant in their reactions to policy and policy-makers.

In Chapter 9 we spoke of Maslow's hierarchy of needs and talked about the need that all of us have for esteem; we are all concerned—to various degrees—with reputation, prestige, and status. The ability of an individual to cope with or assign meaning to some power figure often depends on the individual's own need for prestige or esteem. If that need is high in his value system, he will react differently to his perceptions of another's power than if that need is low or nonexistent. For example an individual may find it more prestigious to be an assistant professor at a well-known university than an associate professor at a smaller, less well-known institution. We often tend to organize our perceptions of power and authority on the basis of our need for esteem, prestige, or status.

A second internal element is our *need for satisfaction* in the organization. Essentially we're referring to the general orientation a person brings to an organization, and the organization's capability to fulfill it. A person's orientation may be altruistic, humanitarian, materialistic, and so forth.

For example we may have a humanitarian orientation toward our particular organization. If we perceive the nature of power to be based on financial gain or rewards, we won't attach too much meaning to that appeal. We all know that college teachers are in their particular line of work for the satisfaction of imparting knowledge and for the opportunity to be involved with students. Appeals from their administrators to do a better job for more money will usually go unheeded.

On the one hand, a need for satisfaction may be *intrinsic*: an individual finds the work is satisfying in and of itself; there are some fortunate people who do the job for the internal pleasure it gives them; for them any other rewards or influences are irrelevant. On the other hand satisfaction may be extrinsic: the rewards of the job have to do with certain factors that exist outside the job. We may put up with the strains and demands of an organization because it allows us a chance to work with a friend or to work in a convenient location.

This notion of satisfaction influences the way in which we make power and authority—in the Trans-Per sense of the term—meaningful. It ought to be clear that if an individual brings either a humanitarian, altruistic, or materialistic orientation with him to an organization, it will affect the way that he deals with the formal power structure of the organization.

We're going to look at the External System now to identify some of those elements within it that may help us better understand the assignment of meaning of power and authority.

Power: External System

We can think of the important public cues of the External System that affect our perception of power and authority as the *organizational norms* and as the *stated means of power*.

Our discussion of norms will focus on the standards of behavior that an organization establishes for its members. In Chapter 9 we discussed norms in the group context, describing them as behaviors that people are supposed to perform—the rules of the group. In the organizational context the norms are again essentially rules, but the rules are now made even more specific. We noted earlier that many of the group norms were unwritten. In the formal organization little is left to speculation on acceptable standards of behavior.

We can think of lines of communication to be lines of authority or power. For the individual, one of the most important positions in the organization is the one directly above him. Stated another way, the individual's level on the organizational chart determines to a large extent the the way that he perceives power. For example, if you're working in a firm in which your supervisor controls your behavior, you can't really change that fact—unless you leave the job or are promoted above him. In a strict sense the structure of the organizational chart defines authority or influence over you. In relation to our earlier discussion of power, we would say that the structure of the organizational hierarchy is a method whereby power and authority are legitimized. Our first external element is then the organizational norms as they affect our perceptions of power.

A different but closely related external element is *the stated means of power*. The organization has certain methods of enforcing its authority that are designed to make individuals conform. Earlier we talked about sanctions that an organization has to guarantee that individuals perform as desired; now we will talk about sanctions as they are used to enforce the power and authority of the organization. In other words these external elements exist for the primary purpose of forcing members of the organization to assign particular significance and meaning to power. We can think of these stated means of power as primarily coercive and remunerative.

Physical means that can be employed to make individuals comply with authority are the infliction of pain, death, punishment, and so forth. In addition, controlling the satisfaction of basic physical needs necessary for survival can be employed as a form of coercion. As a means of reinforcing a power structure coercive methods exist in such legitimate forms as the legal system. Failure to comply with the legal authority that forbids the stealing of another man's property can result in imprisonment for the offender.

When you were younger and didn't do what you were supposed to do, your father might have sent you to your room without dinner. Or you may have found your movement restricted—when you were kept after school —because you didn't do what the teacher, an authority figure, told you to do. Although these examples may seem simplistic, they do point out one of the strongest methods that organizations have of getting us to follow rules. We may even find that in setting up our own family system—our own family as an adult—we have such bitter memories of coercive power that we become very permissive.

Remunerative power is based on some form of control that the authority or power figure has over the material resources of the system. The dean of a particular college or the boss at work has such means of control at his disposal. Each is in the position of having those under his authority conform to the power structure because he controls salaries, fringe benefits, working hours, and so forth. The ability of a state government to withhold an employee's salary until he signs a loyalty oath is an apt example of remunerative power.

Norms and stated means of power are methods by which the organization tells us to pay attention—attach significance—to the positions of authority within the organization.

Power: Trans-Per

We've been told that the person above us in the organizational chart has power over us and that we have power and authority over the person below us. Now that may be—but without the perceptual processes of the people involved, it's simply a matter of a listing on the chart. In actuality, we come to respond to that person above us because we're grown to attach some significance or meaning—in the Trans-Per sense—to his demands. We listen to him because we realize that if we don't we may be fired. Or perhaps we feel that for the unusually generous salary we're getting, we can put up with him or tolerate almost anything. Then again we might respond to his requests or demands because we truly believe in the goals or symbols for which we are working.

We will show in our analysis that power, rather than being something that people just react to, is something that people participate in. As we noted earlier, to put a person in an authority position is to acknowledge those who are subject to his authority. If there's a chairman, there must be a committee; if there's a supervisor, there must be workers.

We noted earlier that an individual's self-esteem is one of the significant internal elements that determines the way he'll attach significance to power within the organizational context. Also we noted that the external element of coercive power contributes to the perceptual process going into the development of meaning. In the case at hand, we want to look at a situation in which two co-workers have similar perceptions. (Remember that we can't have identical perceptions or blends of elements.) Assume we're dealing with two individuals—Gloria and Bella—who both feel within themselves a very low level of self-esteem. They work in an organization directly under the supervision of Bobby, who holds coercive power: unless Gloria and Bella do what they are required to, Bobby can fire them.

We will analyze the kind of communication that goes on among the three of them. Whenever Bobby issues an order, the women start working on it immediately. Each time that the particular job is finished, he gives them another job without providing any words of reinforcement— approval or disapproval. After all, he feels that they get paid to do a job, and that's good enough. Consequently the women are intimidated; they see Bobby as inconsiderate, even ungrateful for their efforts to keep up with the work load. Will they remain? As soon as one leaves, so will the other. What will be the quality of the work that they do? While they decide on a course of action, the work that they do will be only adequate at best.

When they share their perceptions of Bobby, their negative evaluations of him are reinforced. Before long we can expect that the work will drop off in quantity and that one or both of them will leave. We want to stress that for an individual with low self-esteem, an exposure to coercive power will drive his self-esteem even lower, leading in turn to low morale and inefficiency. In any organization the management strives for homogeneity among its workers; in addition, in most enlightened organizations, the management strives to maintain high morale—even if only to operate at optimum efficiency.

Despite the fact that power was assigned to Bobby and that the women were aware of the organizational structure reinforcing this assignment, his lack of response or approval damaged their already low self-esteem; his indifference to them contributed directly to reducing their level of production. The point is that certain individuals in positions of power don't take the effect of self-esteem, an internal element, into account when carrying

out their responsibilities. In Bobby's case, he might try to initiate some social activities, such as tennis, with the women. But even more, he should
discover that workers need approval of their efforts if they are to maintain
their productivity and their interest in the work.

Summary

In our discussion of communication in the organizational context, we have
pointed out some of the internal and external elements that affect our assignment of meaning of conflict, decision making, and power. What we've
been attempting to show you is a new way of looking at communication in
the organization. We've been trying to have you think about communication in the organization as a process of creating meaning. As we said very
early in the book, people create their own subjective and unique meanings.
The meanings that we attach to behavior in the organization are the result of
the individual's perceptual process that blends internal and external elements. Why not reread this chapter and think of communication in the organization as a search for meaning. We think that you'll agree that the
communication factors of conflict, decision making, and power have more
varied meanings for you than they did before.

Additional Readings

Dewey, J. *How We Think*. New York: Dodd, Mead, 1910.

    This source frequently appears in small group communication texts.
Dewey's method of reflective thinking is invaluable to an understanding of decision making in the formal organization. His analytical procedure, which begins
with the recognition of a difficulty and proceeds through the selection and testing
of some solution, is acknowledged by many as an apt description of problem-
solving behavior in the formal organization.

French, J., and Raven, B. "The Bases of Social Power." In *Group Dynamics: Re-
    search and Theory*, 3rd ed., edited by D. Cartwright and A. Zander, pp.
    259–269. New York: Harper & Row, 1968.

    A knowledge of this work in any discussion of power is essential.
Working on the assumption that power is inextricably tied up with influence, the
authors distinguish the principle bases of power: expert, referent, coercive, legitimate, and reward. Their notion of "basis of power" refers to the relationship between the source of power and its subject—an idea discussed in this chapter.

Katz, D., and Kahn, R. *The Social Psychology of Organizations*. New York: John
    Wiley, 1966.

Although this material is not the easiest to read, it is among the most substantive pieces on power and authority that we've seen. Working on the premise that organizations attempt to reduce human variability, the authors develop a number of plausible hypotheses of interest. Since Katz and Kahn take a systemic view of the organization, the implications for Trans-Per will be clear to you.

March, J., and Simon, H. *Organizations*. New York: John Wiley, 1958.

This is probably *the* book on organizational structure and behavior. If you can struggle through much of the complex style, you will find this to be a gold mine of material on organizational communication. The particular section we find useful deals with conflict in organizations. March and Simon identify particular classes of conflict and then analyze conflict between individuals or groups within the organization. Additionally they state some major propositions relating individual and interorganizational conflict phenomena.

Smith, R.; Richetto, G.; and Zima, J. "Organization Behavior: An Approach to Human Communication." In *Approaches to Human Communication*, edited by R. Budd and B. Ruben, pp. 269–289. New York: Spartan, 1972.

This chapter is a good summary of important elements in the organization. The authors distinguish between formal and informal communication channels. Also they examine different perspectives taken by researchers in organizational communication. They conclude by talking about application of communication concepts to ongoing organizations; this "real world" discussion is reason enough to read the article.

Applications

Exercise 1

For at least one organization of which you are a member, watch for two weeks for any conflicts that may arise. Note how these conflicts begin, what causes them, and how they're resolved. Make a chart in which you list the conflicts under one of two headings—Functional or Dysfunctional—whether they contribute to the organization's goals or not.

Then discuss with the class the internal and external elements involved in the conflicts, and why you labeled each as you did.

Exercise 2

Blackstone, Inc., is the United States distributor for Race Masters, a foreign-made ten-speed bicycle. The company has sales of $2 million annually and has at least doubled its sales over the past ten years.

Sam Speed, the salesman for the Texas area, has been with the company for nine years. Although he is only a salesman, he identifies himself stongly with Blackstone; he feels that he has helped the company to become known as a major brand name in the Southwest. He has a reputation for confronting any problems facing the company with a no-nonsense, direct approach.

Bic's Bikes, located in downtown Dallas, and Sy's Cycles in Irving, a suburb of Dallas, both carry the bikes. They are not in direct competition with each other, since the sales area is large and can easily support two outlets. Bic's was one of Sam's first accounts for Blackstone; Sam and the owner have been on very friendly terms for years. Bic's has been until recently the largest dealer in Sam's area.

Recently Sy's Cycles has been ordering more bikes than Bic's. Sy has even decided to open a second store in the downtown Dallas area. Bic has told Sam that Sy should not be allowed to open a main branch in Dallas. If Sy is not kept out he threatens to drop the line and to begin carrying a competing line of ten-speeds. Bic's most recent summer order was $12,000; Sy's was $16,000.

The Blackstone executives discuss the problem but decide not to intervene. They decide to let Sam settle the problem himself since both Sy and Bic are his clients. However Sam is warned that he must solve the problem within two weeks, because the Christmas season is approaching. This is the first time that Blackstone has experienced a problem of this type; therefore Sam's decision will probably set a precedent for future problems of a similar nature.

Discuss possible answers to these questions:

a. What is Sam's orientation toward Blackstone, Inc.? Do you think this problem will generate much conflict within Sam's mind?

b. Considering Sam's relationship with his company and his clients, how do you think Sam will solve the problem? Why?

Exercise 3

Either visit one of the following, or use a previous experience, to discuss these organizations:

a. a military base
b. a large university
c. a prison
d. a large corporation

Now try to answer these questions about the power relationships within the organization:

a. What do you think were the orientations of most of the members toward the organization? Did the orientation differ according to a member's rank in the organization?

b. Does this organization try to "homogenize" its members, or does it encourage individual differences?

c. How does the organization get its members to assign importance to the positions of authority?

Exercise 4

Arrange to ride along with a policeman in his normal rounds. (Most community police departments have arrangements for this.) Observe how the policeman, both verbally and nonverbally, communicates his power to the people he encounters. Also observe how people respond to him. Do they differ in their perceptions of his power? If so, why? Report your findings back to the class.

Research References

Burns, J. "Conflict in the Organization." Paper read at the Symposium on Communication and Conflict, July 1973, at University of Southern California.

Festinger, L. "A Theory of Social Comparison Processes." *Human Relations* 6 (1954): 117–140.

French, J., and Raven, B. "The Bases of Social Power." In *Group Dynamics*, 2d ed., edited by D. Cartwright and A. Zanders, pp. 259–269. New York: Harper & Row, 1968.

Heider, F. *The Psychology of Interpersonal Relations*. New York: John Wiley, 1958.

Hopper, R., and Naremore, R. C. *Children's Speech*. New York: Harper & Row, 1973.

Katz, D. "The Functional Approach to the Study of Attitudes." *Public Opinion Quarterly* 24 (1960): 163—204.

Katz, D., and Kahn, R. *The Social Psychology of Organizations*. New York: John Wiley, 1966.

Leavitt, H. *Managerial Psychology*. 3d ed. Chicago: The University of Chicago Press, 1972.

Maslow, A. *Motivation and Personality*. New York: Harper & Row, 1954.

Newcomb, T. "An Approach to the Study of Communicative Acts." *Psychological Review* 60 (1953): 393–404.

Osgood, C. E., and Tannenbaum, P. H. "The Principle of Congruity in the Prediction of Attitude Change." *Psychological Review* 62 (1955): 42–55.

Rokeach, M. "Attitude Change and Behavioral Change." *Public Opinion Quarterly* 30 (1967): 529–551.

Sereno, K. K., and Hawkins, G. J. "The Effects of Variations in Speakers' Nonfluency upon Audience Ratings of Attitude toward the Speech Topic and Speakers' Credibility." *Speech Monographs* 34 (1967): 58–64.

Shaw, M. *Group Dynamics*. New York: McGraw-Hill, 1971.

Glossary

Anxiety   An interpersonal communication factor consisting of real and imagined fears as well as general and vague feelings of tension, uneasiness, and uncertainty

Attitude   An internal element; the tendency to evaluate any object or issue or person in a favorable or unfavorable manner

Attitude functions   Adjustment, ego-defense, value-expression, knowledge; the four functions attitudes serve

Attitude object   The object toward which an attitude is directed

Attraction   An interpersonal communication factor consisting of affection, respect, and love

Attribution   Making judgments or inferences from the actions of another person about the person's motives

Communication factor   Meaning typical of particular communication contexts, such as anxiety and trust for interpersonal communication or conformity and leadership for group communication or power and conflict for organizational communication

Conflict   An organizational communication factor consisting of incompatible perceptions and behavior of individuals

Constructs
       Components of a theory; concepts, abstractions, or generalized terms

Context   The situation or setting in which persons engage in communication; intrapersonal or interpersonal or group or organizational

Co-orientation   A concept from Newcomb's Balance Theory; simultaneous focusing of two communicators upon each other and the thing being talked about

Decision making   An organizational communication factor consisting of the ability to make judgments with the most efficiency and least cost

Dogmatism   A personality trait identifying an individual's tendency to be either rigid (strongly dogmatic, close-minded) or flexible (weakly dogmatic, open-minded) in his judgments of messages and individuals

External elements   Public cues or stimuli, such as words, gestures, weather, that are potentially available to all persons in a communication setting and that in sum constitute the External System

External System   One of the two basic systems of Trans-Per; the sum of those elements or stimuli both verbal and nonverbal that exist in the environment outside the individual

Games   Struggles, within the boundaries of accepted rules, in which people oppose one another and participants seek incompatible results as each person seeks to maximize gains while minimizing costs

Group context   A communication setting—characterized by norms, enduring nature, and roles—in which persons attempt to share meaning through a social-emotional or task orientation

Information sharing   A group purpose calling for members to acquire and share knowledge

Internal System   One of the two basic systems of Trans-Per; the sum of an individual's internal elements or stimuli, that is, his inner psychological and intellectual complex

Interpersonal context   A communication setting—characterized as informal and rather unstructured—in which two people attempt to share meaning with each other

Intrapersonal context   A communication setting—characterized by individual creation of meaning—in which one person communicates with himself

Involvement   An individual's perception of the significance, importance, or salience of an attitude object to him

Leadership   A group communication factor consisting of a set of behaviors arising out of a specific situation performed by the individual to assist the group in its operations

Meaning   The attachment or assignment of significance to stimuli as the consequence of perceptual blending

Model   A means for showing what is fundamental to a process under study

Nonverbal cues   All external stimuli other than spoken or written words and including body motion, characteristics of appearance, characteristics of voice, and use of space and distancing

Organizational context   A communication setting—characterized by complexity, coordination of groups, predictable tasks, and structured responsibility—in which persons attempt to share meaning

Perception   The individual's subjective, creative, active blending of internal and external stimuli through the three activities of selection, organization, and evaluation

Perceptual organization   The perceptual activity of arranging stimuli into simplified, unified wholes

Perceptual interpretation   The perceptual activity of making judgments or inferences about stimuli

Perceptual selection   The perceptual activity of neglecting some of the stimuli of the environment and focusing on a chosen few

Personality   An internal element; traits, such as degree of self-esteem or dogmatism, that make up a unique individual

Power   An organizational communication factor consisting of the potential ability of one person to influence another within a particular system

Problem solving   A group purpose calling for members to carry out a particular job, resolve a problem, or accomplish a given task

Process   An ongoing, always changing system that produces communication

Propositions   Components of a theory; sentences from a theory expressing relationships between two or more constructs

Roles   A group communication factor consisting of sets of behavior expected of each member of an established group

Self-esteem   A personality trait identifying an individual's underlying perception of his worth

Social comparison   In the absence of objective criteria evaluating the "correctness" of personal opinions and the approximate level of personal talents by talking to others

Socialization   A group purpose calling for members to focus their attention on being together and on each other as individuals

Strain toward symmetry   A concept from Newcomb's Balance Theory; the drive or psychological force upon two communicators to move toward a similarity of co-orientation

System   The part-to-part, part-to-whole interrelationship and interdependence of communication elements

Theory   Possible or proposed general explanations for observed be-
     havior; more specifically, a number of interrelated constructs and
     propositions used to predict and explain a phenomenon
Trans-Per   A model of the fundamental process of communication
     consisting of an External System and at least one Internal System
Trust   An interpersonal communication factor consisting of feelings
     that the other person will not take advantage of you and has your con-
     cerns at heart; crucial to the development of meaningful, intimate
     communication
Understanding   An interpersonal communication factor consisting of
     the ability to know empathetically how a close friend feels, thinks, and
     sees the world
Verbal cues   All external stimuli consisting of spoken or written words
     and including logical and emotional content, sequential arrangement,
     and style

Index

Bodily actions, 52, 94, 183
Burns, 245

Capability, leadership, 229
Caring, component of love, 180
Climax order, 88
Close-mindedness, 74–76
Closure, perceptual, 26–27
Coercive power, 263
Cognitive dissonance theory
    (Festinger), 142–146
    deficiencies, 146
Cognitive elements, 142–144
Commitment, to attitudes, 70–71
Communication
    contexts, 15, 103–120
    and creation of meaning, 12–
        13, 15, 103
    effectiveness, 3
    groups, 111–117, 205–232
    as interaction, 7–8
    interpersonal, 56–59, 108–111,
        161–200
    intrapersonal, 54–56, 105–108,
        125–157
    model, 43–59
    as one-way action, 7
    organizational, 117–120, 237–
        268
    perceptual nature, 11–12, 15
    process, 13–14, 15, 42–43, 63
    systemic nature, 10–11, 15,
        42–43
    as transaction, 8–16
Communication, study of
    frameworks, 6–16
    value of, 5–6
Competitive orientation, inter-
    personal communication, 193
Conflict, organizational communica-
    tion and, 243–251
    nature of, 243–245

Conformity, groups and, 210–221
    defined, 210
    and needs, 214–217
    norms and, 210–212
    and self-esteem, 213–214
    and Trans-Per, 219–221
Congruity, Principle of (Osgood),
    135–142
    deficiencies, 142
Connotation, 51, 85
    defined, 51
Conscience, 246–247
Consonance, 143
Constancy, perceptual, 33
Constraints, interpersonal, 173
Constructs, theory and, 130
Content, verbal, 86–88
    emotional, 87–88
    logical, 86–87
Context, 15, 103–120
Cooperative orientation, interpersonal
    communication, 193
Coordination, organizational
    roles, 240
Co-orientation, interpersonal
    communication, 171–172
Credibility, intrapersonal communica-
    tion, 148–151
    and authoritativeness, 150
    and dynamism, 151
    dimensions of, 150–151

Decision-making, organizational,
    251–262
    leadership style, 259–260
    motivations, 256–258
    nature of, 254
    and policy-making, 254
    and Trans-Per, 260–262
Defense mechanisms, attitudes
    as 46–47, 67
Denotation, 51, 85